I Care About Animals

I Care About Animals

Moving from Emotion to Action

Belton P. Mouras

South Brunswick and New York: A. S. Barnes and Company
London: Thomas Yoseloff Ltd

© 1977 by A. S. Barnes and Co., Inc.

A. S. Barnes and Co., Inc.
Cranbury, New Jersey 08512

Thomas Yoseloff Ltd
Magdalen House
136-148 Tooley Street
London   SE1   2TT, England

Library of Congress Cataloging in Publication Data

Mouras, Belton P   1923-
    I care about animals.

    Bibliography: p.
    Includes index.
    1. Animals, Treatment of—United States. 2. Wild
life conservation— United States.   I. Title.
HV4764.M68   1977   333.9'5   76-58590
ISBN 0-498-02113-0

To Frances Gayle Lee,
who pointed an ignorant, young Army private toward broader horizons

Contents

Foreword

Is it really possible? — A million and a half porpoises massacred by our oh-so-civilized nation in a bit over ten years? Yes, and this book by Belton Mouras will tell you how and why it was possible and the high-flown words that its perpetrators were using to disguise the tragedy.

Is there anything that *you* can do — right on the spot — if you find an animal sick, suffering, wounded, needing aid? Yes, and this book will tell you that, too.

Have you had it vaguely in mind that you *want* to take some personal action about America's threatened species but you wouldn't know how to start or, then, how to proceed? Duck no more; read right on; this book will relieve you of your dilemma. The experiences of ever so many of us — the mistakes we made and the pathways we found — are told in this book in a way that they really have been told nowhere else.

I Care About Animals cries out to be read by those — and this includes most of us, or at any rate the *better side* of most of us — who have known that rapturous instant when we could see the beauty and wonder of allowing animal life to exist very much as Nature itself intended. Here at last is a book that makes us see the rapture and the tragedy at the same time, and does not stop with showing it to us but tells us what to do about it — what *we* can do. It will be a great unfolding to those who want a truly knowledgeable view of the problems and paradoxes confronting the porpoise, the great whales, the wild horse and burro, dog and cat — the whole animal kingdom.

Have you, like the ostrich that hides its head in the sand to avoid confrontation with something not to its liking, been guilty of shrugging off a personal obligation to become involved when you hear of instances of animal cruelty?

Do you then go on to assuage your conscience by self-assurances that "humane societies are taking care of things like that"?

Except for a dedicated few who have taken up the battle for humane treatment of creatures, most people need considerable prodding to realize that humane organizations can't do it alone — there aren't enough people involved with them — the individual must assume a share of the responsibility, must take an active part.

The greatest thing about this book is that it invites you to be with the dedicated few; and it tells you how to do it, skipping the mistakes that even an enthusiast can make in going forward toward worthwhile goals.

I Care About Animals, quite aside from telling some of the most dramatic and heart-rending stories of our time, draws up a plan for action that you can follow — in your home, your neighborhood, your community, your state, your nation, and even in international areas of animal welfare.

The content covers a broad field, from the author's first introduction into humane work to the complexities of present-day political factors. Here is a history of the humane movement that traces that movement into contemporary times. Further, you learn not only startling facts but practical applications — for there is information on the emergency treatment of animals; on the laws that can be leveled against the transgressor; on the ways to band together with others who feel as you do.

Belton Mouras recalls the era when the humane worker's image was projected as a "little old lady in tennis shoes" and contrasts it to the present day when a workable and even businesslike approach is taken to curing the manifold tragedies that eat up animal lives.

There is something better than the jungle drum operating now to tell us when animals are in trouble. We who have been a part of the humane movement for a long time, and are on mailing lists throughout the country, can obtain immediate information on atrocities. We are instructed on how to go about correcting abuses — to whom we should write, where boycotts would be effective.

This information belt is needed, and *I Care About Animals* carries it further by showing how the humane organizations operate and how you can use the information that they collect — or join them — or form your own. It points out the limitations imposed when you function without a broad base of support, wanting to help animals but needing more push. Those self-appointed humanitarians who are the staunch nucleus of the humane movement may work their hearts out and empty their pocketbooks to relieve animal suffering, but they will need the techniques that truly can move the seemingly immovable. Humanitarians must do more than just end up "talking to each other," and this book is resolute in seeking the "action" that must go with the "emotion."

There is a little bit of something for everyone, on every level of humane involvement, between the covers of *I Care About Animals.*

Most importantly, it pricks the conscience of the reader to a point where he finds himself inspired to "pull his head out of the sand" and join that elite corps of men, women, and children to whom kindness to animals has become a way of life.

Velma B. (Wild Horse Annie) Johnston
Chairman of the Board of Trustees
Wild Horse Organized Assistance, Inc.

Acknowledgments

Unlike Winston Churchill, I had help in my literary endeavors. So much so that often I was convinced my name should appear on this page rather than as author. With that confession of a hole in the head, and with great humility and profound gratitude, I acknowledge the following collaborators:

Charlene Rita Heinen — writer, chief editor and organizer (who has compared preparation of this book with an elephant pregnancy);
Susan (nee Heinen) Lock — writer and researcher;
Ted Crail — writer, researcher, and all-round idea man;
Michelle Losornio — researcher and writer (first aid);
Belton Mouras Jr. — researcher (anticruelty laws);
Sheila Grant — graphic artist (cover design and photos);
Larry Racoma — graphic artist (photos and first-aid sketches);
Charlotte Newbill — illustrator (first aid);
John V. Lemmon — legal advisor;
Bruce Max Feldmann, D.V.M. — first-aid advisor;
And others, who helped where needed — Sylvia Hunt, Tom Ann Greene, Susan Haas.

Introduction

Sooner or later, if not already, you will be asked, as I am, why you care about animals. It is not an easy question to answer. A simple answer for me would be and often is, "I don't know." When I do attempt to answer, I first try to evaluate the questioner's interest. Is it idle curiosity — part of a passing conversation — is it genuine interest; and, if the latter, what precisely is the area of interest?

Shortly after my retirement from the United States Army, I was employed by a then rather new national humane group. The organization had recently received a sizable bequest, dictating that part of the funds be used for protection of livestock and of animals in the Rocky Mountain Region; a director for this regional office was needed. When interviewed for the job, I explained that I knew nothing about livestock save for my boyhood chores of cleaning up after our one and only milk cow, Flossy. My father was a cotton sharecropper in a small, French-speaking town in central Louisiana, and Flossy was loaned to our family by the landowner.

My application to the organization resulted from a life-long interest in four-legged creatures (the base adoption/lost dog/animal care program always seemed to issue from my quarters). My total lack of professional humane experience could possibly be waived, I thought, in the face of this dedication. Imagine my surprise at learning that my lack of expertise was an excellent qualification for the task of heading a livestock-protection office. There were many experts in this field, as everyone knew, but it was believed this expertise inhibited the sympathy and empathy needed to promote, encourage, and foster protection for millions of head of livestock used each year for food at home and abroad.

Nonexperience with livestock was an important characteristic but only one of my two great qualifications — the other was naiveté, resulting from living for twenty years in a military vacuum, regulated at the whim of personnel officers. This naiveté equipped me to face, with unquestioning loyalty and obedience, the political, social, and economic quagmire comprising the loose and fragmented humane movement in the United States.

Armed with a dictating machine and *Roget's Thesaurus*, I was ensconced in a Denver office, complete with secretary, by late spring of 1960. My position was a dual one — director of the Rocky Mountain Regional Office and of the organization's National Livestock Department. But there was little to do in those early weeks. I became acquainted with other executives in the building, who turned out to be curious about humane work and curiously ignorant about the people involved in it. To them I was a paradox. Hadn't I been a paratrooper? been decorated? killed people? "But you don't hunt or fish!" "Why are you interested in animals? You look normal to me!" All of this dialogue took place on an elevator going from the eighth floor to the basement cafeteria. How do you answer a friend or acquaintance who compliments you on your physical appearance and insults your intelligence at the same time? And how do you explain your deep feeling and concern for animals in the space of a brief elevator ride? You don't. You don't even try. I evolved a standard reply that can be useful for you who are or will be hit with the same quiz question: "When you have

13

time, I'd like to share some of my thoughts about animals with you." If the inquirer is genuinely interested, he will seek you out later, when you've had a chance to marshall your thoughts and aren't under time pressure or feeling defensive.

When I was a young boy, I used to cringe when I saw straining team horses or mules being lashed with a whip. I cried uncontrollably during butchering season and once even ran away from home. I used to wish that the person inflicting pain on an animal would himself suffer in the same way. Abuses to animals elicit an intense feeling of anguish and frustration inside me. It's a hex, a curse. I care about people, too, but I know more can and is being done for them. I care about animals. I don't know why.

Can animal suffering be eliminated? While I may root for the underdog — no pun intended — I'm not a believer in lost causes. Animal suffering can be, if not completely halted, greatly alleviated. There is a job to do in reaching people hitherto unaware of the problems (an unawareness those already in the movement often find incredible), but there is an even more important mission in informing the hundreds of thousands of Americans who feel as I do, how they can further the animals' cause. This book is intended as a guide for individuals who want to take action, privately or publicly, individually or through groups, toward this end.

Belton P. Mouras
Sacramento, California
June 1977

I Care About Animals

1

The Grenade at the End of the Harpoon: Why Animal-Human Relationships Are Exploding

And Man so loved the animal world that many centuries after he took to tattooing his own skin, he found how useful it would be to put corrosive chemicals on the feet of the horse. These chemicals effected a shortcut in achieving the valued Tennessee Walking Horse gait—by making it painful for the mount to put his weight down. The Tennessee Walking Horse is a dream walking—when you don't know that it was all done by pain.

Now who could get upset over that? Far worse exists in the world. Particularly the animal world.

"Harvesting a whale," to use a phrase of wonderful neutrality that makes the mightiest of earth's mammals seem like a grain of wheat, has always called for a thundering sort of ingenuity on the part of the whale's pursuers. Nowadays the whale comes to an end with a devastating demonstration of man's mastery of a varied technology.

The harpoon finds its mark—then a grenade, located at the end of the harpoon, explodes.

This is far more purposeful than that myriad of accidents that befalls the bald eagle, a bird that had little trouble becoming the symbol of American mightiness, but has had a great deal of trouble staying alive while this country stumbles around like the wistful brute, Lenny, in *Of Mice and Men*, who killed whatever he touched. The eagle flies down to his old proud territories—and finds himself caught in a trap set for wingless animals. Or he gets mixed up with the same crop poisons that Americans have belatedly begun to suspect may have something to do with the rising rate of cancer. Eagles don't have time to die of cancer. Man has devised so many accidental forms of death that any eagle is lucky to get past adolescence.

Animal-human relationships have exploded all over the globe in recent years and the most common factor is outrageous cruelty, witting and unwitting.

Are you pesonally acquainted with it? Can you think of the last time you witnessed a case of animal cruelty? Or, indeed, have you ever?

It's entirely possible that your sympathy for animal suffering is based on hearsay— hideous and no less true, but secondhand. With the exception of a few birds, maybe some squirrels in a park, the neighbor's dog, the average person can go for weeks without seeing an animal in the flesh. After all, horses no longer pull city coaches, slaughterhouses have discreetly removed themselves from city centers, and the popularity of circuses has been replaced by that of sporting events.

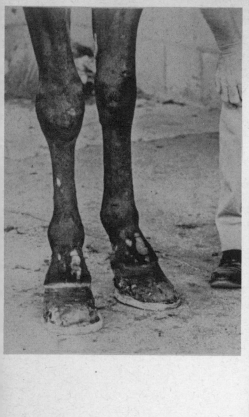

Owner's choice—chemicals or chains. These closeups show the practice of "soring" a horse to achieve the graceful Tennessee Walking Horse gait where the animal puts its weight on the back legs. Chemicals or chains used on the hooves make it painful for the horse to put weight on the front legs. A law to prevent movement of sored horses in interstate commerce helped motivate more trainers to abandon these training shortcuts.

Animals, in general, are out of sight and, consequently, out of mind. It's not un-usual for newly introduced acquaintances to express surprise at my vocation, often because they "thought the SPCA took care of all that."

There has been a traditional and a critical correlation between man's survival and the existence of animals. They've provided us frail humans with food, clothing, shelter, medicine, transportation, companionship, entertainment. Stress on some of these gifts has lessened with increased technology, and different countries take oddly varying views (consider India's reverence for the cow, Korea's irreverence for the dog),

18

but a world devoid of animals is almost impossible to imagine. How unutterably dull such a planet would be and how bereft the humans in it.

Animals are still with us—sometimes, it seems, in spite of our ancestors' best efforts—and wherever they are there is also the plausibility of cruelty, of abuse, of suffering. Why? Because man in his arrogance has assumed proprietorship over all animals (even species not directly under man's thumb—wildlife—are "managed"), often tracing humans' "dominion" to the Bible.

If man does, indeed, have domain—and this could be disputed—he has, at the same time, a moral obligation to use it only when necessary, and then humanely. All too often this is not the case and, whether or not you and I witness it, animal cruelty persists.

The Animal Protection Institute, in planning its programs, classifies and estimates animal populations as: pets—90 million; food animals—375 million; laboratory animals—600 million; wildlife—even more, but impossible to estimate. From this breakdown it would appear that the area of humane organizations' greatest concentration would be wildlife. Not so. Dogs and cats, with other pets following, hold the spotlight of interest according to a membership survey. Odd, perhaps, but understandable. People live with dogs and cats; they can identify and sympathize with them (a 1971 study reported thirty eight percent of all households owned a dog, twenty percent had a cat). It is more difficult to stir emotions about and create interest in animals people never see, though it is done. This parochial emphasis can be viewed cyclically: people identified with pets, protectionist organizations traditionally concentrated on problems of dogs and cats, their followers' horizons remained unbroadened.

A further conclusion, this one correct, is that it would be financially fatal for an organization to spend a disproportionate amount of the membership's dues and contributions on other than dogs and cats. However, there have been two very notable exceptions—trapped furbearers and clubbed harp seals. Millions of Americans have seen the pitiful photo of the now-famous raccoon, broken and dead in a leghold trap. It was used in an anti-leghold-trap advertisement API placed in major United States newspapers and many magazines beginning in 1972; the resultant swell of public outrage was responsible for subsequent introduction and support of federal legislation.

The annual brutal clubbing of harp seal pups in Canadian waters elicited a similar response—particularly when film footage was televised nationally at breakfast time. Whether these are cases of publicity motivating individuals or of hitting on a situation that angers them, is arguable; probably both descriptions apply.

PETS

People respond to pet issues because they live with these animals. Thus, it's easy to assume that dogs, cats, horses, etc., "have it made," that there is little abuse of pets. Not necessarily. If familiarity elicits sympathy, it also breeds contempt. Often the source is unknown: in Houston one month four dogs in a city block were poisoned; in Ohio a dog and two cats were found hanged; vandals stoned two ponies to death in a Pennsylvania stable. At other times pet owners are responsible, either deliberately or through ignorance—one story that made the papers was the near-dead dog whose owner left him in a closed car for thirty five minutes under the Florida sun.

Pet owners can also be held accountable for contributing to the surplus pet population. Estimates of the number of puppies and kittens born per hour range from two thousand to ten thousand. One can actually trace the sequence, from the newspaper ads—"Free, to good homes"—to the animal pounds and shelters, where some fifteen million are killed annually. The answer, simply, is for owners to neuter their pets and not to abandon them. Instead, too many people shrug off their responsibilities, clinging to the illusion that shelters will find—that it's their *duty* to find—homes for the surplus.

Thus, the onus is shifted to animal shelters, which fight a losing battle. They must house, feed, and care for dogs and cats at great cost, sometimes as much as ninety percent of their budgets; and after so many days they must destroy the majority and dispose of the carcasses.

This is not an uncommon scene for puppy mill operations. Animals can't put in complaints about the methods of those who say they're "caring" for them. PHOTO BY R. NORMAN MATHENY, Christian Science Monitor.

Shelter-operating organizations usually depend on private donations, but their jobs are public relations nightmares. Kill rates and methods, if unfavorably reported to the public, can draw community wrath and epitaphs of "slaughterhouses" and "murderers." To compound the matter, if it is generally known that animals are killed, people tend to abandon their animals in a "good neighborhood" or in the country so as to "give them a chance." The abandoned animal then faces an even greater ordeal and, additionally, presents problems of health and safety to human populations. Thus, as a result of a problem they didn't create, societies lose desperately needed financial support and gain additional operating costs. The alternatives are equally grim: deception of the public or refusing to take in animals on reaching capacity.

As an adjunct to reducing—or, at the very least, stabilizing—the pet surplus, API urges people to acquire pets from shelters and pounds rather than from breeders and pet shops, selecting from the already-condemned, so to speak, instead of adding to demand on the yet-to-be-born end. Not everyone, unfortunately, agrees. Wrote one member:

> To the contrary, purchasing dogs from a pound or humane society encourages people to let their mongrels (or purebreds) breed indiscriminately, since these people know that they can always leave the litter at the Animal Rescue League. . . .they do not have to feed the dam right, worm her, worm the puppies or inoculate them, since they will be held responsible by no one. . . .On the other hand, a breeder is very concerned that the puppies be healthy and stay healthy. . . .

The writer concluded that it was far better for a customer to get a "carefully reared, healthy, paper-trained, and affectionate animal than a mangy dog from the pound," and that "there are too many sick and ugly dogs being foisted off on the unwary by well-meaning 'humane' societies."

One point to be taken from all this is that no shelter or pound should adopt out animals at no charge. It's easier to invest in proper care of pets if they have had a value placed on them initially.

Other elements, however, need contradicting: (1) An "ugly" animal is no less lovable and a mongrel often makes a better pet than a purebred; (2) Simply because a puppy is healthy and purebred does not guarantee it will not end up on death row; (3) Not all breeders are conscientious. There are those who perpetrate the evils of puppy mills: bitches, housed in unsanitary conditions, are bred exhaustively and the pups—often sick or of undetermined breed—are flimsily crated and shipped off for pet shop sales. In fact, many of them die in transit, in pet shops, or in the homes of new owners.

Pets sometimes change hands through public sales, and the exchange procedure can be an uncomfortable one. In Ripley, Mississippi, such an event is held each month and the merchandise includes dogs, cats, horses, and ponies. API National Advisor Ed King of Indiana attended the sale one September and saw dogs without food or water and cramped in too-small cages, all suffering in 110-degree heat. Unsold dogs have reportedly been shot or beaten to death by their owners.

Many times pets are sold not to other pet owners but to laboratories. They can be bought under false pretenses or even stolen, transported across state lines if necessary to join other guinea pigs in medical testing and experiments completely uncontrolled by law.

Add to the list dog racing, where the animals' instincts are "honed" on live (for a time) rabbits and losers are not tolerated, and dog fights that persist though illegal. API has even uncovered a market for domestic cat fur—twenty to fifty cents a pelt.

Pets, of course, are not always dogs and cats. Tame rabbits, horses, tropical fish, caged birds, mice, rats, hamsters, and guinea pigs also qualify. API discourages keeping pet turtles because: (1) they are sensitive creatures that usually survive only a few months in captivity; and (2) they can carry the organism salmonella, which can cause human illness.

Actually, people tend to make pets of whatever animals they can lay hands on, be they tame, wild, or exotic. Wild animals are best left that way—even injured ones can be treated without being domesticated. Making pets of wild animals imported from other countries is a tragedy. Reports abound of humans attacked by usually docile exotics, of household furnishings destroyed, of declawed, defanged big cats offered to "good homes," of nocturnal animals upsetting human schedules. But these are the animals actually acquired by owners—about one-fifth of the total take from foreign plains and jungles. The other eighty percent? They die along the way—in capture, in transit, within weeks of purchase. In addition to the suffering of individual animals, foreign populations are decimated and potentially damaging species are sometimes loosed to affect American wildlife and crops.

FOOD ANIMALS

From the grey dawn of human history, we are told, animals have provided man with food. Indeed, so ingrained has become the practice of meat-eating, I'd guess most of its adherents, if they stop to consider the animals killed for this market at all, look on this humanized predator-prey relationship as natural law. API itself does not propound vegetarianism as a requirement for protectionists, even though its publications have reiterated the advantages and ten percent of members and several staff people forego meat. Practically speaking, such a stipulation would drastically undercut the organization's size, strength, and effectiveness in dealing with the hosts of other animal problems.

Many people are not overly concerned about food animals because of the common idea that our meat and dairy animals are raised on picturesque farms and spend their days leisurely munching grass, the friendly farmer hovering solicitously in the background. Careful consideration reveals the flaws in this concept. With increased population and living standards, the world's food needs have expanded enormously. At the same time, there is less space available for raising livestock and feed crops. Money-making is the name of the game, and the solution is to raise as many animals as possible in as little space as possible in as short a time as possible using the least possible food.

Poultry production has taken a leaf from the assembly-line book. Sometimes all operations, from egg production to finished broiler chickens, are accomplished by one establishment; or, one entrepreneur produces eggs and hatches chicks while another raises day-old chicks to broilers. If the latter is the case, the following outlines what these birds have to look forward to.

Day-old chicks are boxed and shipped to a feeding farm. Handling along the way may be rough, so a percentage (usually one to two percent) of the whole order is added to replace the chicks that will die. Upon arrival at the feeding farm, the chicks are placed in dark, artificially ventilated and heated buildings (cooling is considered expensive and thus unnecessary). Large numbers of birds crowded into confined quarters will fight after a certain age—keeping the buildings dark so the birds cannot see each other forestalls this. Some establishments clip the birds' upper beaks to prevent pecking at their neighbors, while others use tiny spectacles so the animals can't see straight ahead. The chickens are continually fed and watered automatically, thereby allowing for maximum efficiency with a minimum of effort. Conditions vary at different establishments, but for the most part the nine to ten week lives of these birds will not be particularly comfortable or pleasant.

Laying hens are not afforded better treatment. Production is pushed to its maximum with individual hens producing over two hundred eggs annually. The birds are kept in small, wire cages with bright lights trained on them almost continuously to simulate daylight and thus continuous egg-laying.

Veal may be considered a delicacy, but the meat is produced under what can only be described as abhorrent conditions. The calves are taken from their mothers when only a few hours or a few days old, even though the milk produced by the cows for the first four or so days after calving is not used for dairy products. Male calves born to dairy farmers are considered virtually useless and often end up as veal.

At the producing farm the calves are installed in their new living quarters, which will vary from solid-sided crates to slat-floored pens. In most cases, the animals are either placed in stocklike structures or closely tethered to prevent excess movement and other undesirable activities. Various methods are resorted to in order to produce the desired "white" flesh. These include: bleeding the calves at intervals; feeding iron-deficient diets composed exclusively of milk or milk replacer; decreasing mobility and rearing in total darkness. Not unexpectedly, the mortality rate is quite high even though most calves are marketed after only twelve to fourteen weeks of life.

Beef cattle calves are allowed to stay with their mothers for a longer time after birth, but this merely postpones their first painful encounter with man. The calves are caught, branded, given several immunizations, dehorned and castrated, all within a very short time. Virtually no follow-up care is given, so infection is common. After gaining a certain amount of weight, the cattle are prodded into transport trucks or trains and shipped to the stockyards for "finishing" and, finally, slaughter.

Pigs, dairy cattle, goats, and other food-producing animals each suffer particular types of pain and discomfort during lives of varying duration. Transportation to the

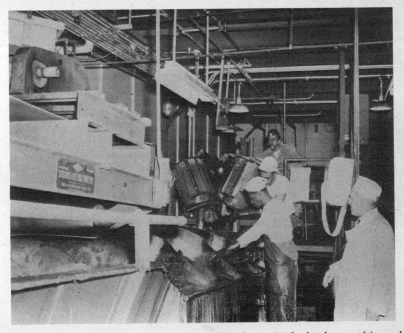

The killing of food animals is on an assembly line basis. In the background is an electric stunner in action; hogs on the conveyor belt are being bled. PHOTO BY HOWARD OBENCHAIN, USDA.

slaughterhouse can be a frightening and sometimes painful experience, with animals crowded tightly into vehicles. Producers have no incentive to prevent crowding when they can recoup losses due to bruised or dead animals through insurance.

Due to the intensive living conditions found on most livestock-raising farms, chemicals and drugs need to be added to feeds to prevent sickness. Many additives are used even when they're not necessary for health purposes. In a pamphlet explaining the merits of his milk replacer for calves, a well-known feed producer boasted that this particular product contained "fifty grams" of a certain antibiotic "per ton for disease control and *feed efficiency*" (emphasis mine). The questionability of this practice can be demonstrated by the recent decision of the federal Food and Drug Administration (FDA) to impose tighter controls on the use of the widely used chemical additive, Diethylstilbestrol (DES). Studies revealed that residues of DES and other chemicals can sometimes be found in slaughtered animals destined for human consumption. The effects of such chemicals on, initially, livestock and, secondarily, human consumers are, at best, dubious. Long-term effects are even less understood.

One keen observer has noted that if slaughterhouses were made of glass, we'd be a nation of vegetarians. But as long as man eats meat, it seems only reasonable for him to ensure his victims a painless death. The attempt was made in the Fifties, but the federal Humane Slaughter Act passed in 1958 contains large loopholes.

Previously, animals were brought in, shackled by a hind leg, hoisted above the ground — all while conscious — then slaughtered. In addition to intense fear and pain, the animals suffered broken legs, torn muscles, and dislocated joints. The Act stipulates that animals be rendered unconscious before slaughter, but it has two major flaws: (1) The law applies only to packers who contract with the United States government or, if state humane slaughter laws prevail (they do in twenty three states), with state agencies. Other packers are not required to follow the federal law, although some do; (2) An amendment was added that allows the shackling and hoisting method to be applied to *conscious* animals in the case of Jewish ritual slaughter (cutting the throat). Jewish custom dictates that an animal be conscious at the time of slaughter, and federal law prohibits the cut surface of a food animal coming in contact with the ground. In spite of this, Canada, Britain, and other European countries have managed to retain ritual slaughter without the preliminary shackling and hoisting.

LABORATORY ANIMALS

Few people realize that the prescription drugs we take, the shampoos and cosmetics that promise to beautify, the helpful drain cleaners, all owe their market existence to the millions of animals that gave up their lives in product-testing laboratories.

Laboratories all over the world use animals of all species by the millions for experiments, many of questionable validity and application. A great deal of these experiments are of a nature that prohibits use of anesthetics or post-operative pain killers (so the researchers say). Some are so painful that normally silent animals scream in agony. In one laboratory testing shampoos for eye irritation, rows upon rows of rabbits are kept in apparatuses similar to the colonial stocks. The rabbits' eyes have been surgically altered so they are constantly open, and a researcher travels the rows of rabbits, placing samples of concentrated shampoo in one or both of the animals' eyes. We are all aware of the pain involved when even a minute quantity of dilute shampoo comes in contact with our eyes. Even more intense is the rabbits' pain — some actually cry, making sounds like human babies.

The FDA says that a certain amount of animal testing must be performed on virtually all products. Many companies far exceed governmental demands to add a margin of safety in case they are later sued for product damages.

The effectiveness of these tests on animals is debatable, for present scientific knowledge notes numerous physiological and anatomical differences between the common laboratory animals and the humans who, in most cases, will be the ultimate users of the tested products. Thalidomide was completely animal tested in several countries before being marketed, but the researchers were unaware that normally used laboratory tests did not reveal the fact that thalidomide used during pregnancy could cause deformities in the child. Even today it has been extremely difficult to reproduce the effects of thalidomide in laboratory animals, including monkeys.

There are other examples. Insulin was found to produce deformities in the offspring of chickens, rabbits, and mice — but only *after* the drug was deemed useful in treating diabetes. Had the negative finding been made earlier, it's possible the beneficial uses for insulin would never have been discovered.

Another aspect of animal research is experimental surgery. These surgeries, of innumerable design and "purpose," are performed over and over even though the results have been previously documented. Some claim practice operations on animals are necessary practice for surgical students. In Britain, however, surgeons learn their techniques almost exclusively by watching and assisting established doctors, and the skill of this country's medical men does not seem to have been impaired. Yet, not all experimental surgeries are done for practical experience. Some are undertaken "purely for the sake of research," as noted by Robert Van Citters, Dean of the School of Medicine, University of Washington, in a government publication. Many researchers work under federal grants, using money collected from taxpayers who may strongly disagree with a laboratory's approach (or lack of approach) to questions of ethnics.

The categories of animal experimentation are as numerous as the numbers of animals used — chemical testing by defense agencies for possible chemical warfare; pharmaceutical testing; toxicological testing; even psychological testing. Everybody can get into the act.

The Animal Welfare Act of 1966 (amended 1970) was enacted with the hope of providing a measure of protection to the animals used for experimental and exhibitional purposes. Even following its passage, however, conditions for the animals have not improved significantly. Housing conditions in many cases are still substandard. No specified exercise time is allotted; consequently, animals may be kept continually in cramped cages for years. Dogs seem to suffer the most from this plight, but other animals are not exempt — even exotics such as giraffes and armadillos are closely confined.

The Animal Welfare Act provides for inspections of laboratory facilities, but there are thousands of institutions using experimental animals and an insignificant number of qualified inspectors to look in on conditions in them. The inspections, when made, are supposed to be unannounced, but most can be anticipated and problems covered up. This lack of enforcement is one of the main problems, but there are others — wording, trivial penalties, limited applicability.

Veterinarian Pierre Chaloux of the Department of Agriculture reports: "The registration, inspection and reporting provisions of the Act applicable to research facilities and exhibitors are not applicable to research facilities operated by federal agencies. Accordingly, no inspections of federal facilities for their compliance with the Act are made by the U.S. Department of Agriculture employees."

WILDLIFE

By this time it's obvious that contact between man and animal is often disadvantageous for the latter. Yet there is no assurance even for wildlife, for man is an arrogant, determined, and mobile creature — evading him is impossible.

Humans kill many animals "for their own good," i.e., destruction of animals by man to prevent their overpopulation and starvation by nature. This is one of the first defenses trotted out by hunters—this and the idea that hunters finance "conservation" through license fees and arms taxes. Some comments are in order: (1) A broader base of support for state fish and game departments is needed, for where hunting and trapping fees are the revenue source, it's only natural that these are the people catered to as beneficiaries of the bureaucratic system of (2) mismanagement—whereby natural predators are killed off and animal populations are managed artificially to provide targets for "sportsmen"; (3) arms taxes are levied on *all* guns, not just those used for hunting.

The woods are invaded in early fall by bow-and-arrow hunters. Where gunshot, accurately aimed, can mean instant death, bow hunters' prey must suffer through internal hemorrhage before dying.

Gun-toters follow later in the season, and in the so-called competition between animal and man the latter is given the advantage via high-powered rifles, binoculars, walkie-talkies, dog packs, lures, and decoys. Except in a couple of states, hunters are licensed without any regard for shooting accuracy, ability to identify target animals, or strength of eyesight.

Ironically, hunters can sometimes cause more destruction through default. Two to three million waterfowl die each year from lead poisoning contracted because the birds find and eat shotgun pellets that have missed their mark and fallen to earth.

Trappers also roam the forests and they, too, are looking for trophies—not to decorate homes or clubhouses, but to adorn fur-wearing men and women ignorant of the animal suffering inherent in their status garments. Over twelve million wild furbearers are trapped annually (this does not include discarded "trash" animals). The device usually in play is the leghold trap—two viselike clamps that spring shut on an animal's leg or paw with enough force to hold him immobile until the trapper comes—whenever that might be.

The ordeal has been compared to a human's catching a hand in a car door, but trappers insist they often find trapped victims "sleeping peacefully" rather than suffering any pain. Other defenses are equally imaginative. One sportsman envisioned unculled furbearers multiplying to the point where "they would soon chase man away from that part of the country."

The wearing of furs also occasions the annual slaughter of seals. Under the auspices of the U.S. Department of Commerce, each summer twenty to thirty thousand northern fur seals are clubbed on the Pribilof Islands off the Alaskan coast; the skins are processed by the Fouke Fur Company of South Carolina under a long-standing federal contract.

Canadians and Norwegians kill seals in the spring. The prey here is the whitecoated harp seal pup. Norwegian factory ships operate on "the Front," an area off the Newfoundland-Labrador coast; and the seals taken are divided between the two countries. More pups are taken farther south, in the Gulf of the St. Lawrence, by Canadian landsmen. (In an astonishing move—that was a slap in the face to 10 + years of world protest and went against scientific evidence—officials *raised* the 1977 quota by 40,000 to 170,000 seals. The allotment was: 35,000 to Norwegian vessels; 62,000 to Canadian vessels; 63,000 to Canadian landsmen; and 10,000 to Greenland and Canadian Arctic natives—the first time this part of the kill was included in the "total allowable catch.") Tens of thousands of seals are brutally clubbed for frivolous luxury items.

Some animals are destroyed not because they are of positive use to man, but for the sake of pest removal. Predators—coyotes, bobcats, wolves, etc.—have been subjected to intensive wholesale eradication programs utilizing poisons, traps, clubs, and guns. Why? Because, charge western landowners, they prey on cattle and sheep. We do not

"Coyote getters" get more than coyotes. Also called M-44s, these devices are designed to release, when disturbed, a spray of cyanide down a coyote's throat; this time a dog was the victim.

deny domestic animals protection, but it can be had in a reasonable manner. Conservation departments in Kansas and Missouri have established the principle of removing the specific marauding predator rather than attacking entire populations. Oregonian Dayton O. Hyde, rancher and author, welcomes coyotes; by not allowing poisons to be used on his land, the scheme of nature—involving prey *and* predator— has been maintained.

Western stockmen also disagree with protectionists on the subject of wild horses. These hardy descendants of Spanish ponies were, until just a few years ago, rounded up via buckshot and aircraft and shipped off to meat-processing plants to be transformed into pet food. Because wild horses had no trophy value and were viewed as competitors for grazing on public land, they were declared worthless. Even after the 1971 passage of protective federal legislation declaring them a part of this country's history, freedom from harassment is not ensured. One ruse is for ranchers to cut feed costs by turning privately owned horses loose on public land; when it's time to round them up, there just may be some truly wild animals caught as well. More importantly, western landowners possess considerable political clout—in 1975 a federal district court in New Mexico declared federal law P.L. 92-195 unconstitutional, forcing the Department of the Interior (the administering agency) to appeal the matter to the Supreme Court. (A year later the high court upheld the statute.)

Endangered species seem to be the rallying point for a great many organizations, and this could even be viewed as common ground for protectionists and conservationists (it's what happens to them *after they're unendangered* that causes dissent).

Since 1895 more than 17,000,000 harp seal pups like this one have been killed in Canadian waters.

The United States lists over one hundred species as endangered, and foreign countries add considerably to that number. Causes include habitat destruction, environmental pollution, and the demand for furs, exotic pets, and trophies. Commerce and politics often work hand in hand to prevent remedial measures. The Japanese and Russian whaling industries, ignoring or disputing scientific evidence testifying to the critical decline of great whale populations, continue to set their factory ships, sonar, and grenade-headed harpoons on these marine mammals. Only the force of world opinion and a citizen-instituted boycott of products imported from the offending nations force the slightest concessions to International Whaling Commission agreements. Meanwhile, federal resolutions calling for an embargo of Japan's and Russia's exports languish in House and Senate committees.

Dolphins, like whales, are of the order Cetacea. While both species are highly intelligent, dolphins, perhaps because they are smaller and more visible, seem to possess a universal appeal for humans. Three species of dolphin, however, are having difficulty staying alive—the spotters, the spinners, and the whitebellies, which associate with schools of yellowfin tuna. As fishermen gather the deeper-swimming tuna with huge nets, the dolphins on the surface become entangled and drown (these air-breathing mammals can remain submerged for only a few minutes, and they cannot swim in reverse to extricate themselves from netting).

In the early 1960's the tuna-fishing industry changed from a hook-and-line fishing method to that of netting, using purse-seine nets a mile or more in length. Since the transition, 100,000 to 300,000 porpoise suffocated each year, "incidental" to fishing operations. The situation remained undiscovered for a time; when it came to light toward the end of the decade, there was no formal forbidding of the massacre until 1976. Tuna fishing is commercially important, and tuna fishermen maintain that any moves to drastically reduce porpoise deaths would wreak economic havoc on the industry.

ANIMALS FOR ENTERTAINMENT

Man has found that animals can also be used for purposes of entertainment—his, since their roles are not particularly comfortable. Aside from the very real attraction of making money, some of these functions are justified on the basis of heritage/culture. Rodeo cowboys testify to the event's cruelty—to them; the animals, not unexpectedly, are well treated, practically living in luxury. These are the same horses that buck only under the spur and when a strap is tightened around their flanks and genitals ("horses like to be tickled"), the same calves that are lassoed when traveling twenty-seven miles per hour and slammed to the ground, the same steers that are flipped, twisted, and stretched by roping-event contestants.

One protectionist noted that if the animals are well treated outside the arena, it's like feeding your dog well so you can beat him every day.

Other countries can be denigrated for staging bullfights, but the demand is not wholly internal; tourists are also to blame for patronizing such events and West Coast viewers subscribe to fights televised from Mexico. Unequal though the contest looks, it may, in reality, be even more so. Special treatment before the bout helps ensure the outcome: vaseline in the eye for blurred vision, cotton up a nostril for shortened breathing, beating with sandbags, which exhaust but leave no mark.

Cockfighting, where trained birds equipped with gaffs and spurs stab and slash at each other until one dies, has been called "sophisticated cruelty." It is not illegal in some states, however, due to the heritage ploy. In a Louisiana debate one legislator declared, "This is ingrained in the Cajun culture. Next year you might prohibit us from having a crawfish festival." One of Oklahoma's state representatives saw cockfighting as "the sport of all free countries"; in his opinion, the first thing communists do in a takeover is outlaw it.

For movie producers and directors, the cheapest and quickest way to film scenes involving animals is without fakes. Thus, in this self-regulated industry, chances are some of the shots of animals being tripped, mutilated, and even killed, are not make-believe. And there are other instances of cruelty for fun. Animals in roadside zoos are often painfully confined and ill-treated; in legitimate but unenlightened or poorly subsidized zoos, animals can be sentenced to a life of pacing a minimum-footage cell. And the economic pressure on circuses does not always make for kind treatment and training of their animal attractions.

THE SAVING PHILOSOPHY

Species, reasons, settings vary, but in any confrontation with humans bent on destruction, animals are the losers. Is there a solution? Definitely. It's to organize human spokespersons for animals, to initiate and continually regenerate the concepts of recognition of "four-footed rights" and a human-animal sharing of this earth.

The philosophy of API toward this end is echoed by many national and local organizations: If a large enough segment of the public becomes aware of particular problems, a concerted effort, and thus pressure for change, can bring about correction of problems. That is the goal; the vehicle is *public humane education* — using all communications media to gain publicity for specific cruelties and to apply pressure where it's needed.

An illustration helps. Shelter operations and individual rescue efforts are important and necessary. Yet, they treat the *effect* of a problem — overpopulation of, and callousness toward, pets. If the cause of that problem is not attended to, the effect will continue and increase indefinitely. Educational organizations don't handle animals directly but, rather, address themselves to the *cause* of the problem on a massive scale, educating present and potential pet owners to take proper care of their animals and have them neutered. Similarly, we don't set employees loose in the woods to free trap victims, but we do influence the public to an abhorrence of furs and the animal suffering they represent.

As implied, public humane education has a ripple effect. For example, from one ad or television announcement ten-thousand people will be alerted to the fact that dolphins are dying needlessly; five-thousand will express their views to the federal regulating agency; two-hundred will notify their neighbors via a letter to the local paper; one-hundred teachers will request supplemental information for their students. The most important asset of any organization is a supportive, active membership.

Humane education works to change attitudes; but, you say, what about those who know and don't care, who have a permanent, and incompatible, mind-set? This is where laws and regulations are valuable. And, here again, it is the squeaky wheel, the loudest lobby, the informed and active protectionist who gets results.

All is not peaches and cream, of course. Often in the past, after achieving a political victory requiring careful planning and long hours of hard work — a victory that would have a vastly beneficial effect for great numbers of animals — I have been asked, "Yes, but have you rescued a single dog yet?" This is the discouraging thing about education — immediate results are often not visible. And to a culture imbued with the desirability of quantifying results, it's all too easy to demand a magic figure of "fifteen-thousand less animals trapped" as a measure of a movement's worth. It's like asking a church how many souls it saved last year.

The API staff sees evidence of effectiveness in membership growth, in reports of member activities, in favorable votes on legislation; but pulling out a manipulated figure reduces all efforts to the local adoption program's "twelve-dogs-adopted-today" level.

An advancing ship means death to a harp seal pup. The pelts of these animals are most desirable when they are about three weeks old; the pups are killed annually by clubbing.

2

God's Will and the Glory of Leopard Coats: An Almighty Uproar over Trapping

If you want a good reason for not believing in the Abominable Snowman, here's a very simple one. If the creature existed, some trapper would have figured out, by now, a way to trap it. Trappers know how to trap everything and they find their way to every animal that's in any kind of demand.

Also — and assuming that fur customers could wrestle it away from the museums that would want it — there are a good many people who would be there, vying with each other, bankbook against bankbook, for the honor of buying the first Snowman coat.

Does this seem bitter?

It is slightly out of date. People aren't nearly as anxious to buy exotic furs these days as they used to be; under the Endangered Species Act and another law that applies at the nation's fur center in New York, the furrier is sharply limited in what he can sell. A significant element in the fur trade also exercises voluntary restraint for fear of "bad publicity" — and so the great public outcry has done a part of its work in making unfeasible the flame-harvest of the furrier when jaguar, tiger, and others were trapped and gunned to near extinction.

Yes, the fur trade is on the run — running to see what other animals can be caught since some of the old favorites have so many champions and wearing a *real* fur instead of just a fake fur can make you a social disgrace. This floundering after new products is serious enough that only four years ago API, working by telephone, had no trouble reaching fur dealers who were willing to consider the purchase of domestic cat skins.

One of the more poignant moments of recent times (especially poignant to fur dealers who treasure the price they can get for a really fine group of animal pelts) occurred in 1972 when a New York furrier in a four-generation firm that has survived a hundred flip-flops of the fashion world, rather proudly cast before his customers six leopard skins.

These, he declared, would be for the last leopard coat made in America.

The furrier paid his respects to the glory of leopards and he remarked that these skins had come from Somaliland, and that "Somaliland has always been known for having the best leopards in the world." It had also been known for having quite a few of them. But that had changed. Trapping, spearing, and shooting had the leopard seriously decimated by the early Sixties; the animal's only "good luck," if you want to call it that, through another full decade, was in finally becoming so scarce that the government declared it officially endangered.

Even now the furrier did not think his customers ought to feel bad if they had an urge to seize those tawny skins and make themselves an utterly divine leopard coat. Why no, he said—"These animals were killed before we really knew what was happening. The woman shouldn't feel bad because they are already dead. Ten years ago nobody mentioned these things; we were not aware of it."

The story stays remarkably the same from generation to generation, from animal to animal—the trapper traps, the furrier befurs, the animal scrambles against this homicidal tide with less and less luck and then, at length—"These animals were killed before we really knew what was happening. . . ."

The grandness of trying to save the leopard—and it was grand that something finally had been done—did not truly end the problem, not even for leopards, but it did establish that outcries mean something. The shouting, when it got loud enough, was heard.

In America it proved far easier to protect animals of Somaliland than to lay down some basic rights for animals out in the American countryside. Traps by the millions were concealed in those byways where the fox runs, the wolf howls, and the beaver chugs through the water toward his dam. An all-devouring fur industry was interested in every hide, but the drama of the beaver, compared with the drama of the leopard, is almost too close to us to be of interest.

Only here and there did someone become aware that when a beaver dies—near a typical pond in a typical trap to provide some spending money for a reasonably typical lad out of an American high school—it may die in wallowing pain that can go on for days and the hide (since it is not a mighty prize like the leopard's) may not induce a rapture of skinning and an urgent trip to the trading post. The professional trapper might attend quickly to his trapped beaver—the amateur, not so quickly. And a beaver who is half caught and half free—taken in a leghold trap that holds out the promise of freedom but does not free him—dies a death of astonishing cruelty. This is America's most common story.

Only as we began to open this subject did API discover that it was stabbing with a poker the touchiest nerve in America. Trappers fight with wild and tigerish violence to deflect the faintest reform. They are a breed committed—powerful antagonists—*righteous* antagonists. They view themselves as true inheritors of an American dream. They battle any suggestion that the level of cruelty be lessened, by arguing that when coondogs kill their prey they "munch and crunch him to death," and that this is far more ferocious than what traps do. In stinging and righteous rebuke, the trapper brands the "meddler" as scoundrel, tyrant, destroyer of the dream; and Animal Rights, he declares, is a puny cry which all the puny city people should apply to their pekingese and not to him.

Who *are* these trappers, then? They are a multitude. But one in every four of them, here in the United States, is a boy of high school age or younger. A boy alone, a boy in the forest, a boy as swift as foxes who sees himself as a New Pioneer.

A CLOSER LOOK AT THE OUTDOOR BOY'S DELIGHT

Enrapturement is an important part in the transformation of an eight-, ten-, or twelve-year-old into a steely-fingered trapper.

"Fortunately," wrote a writer for *Fish and Game* magazine, "I was well acquainted with an old man, who frequently smelled like mink lure, that knew mink and muskrat as well as the cracked and wrinkled backs of his hands. 'Son,' he asked me, 'what does an old boar mink do when he's hungry?. . .Well, sir, about dark that customer is gonna come out and start off down the creek. He's gonna stick his head into every hole in the bank he comes to that's likely to have a rat or crawdad in it 'til he gets something to eat.' " The boy could catch the toe of a mink—But no mink, and the old man said, " 'Son, how do you set your traps?'. . .I told him how the trigger was carefully brushed free of rust and the pan set so lightly that a wet maple leaf would trigger it. 'Well then,' says he, 'there's your problem. A mink is quick as lightning and light-footed as a falling feather. If your trap springs before he puts his full weight on the pan, he'll jerk his foot out before the jaw shuts.' "

And so the boy is enticed by the mysteries of a craft—by the test of pitting his wits against an animal's wits. If he doesn't leap away at the beginning—appalled by

This wall of fur represents eighty thousand dollars worth of pelts—one fall's catch by 150 Maine hunters and trappers. UNITED PRESS INTERNATIONAL PHOTO.

the torture that the trapper has learned to ignore—he may soon adapt to the sadness, not even feel it. His grizzled mentor aims to show him that life is full of killing; killing is everywhere.

More killing, in fact, than a trapper ever aims for. Once the boy is a bonafide trapper—and even in that tiny percentage of United States trappers who are actually "professionals," nearly all have been trapping since earliest boyhood—here are just a few of the things that can happen from everyday trapsetting:

•Three bald eagles were caught in Michigan in traps set around beaver ponds. The eagles had developed the bad habit of "hanging around beaver ponds in the Spring."

•Near Convington, Illinois, an amateur trapper named Wayland Middendorf caught something rare and special. An albino raccoon. You can go a lifetime and never see an albino raccoon so this was a remarkable catch. The raccoon, of course, came into town dead. They mounted it.

•In Hightstown, Carlton Lawrence recovered his two-year-old foxhound, Sue. He had been searching for her for three weeks and two days. Dr. Ellen Friedman, a veterinarian, said, "The trap sprung on both sides of her head, about one and a half inches behind her ears. The flesh was eaten away to the bone on both sides of her neck; another few days and her head would have fallen off."

•In a seven-county area of Nevada in September, 1973, it was reported that more than six-hundred bald and golden eagles had fallen as accidental victims of trappers trying, with jackrabbit bait, for bobcats and coyotes. This indicated why most sources now believe that the bald eagle, in spite of efforts to protect it, cannot last much longer and will become extinct. By 1976 only a few hundred bald eagles were left in the United States.

•In Williston, North Dakota, a dog named Chico was never going to catch up with the man whose traps had seized her. Caught by her two front paws in two different traps, she was found buried in the snow. She had gone through a blizzard that way. It was hard to know whose traps had caught her—in Williams County, where Chico lived, some nine-hundred licenses had been issued to trappers.

•In the Coos County Forest, Mrs. L. N. Morris was with some 4-H boys when they found a cat caught in a trap. They worked for several hours to free it and couldn't—the mechanism was too much for the animal and too much for the 4-H boys. "Looking around," said Mrs. Morris, "we found many traps set—all unmarked—under dead leaves, under rocks and many places where a person might also get caught." Back in the same woods a week later, they discovered the cat was still there, the trap untouched. "Nobody," she said, "had checked any of those traps in that time."

Trappers frequently write the Animal Protection Institute to claim that all traps in this country are visited once a day, or several times a day, to collect the furbearers and release the innocent. The file also bulges with incidents like this one that show it isn't so. The professional trapper checks his traps with regularity? All right. But it's a trade bursting with amateurs. When your living doesn't depend on it—and it's hard to get your living out of trapping alone, especially in those places where dogs and cats are plentiful and wild game more scarce—how often you make the rounds of the traps is apt to depend on your mood at the time. Laws seek to enforce this. But the trapper is out there in creekland and snowland where the first sign of his presence is apt to be a sudden *thwank!* and a yowl of pain as trap crushes leg.

"City people are the ones who're against us," muttered trapper Alvin White to a Michigan reporter named Bonnie Stowers. "They don't understand much about animals in the first place and they certainly don't understand trapping. Everything leading up to the kill is what makes trapping a great sport. People say we're killers, murderers. That's just a bunch of nonsense. Most of us, the majority of us, eat the meat we trap. So it's all just a bunch of nonsense as far as I'm concerned because every American who eats meat is involved with killing in some way. Just because you get your meat under cellophane doesn't make you pure."

Dave Scadden, an eighteen-year-old Utah boy who dressed like a cross between an Indian and Daniel Boone, tried trapping near the Snow Basin Ski Resort because there was beaver there; but people raided his traps, so he staked out an area near Monte Cristo where he needed first a snowmobile, then snowshoes to take him deeper.

Dave told reporter Vandra Webb, "I like the feeling of aloneness. Back in twenty or thirty miles, you can really think. Everything comes alive. You can hear a bird whistle, stream chortle, or animal running." Dave has a buffalo robe he stitched himself and that buffalo robe probably does not mean to him what it would to many others—people who sorrow that as the fever for buffalo robes grew in this country, between 1850 and 1870, a total of sixty-eight million of these great old beasts were slaughtered in just one twenty-year period. Dave likes the feeling the buffalo robe gives him and perhaps does not relate his actions to what was happening in the world before he came along. Dave traps beaver—the same beaver that are making a painful comeback after the great homicidal hat-making that almost wiped out the animal.

"Heck, I've been trappin' something or other," Dave confesses, "since I was knee-high. It just becomes a part of you. It's something I've got to do, breathe new life in something that's almost died out."

Died out? Not quite.

The Department of Commerce estimates that two million trappers exist in the United States—admittedly a figure hard to be certain about because many states don't require licensing of the under-14-year-old amateur.

Died out? Well—no. But practiced more efficiently—more killingly—than it used to be? Indeed.

The snowmobile is the trapper's chariot and he can now cover great territories never reached a century ago. For all the outcry against the trappers' cruelties, amateurs are regularly lured into it as "a sport," as "a way to enjoy the outdoors," for "pocket money," for "a chance to get out of the house." Just over a quarter (26.4 percent) of all United States trappers are believed to be youngsters, mostly high school students; another quarter are laborers and farm-hired men; another quarter are proprietors and farmers. The "professional" trapper represents a minor percentage of the remaining twenty-five percent, and just how small a percent is anybody's guess. A study made in Colorado in the late Forties indicated that only about one percent of the kill in that state could be attributed to the professional trapper. There is reason to think that this stakes out a truth for the United States at large "with the exception of Louisiana."

While plumbers and doctors and other professionals actively discourage recruits, it's common for trappers to welcome the lad who would like to do some fooling around with traps; for the trapper fears that this great tradition of his may well die out—so many things are against it in the modern world. It is a truism of the trapping trade that you nearly always have to interest a boy before he's eighteen or you never will. Beyond that age, he's apt to be overconcerned at the naked punishment he sees for trapped animals. He may not be able to handle philosophically—as just another hazard of the trade—the god-awful uproar that breaks out when somebody's dog or cat goes hobbling home on three legs and another kind of pursuit begins: a pursuit of the trapper himself.

A boy—well, a boy begins to feel that he is learning all sorts of magic. He spots muskrat dung on a log and feels a surge of joy—a good place for a trap.

A narrow place in a stream makes a fine place to put your mink trap—you put it underwater on the mink's swimming path and, naturally, once caught, that mink has to drown because he can't get air. And drowning, as the experienced trapper is apt to advise the novice, is one of the pleasantest of deaths, an easy way to go. Put a rock on either side of that submerged trap, advises the wily old coot who teaches these tricks, so the derned mink won't slam off around the trap 'stead of right into it.

Now, many a boy was not up to drowning minks for a living. He skedaddled right out of the trade again as he learned what was expected of him. But many did not.

Trapping remained an esoteric art, particularly to city dwellers, and questions of investing in quick-kill traps or the study of baits were very far removed from the life of the average citizen. But along came that critical campaign to stop the killing of some large, fur-bearing animals before the fur trade had driven them to extinction. And with this came a new and closer look at trapping.

The drowning of animals—a quick death, drowning—was so humane in comparison with what went on elsewhere in trapping that the trap that merely held its victim helpless underwater began to be treated at public hearings like "the good example"; trappers tried to prove that, as often as possible, they simply drowned their prey. The crushing and stomping of half-dead creatures who were taken on land and did *not* drown made for some really ugly descriptions, even though a trapper tried to explain how he could break an animal's back and take its life away all in a single, skillful, life-crunching kick.

To win any battle at all, the anticruelty faction had to concentrate. It began—in the late Sixties and early Seventies—to concentrate on the torturing violence of the steel-jaw leghold trap.

When API began to publish its famous "Grisly Death" advertisement—a ghastly view of a raccoon caught in one of those steel-jaw traps (see illustration, page 149)—the most outraged attacks on us came from those old woodsmen and boy trappers who continued to think of trapping not as a game of cruelty but as a game of wits.

For a game of wits, it held strange and grisly terrors—if you accept (as many trappers did not) that grisly terror is possible to animals like fox, raccoon, and skunk.

No human, for instance—not in any game of wits he's subjected to—has occasion to chew off his leg as a way of outsmarting his opponent. A man's leg is too thick and his teeth aren't sharp enough. But there are a good many animals with thinner legs and sharper teeth.

One of the first alternatives considered by the animal caught in a steel-jaw trap is self-amputation. Teeth flicker in the fur, teeth often broken against the steel of the trap. The amputation is accomplished in a frenzy of gnawing. Or—with too much shock setting in—the animal slides toward death while the amputation is only half-accomplished. If the leg does give way, the animal may hobble off, to die or to live.

If he lives, the same animal can be caught again. A trapper tells, in wonderment, of catching these three-leggers when they would fall into the same desperate predicament all over. And another trapper tells of one of the rarest of his catches: a beaver that was, by the time this final capture came about, "a one-legger,"—a beaver that had lost three legs to traps and at last died just before it became a basket case.

Who could stand to hear the true story of that beaver's bewildered and frantic effort to somehow hold out against the trapper who never relented, who never went away?

If you start young and develop a sense of triumph about anything caught in a trap, perhaps you don't worry unduly about making those animals for whom you protest your love into three-leggers, two-leggers, and one-leggers.

"My first season's catch (at age seven)," recalled a Canadian trapper, "consisted of one muskrat, two raccoons, and one mink's foot—the mink had long since left the scene when I arrived at the trap. However, a mink must have been on the end of that foot before I got there and I was just as pleased as I would have been with the whole mink. Needless to say, the foot was a treasured possession for a long time afterward."

In the trapping trade, they call it "a wring-off," the paw that's left behind when the crippled animal frees itself from a leghold trap. The trapper hates to see a wring-off but, encountering a three-legged animal in the wilds, he may have a glint of admiration for it—now *there* was a critter that knew how to fight!

The trapper finds himself living in a turned-around world where "sportsmanship" takes on a very odd quality. When he brings his furs in to sell them, he can hear some weird stories that wouldn't be told with the same crackle of laughter around most dinner tables.

"These two coon-hunters," begins a fur-buyer, "—well, these two coon-hunters were out one night after an ice storm. Crystals on the ground started cutting their dog's feet so bad he couldn't run anymore. They carried him to a farmhouse where they borrowed a wheelbarrow, put the dog in it and pushed him around all night in whichever direction he bayed."

Now a boy who sticks around with the trappers and the gruffer hunters until he begins to see something admirable in open suffering—and sometimes he does—well, that boy may decide it's gutsy and pioneersy to prowl the wilds ceaselessly for game. If he takes up trapping as trapping is routinely practiced, he's going to cause an almighty amount of pain as he goes about it. He will cause it, in large part, because he does not ask what an uncaught fox can do for the wilderness—he asks what the fox who is caught might do for *him*.

THE TRAPPERS: NOT ALWAYS WHAT YOU EXPECT

And the other trappers, the ones who are *not* young boys—who are they?

In Monson, Massachusetts, one of the notable local trappers turned out to be a schoolteacher named Mrs. Theresa Jurczyk, who, with her husband James, serviced a trap line of two-hundred traps, each of which had to be visited at least once a day according to Massachusetts law. The traps were spread out for twenty miles through the outlands of three different communities. The Jurczyks started trapping when they married. No leopards around Monson; but less than a year after the marriage, on a possibly representative day, their storehouse included twenty-four red fox, 140 muskrat, four beaver, six raccoon. Theresa rose every morning at 6 a.m. and hit the trap lines until it was time to go teach school.

Over at Rutland, North Dakota, three local trappers with an excellent catch in muskrat, fox, mink, and beaver, were women like Doris Holstad, Arlene Skogen, and Mrs. Marshall Taylor. They seemed to enjoy it, but at the same time trapping *does* give you mixed thoughts.

"Trapping is cruel, no doubt about it," said Doris. "One woman asked me if I just thought of the dollar signs. . . .Sure, the money is nice, especially at Christmastime. But it's the sport, too. It grows on you. It's being outside and it's animal control."

Said Arlene: "Trapping may be cruel but I know there gets to be too many of one animal if you don't trap them. There are a lot of cruel things in this world. Trappers were awfully hard on fox this year, however. I don't think I'll trap fox for awhile because of it."

And Mrs. Taylor said, "I don't think it is a humane thing to do, but I feel I was conscientious about checking traps often enough so they don't suffer."

Who *are* these people who trap?

Theresa Jursczyk of Monson and the somewhat apologetic women of Rutland are not all that atypical—for "the trapper" is not, for the most part, who you think he (or she) is. Most people would probably see Conie Raymond Humphrey as a more likely trailsmith in the trapping trade.

Out on the Papago Indian Reservation west of Tucson, Conie Humphrey wangled the permission of the Indians to trap off game. It's not hard to sell coyote skins these days. Since the fur merchants find no excessive shedding of tears for certain animals that are believed to be plentiful and have reputations as marauders, it was the coyote who received most of trapper Humphrey's attention.

The coyote, before it becomes entangled in Conie's snares, knows a single moment of glory. It twitches its nostrils, for adrift on the air comes the rank smell of something marvelous. The coyote begins to trot toward the source of this smell. If there's no warning, the coyote will soon be caught, by starlight, in a fierce instrument—an offset-jaw trap with drag chains—which is the true bane of coyotedom. Now, the coyote is clever—as clever as the Indians thought and far more clever than most humans can imagine—and Conie is aware that if he simply attached the trap to a stake, the coyote would figure it out and dig up the stake and lope away, oddly shackled, to nurse its wounds. The drag chains let it lope—but not far. They are designed to catch on rocks or the plants of the desert and hold a coyote and wear it down until Conie catches up.

Douglas J. Kreutz, the writer who caught up with Conie Humphrey out there on the Papago, discovered that the bait the trapper used to attract his prey is one of those professional secrets. But Kreutz did get a hint of what the magic potion is that sets the nostrils of the coyote aquiver. You start, Conie told him, with "rotting rattlesnake guts, aged dog urine, and commercial fish bait." Since few people care about the coyote, believing that if it really goes wild over rotting rattlesnake guts it deserves what it gets, Conie Humphrey finds it far easier to trap down here on the Papago, than at Willow Springs Ranch. He left Willow Springs Ranch because, he said, "Those animal lovers were stealing my traps. They stole the traps and left me a note that said, 'We've let your catch loose,' and then it said some obscene things about me. . . .I lost twenty traps up there. . . .Those traps cost $4.50 apiece from the government. It finally got so bad I left."

Peter Wild, a conservationist who lives in the same area, objects to the killing of coyotes on the ground that the practice upsets the balance of nature, but Conie—having no magic bait with which to finish off the exasperating environmentalists—calls Wild and all the rest of them "crazy" conservationists and lets it go at that.

Even Conie Humphrey worries, though, about what he sees as a bad trend. "There's a lot of fellows getting into the business," he says, "who don't know anything about trapping." But in his part of Arizona, at least, the environmentalists who jump on the traps and free the animals don't seem all that discouraging. As far as trappers go, he says, "There are ten times as many now as there were three or four years ago."

HOW THE TRAPPER JUSTIFIES HIS TRADE

Roy Johnson described himself as "just a country preacher" and he shouldn't have been so modest because there have been few country preachers like Roy Johnson. His sermons had a great originality. He managed to combine, as someone noted, "a sermon on salvation with directions for setting leghold traps."

For Roy Johnson was sure that he would have been no trapper at all if it hadn't been God's will. In his privately published work, *Trapline Ramblings*, he tells how he used to skin muskrat in the basement of the boys' dormitory at the Providence-Barrington Bible College in Rhode Island.

It was for love of God that he did this, and God's love came back to him in the form of great numbers of animals whisked into the traps Rev. Johnson set for them out there in the God-given wilds.

In a statement a bit different from what Billy Graham and other evangelists elicit from the reformed sinner, Roy Johnson declared, "I would like to acknowledge God as my partner on the trapline and in all of life. Some of the catches would never have been made without His wisdom, strength and help.

"I said, 'Lord, it is nothing with you to put a wolf in each trap the same night if it pleases you.' Sure enough, one morning there was a triple catch. The muskrat catch last spring was one of the largest in the area caught in a short time, with practically no Sunday trapping. Again, God must receive the glory. . . .But in all of life, whether on the trapline or otherwise, what could be more satisfying than to know that God is my partner?"

The impression could easily get about that trappers are different from other people, that they march to a different drummer—or, to put it more appropriately, they glide these days on snowmobiles to the snap of a different trap.

I readily concede the peculiar strength and hardiness of the trapper. Making his living in an elemental way and turning his furs over to some other folks who are not quite so elemental (John Jacob Astor was one of many Americans whose millions originated in the great stampede after furs), the trapper finds an elemental way to cope with the great questions of life and death he finds everywhere about him. To endure his life, the trapper needs a jaw set as forcefully as those traps he will spring upon his prey. Even with the coming of that snowmobile which makes it possible to tend traps over an area that may run through a hundred square miles of ice-covered streams and deep drifts of snow, the successful trapper needs sinews of steel just like the game he hunts.

Up in Ontario, a mere 120 miles from Thunder Bay (the nearest city) and on the shores of the Wawang Lake, Terry Kaliski and his wife, Margaret, a pair of twenty-three-year olds, found, in 1973, a life that closely approximated the life thousands of westward-moving Americans knew just about a hundred years ago. A log cabin was home and the forest their living. Rugged, yes. But 1973 proved to be a great year for them. Suddenly the red fox pelt-price, which interests the trapper in the same way a price-quote on General Motors stock interests the investor, soared to fifty dollars from the low a few years before of five dollars. The price of a lynx pelt doubled in a year and reached one-hundred dollars. Pierre Trudeau, the prime minister of Canada, did not let the cussing and feuding over the worldwide slaughter of furbearing animals interfere with his public relations work. Helpfully, he posed for photographs in an otterskin coat—and, whoops, otters were up to eighty dollars a pelt. All very nice for the Kaliskis.

Despite the eighty traps they tended in their one-hundred-mile area around the Wawang, trapping had been netting them only about two-thousand dollars a year until the great '73 upswing in prices. Even in the Canadian wilds, two-thousand dollars a year is nothing to get excited about, though there were American housewives who would envy the price the Kaliskis paid for meat. According to Margaret, the cost for one thousand pounds of moose meat was thirty-three cents—the cost of the cartridge that felled the moose.

The Kaliskis were apparently good shots. They certainly felt they had a good life. They lived in their log cabin on the Wawang, eating moose meat and feeling a thrill

Traps catch the wanted and the unwanted alike. An estimated seventy-five percent of trapped animals are "trash"—unwanted and unsought by trappers. UNITED PRESS INTERNATIONAL PHOTO.

when their Norwegian elkhound, Trygve, managed to chase another marten up a tree (Margaret could easily finish the marten off with a bullet).

Like twenty-five thousand other Canadian trappers, they were well removed from the horrible commotion of the cities. Little to trouble them; very little at all except (and it must have seemed rather unbelievable to the moose-eating Kaliskis) the far-off battling over traps and the ethics of trapping. This was the single fly in their ointment.

As far off as it was, the trapping battle plagued them and they worried about it. When you're riding an eighteen-hundred dollar snowmobile and you've worked traps for three and one-half years while waiting to see the market suddenly soar so you can finally make more than two-thousand dollars in a season, a verbal battle in the cities that threatens to interfere with that livelihood is certainly a punch in the groin.

Canadians actually had little to fear compared to the trapper in the United States, because it was far harder to make the case that the supply of animals is limited in the Canadian wilds than to demonstrate in a fast-growing Florida that very few animals can adapt to the highrise.

That the trapping controversy had percolated even to the Canadian backwoods was a sign, I suppose, of the overwhelming ardor with which this particular issue has been discussed wherever raised. The trapping fight is different from the porpoise fight, and the whale fight, and the grizzly fight, and the fight for the Rocky Mountain bighorn and the wild horse. No one who kills the porpoise puts himself forward as noble. No one who has shot or poisoned the grizzly, on grounds that it is a killer of coeds and a threat to the territory, has been full of apologies.

The trapper who joined in what swiftly became the most monumental of all the great animal debates was doing a ricochet between these two extremes. He wanted to argue not just the utility but the nobleness of what he was doing—ridding the world of chicken stealers, keeping the animal world in balance—and he also wanted to establish that a backbreaking stomp on a quivering, caught animal was—well, maybe not a nice thing to contemplate—maybe a kind of frightening act if you looked at it in the abstract—necessary, though—my God, is a woman supposed to shiver through the winter because she can no longer buy a fur coat?—oh, a terrible thing in its way and yet look at the skill it took for a trapper to dispatch the animal with one perfectly aimed stomp!—imagine, if you could, the benefits that had accrued to civilization because a shrewd old trapper out in the wilds had learned to lure the crafty coyote with his splendid secret bait-formula concocted out of rattlesnake guts and dog urine!—what city-bred fella, drinking his secret-formula Coca-Colas and basking through the morning coffee break, could possibly appreciate the paradoxical *rightness* of that grand system by which God both giveth and taketh away from man and beast alike—way out there on the trapline!

The trapper could chase himself in mystical circles, trying to explain this to the outsider or even to himself; and when the Animal Protection Institute began its campaign not to eliminate trapping altogether but to lower the level of cruelty by eliminating certain kinds of traps, we received a reaction—from both sides of the controversy—that can only be described as awesome.

Thomas Timken, a trapper of Boulder, Montana, was one of those who had been in an almighty wrestle for much of his life to understand the paradoxes of trapping. And this is what he wrote to us:

"Let me say that your basic idea that trapping is cruel happens to be true. I, too, have felt sickened, seeing an animal writhing in pain in one of my sets.

"Then why do I trap?

"Believe it or not, it's because I have a great love for wildlife. . . .It is possible to watch animals suffer and yet love them at the same time. The Indians did it for thousands of years. They killed more wildlife in one year than a modern man will kill in the next century. They killed countless numbers of animals and oftentimes in a cruel manner, but they never did any harm at all.

"Why?

"They killed the animal, not the habitat.

"Death isn't so bad — it's great. For every life, there must be a death. And this death in a natural way isn't as pure as one might expect — it involves predation, starvation, disease, or a combination of all three — and believe me is seldom painless.

"So Nature is cruel? Yes. And the trapper is cruel? You're right.

"The trapper is the predator, making a part of his living in a barbaric, adventuresome sport where his wits are matched against instincts of wild animals. He enjoys the thrills in Nature, whether it be a footprint in the sand, a glimpse of a buck, or the sight of an animal in his trap — [a sight] that will bring a little money, enough to make this adventure possible. The trapper rarely hurts an animal population. You can trap an area only so long, until it is not profitable — and you wait until next year when the population will be back to its normal level. Unless the fools have done it again with progress — stamped all over the area.

"I used to trap this swamp where I always caught around one-hundred muskrat and three or four mink per year. Then, one year, the owner of the swamp drained it and filled it in. There will *never be* another muskrat, duck, fish, or hundreds of other organisms that used to live there and nobody cared about that old swamp — except me, a trapper.

"Nobody looks upon a new house or a planted field as being cruel to wildlife, and yet they are the reason for the destruction of a vast and rich wildlife area. . . .

"I admit there are trappers who might fit your description but every time I see a new housing development, a four-lane highway, a channeled river, a wife with ten kids, I can see clearly where the cruelty lies. The problem is that few people can see it."

Thomas Timken, torn in two directions by an obvious love of the wilds and a confirmed belief that the avoidance of cruelty is not possible (one of the attitudes that makes cruelty so hard to erase), represents an important link that has in some measure determined what we are as a country. He represents the trapper and the trapping defender at their best. As the campaign against the steel-jaw trap proceeded and was embodied in a federal bill (still not passed), we heard from hundreds who represented the snarling worst.

Didn't API know that "animals do not suffer" and have no God-given soul and therefore, for all their writhing around in apparent pain, are not "suffering" in the human sense at all?

Didn't we see that rabies would enter the cities like a scourge the moment the trapper let up for a moment?

Didn't we have the practical sense to realize that those animals caught in traps weren't pained, just "peacefully sleeping" while waiting for the trapper?

How un-American, how communist, how money-grubbing, how dirty-dog, sneaky, snaky, vile, rotten, lowdown, pitiful were we, anyway?

His buried sense of guilt made the trapper screech like — well, like someone trapped. It was becoming clear enough, even in the midst of a million hurled charges, that the trapper could not forever retain the right to cause cruelty unending to any living creature that happened to prowl his trapline.

Congress has not been courageous in dealing with the issue. It has not been quick. Yet, sooner or later the old, bad ways must end. The trapper sees Doomsday; the Doomsday being that day when he will have to invest in a somewhat kinder trap.

A bill against the wilder excesses and the more moronic manifestations of torture-in-trapping will assuredly, some day, become the law.

In their desperation the trapping defenders began to fill the mails with scarifying leaflets. Western civilization, it seemed, was going to fall on its face if the trapper had to give up his God-given right to torture and maim without accountability.

The domino theory, as applied to the American outdoors and the insidious plans of the Animal Protection Institute and other devil-inspired groups, held that if we were successful in stopping the heedless use of traps, soon we would ban trapping and animal killing in all its forms.

"Are you AWARE that there are certain organizations working actively to eliminate first TRAPPING, then HUNTING, and then FISHING?"

—and *then:*

"Food prices will accelerate because of loss of crops by raids of coon, skunk, opossum, fox, etc. . . .Bird life will be endangered by increased numbers of predators. . . .Farm revenue will decrease so overall taxes will increase as a result. . . .Revenue from fur pelts will be eliminated—again a raise in TAXES. . . . Young men who depend on cash from trapping will have NO pocket money and those who depend on this revenue for college will be SHUT OUT of higher-education. . . .Small gardens (even in large cities) will be raided by coon and opossum. . . .What will happen to the legacy due our children if they have no incentive to trap, hunt, fish, and get exposure to nature?. . . .Why don't these do-gooders try to help solve some of today's dangers—dope, crime, dishonesty? Surely the young people are worth saving?"

Taking a lofty view of all this from an editorial perch in *Game News,* a gentleman named Bob Bell made history of sorts when he lashed out with an essay called, "Bambi Must Die" (and really meant it).

"If there ever was a bigger problem in wildlife management than dealing with the 'Bambi syndrome'—that emotional situation created by movies which make appealing near-humans out of animated cartoon animals—I haven't heard of it," he said.

In Bell's opinion, Americans had been subjected to an "effective, if unintentional, brainwashing by Walt Disney" and were now cluttering up the entire field of wildlife management with their sentimentalizing.

". . .With the movement to urban life over the last several decades, most Americans lost contact with reality, insofar as animals go, and the 'facts' that now clutter their thinking grew out of the nonsense of Bambi. As a result, today's wildlife managers, professionally trained biologists with several university degrees and years of personal experience for the most part, often find it an impossible task to implement valid programs for this country's game, simply because of the Bambi-imprint on countless minds. . . ."

He was not writing about the trapping quarrel but he might as well have been. He was right in the sense that there *is* a Bambi syndrome abroad in the world: there's a great strike force of people who believe (they would not agree that they believe foolishly) that the Bambis of the animal world, and the Bambi mothers and Bambi fathers, and tens of thousands of animals that cannot be confused with Bambi and needn't be, have been given short shrift by humans—and that it has to stop.

Groups that have organized for action in this field are far from preventing "wildlife management." Mostly, they cry aloud for it. But where "management" means managing all the humans in and all the animals out—as it often does—they draw a line. They try, at the least, to force a discussion. It is amazing how many wildlife managers have *not* been brainwashed by Walt Disney and instead act like the loco giants out of Popeye who just want to hammer down anything that yelps.

When it comes to the "management" of trapping, what API and a good many organizations have been working toward is simply a new set of rules that requires the trapper to move on, and away from, a trap that was invented in 1820, hasn't been seriously improved since, frequently maims, tortures to no purpose, and has a year-in, year-out record — by authoritative, and not just sensationalistic, estimate — of catching three unwanted animals or birds for every wanted animal the trapper actually has an interest in.

Traps that kill instantaneously, traps that harbor animals without injuring them, traps that drown: all of these do cause Bambi-people to wince or to worry. But they do not lift them to the same level of outrage as the unconscionable steel-jaw trap that, as it happens, is the norm for American trapping.

Without doubt, animals need a Trapping Bill of Rights to protect them from the very miscellaneousness of Man's attack — an attack so indiscriminate that you can go for beaver and end up with bald eagle — but the first plank of that Bill of Rights would at least have to be: Freedom Forever From the Steel-Jaw Leghold No-Surcease No-Safety-Factor Trap.

HOLDING A LAST FRONTIER

One of the first "ecologists," at a time when that word hadn't been invented, was the western artist Charlie Russell. Russell's crusade was to save things. He couldn't save them in fact so he tried to save them on canvas. A cattle skull was his signature and the whole Wild West his range. Nobody has ever regretted more than he did that the Wild West got tamed.

Charlie Russell rose to his feet one night at a meeting of Montana boosters and said something that couldn't have hurt his listners worse if he had been an Indian filling their chests with arrows. He tried to tell these pioneers what, in their boosterism, they were doing.

"In my book," Charlie Russell said, "a pioneer is a man who comes to a virgin country, traps off all the fur, kills off all the wild meat, cuts down all the trees, grazes off all the grass, plows the roots up, and strings ten million miles of bob wire. A pioneer destroys things and calls it civilization. I wish to God that this country was just like it was when I first saw it, and that none of you folks were here at all."

We already know, by the letter from Thomas Timken quoted previously, that there exists a type of trapper who sees himself as the last apostle of the wilderness. He is partly wrong — that position is bought at a cost of too much cruelty — but he is partly right. He feels a tremendous moral superiority to the real estate developer who does not torture *some* of the game *some* of the time; but drives out *all* of the game *all* of the time.

And who can argue with this? Certainly Thomas Timken is right about being one of the few who would shed a tear over an "old swamp." There are trappers who are closer to the position of Charlie Russell than the conservation-spouting "city planner" whose plans are so all-encompassing that few self-respecting squirrels, let alone a raccoon or a fox, could ever find cover and sustenance within those beautifully kempt "greenbelt areas" that give us the pretensions of an American wilds — with no wilds left.

All this can be said in agreement, for destruction of habitat, for man and beast alike, has been the twentieth-century specialty.

But the Timken position is only a part of the story. The trapper cannot get off clean. He cannot say he alone cares about Nature — and find a rationale for cruelty out of the folklore of the American Indian. This, too, is a dodge. When the trapper is finally able to look beyond his own swamp, his own snowy stream, and begin to

45

take a personal responsibility for *saving* animals and not catching them — only then does he become a genuine stalwart in America's struggles to keep some final hold on her last frontiers.

3

Is a Porpoise a Tree or a Person?
A Congressional Dilemma

"I guess the question is," said Congressman Robert Leggett, "are porpoises like trees or like people and what you are saying is that they are more like trees."

Surrealism, stark and raving, had entered the committee room.

The Great Porpoise Debate, which started almost unnoticed in the Sixties but reached a moment of high emergency in 1976, proceeded for a number of years in an atmosphere of surrealism no different than that which must have prevailed in the era of the Inquisition.

It was porpoises,* not humans, true enough, who were on the block. But the arguments and the rationale of the Inquisitors were much the same.

In May 1976, at a hearing convened like a whirlwind because it appeared the cause of the porpoise had at last been vindicated, television talk-show host Dick Cavett came into the committee room where Leggett (at that time a prime obstacle to porpoise freedom) was seeking to frustrate an order from U.S. District Court. Even Cavett became mired in the legalistics that had been used to defend the porpoise-slayers.

This gracefully acidic moderator of the talk shows, whose mind is lightning and whose touch is deft when he exposes the pooh-bahs on TV, had a rough time trying to stick up for the porpoise with legislators who leave loopholes for slaughter by solemnly declaring in the law that killing of porpoises must not go beyond "optimum sustainable population level." These words were the politician's sly way of giving tuna fishermen the right to make a big kill. The murder of the porpoise is arranged, sanctified — made scientific-sounding — by the very words that would seem to mean the killing should stop.

Cavett tried.

Cavett called "optimum sustainable population level" a phrase "so vague as to be virtually meaningless and unenforceable."

It wasn't meaningless to tuna fishermen. They felt that as long as they could get government analysts to agree that the porpoise was somehow surviving (surviving in spite of everything) they could kill at will. As they had been doing. To make the tuna fishing easier.

---

*The "porpoises" referred to are actually dolphins. Both species belong to the family Delphinidae, which is, however, divided into beaked (dolphin) and beakless (porpoise) genera. Fishermen, West Coast scientists, and government officials designate both dolphins and porpoises by the latter term.

Government analysts weren't about to inform the tuna fishermen they were committing a crime against the "optimum sustainable population level" and couldn't kill even one more porpoise. Government analysts had a long record of running to the aid of tuna fishermen whenever there was a chance public indignation over porpoise killing might actually cause the slayers—who comprised ten percent of the United States tuna fleet—to cease their slaying.

There's a reason congressmen get the kind of figures they do from government scientists. When a question of justice is involved, they lean heavily on analysts of the Commerce Department to tell them what justice is.

All this, of course, might seem just another ironic example of politicians being politicians if the Great Porpoise Debate hadn't actually operated to permit the continuation of a historic massacre that may one day be recognized as a chapter of American history as sorrowful as Wounded Knee.

HOW TO KILL 728 PORPOISES AT A SWOOP

The newspaper reader and television viewer were aware of the porpoise debate—but only in a limited way. The violence, the great endless depths of violence glimpsed from the decks of the tuna boats, somehow could not be encompassed in a sentence or two on the evening news.

For stark terror, for a chilling portrait of modern man at work, nothing rivals those incredible log-notes, made by official observers, on the acts of the tuna fishermen who used the friendly, frivolous porpoise to lead them to the tuna and often, then, rewarded the porpoise by causing his death in the process of netting the tuna schools.

Few Americans, few congressmen, could clearly picture the mass-massacre circumstances of this giant porpoise-kill. The net becomes a death trap when conditions are wrong or judgment goes awry. Often it is not the death-trap of a single panicky porpoise—or two porpoises—or even three. No, at times:

"Seven hundred and twenty-eight porpoise killed," states an entry from the log of a tuna boat. "Porpoise set more than I ever thought possible. About one mile long by one-half mile—solid. . . .Now that they are caught, it looks unreal. Where do they come from? They almost fill up the net completely. Skipper says at least 150 tons of tuna. . . .Wind is gusty at twenty knots. . . .It's getting rough and a frightening rip current. *The rip current is making this set a disaster.* . . .Backdown got a lot out but still a lot left. Rescuers could get to very few porpoise."

Another day, another tuna boat: "Sixty-four porpoises killed. . . .The primary cause of mortality was definitely the extremely strong current. The net collapsed and many porpoise were trapped in big canopies. We killed eleven alive in net."

Another. "One hundred and twenty-three porpoise killed. . . .The usual panicking after dark coupled with poor visibility and sharks contributed to large mortality. About fifty porpoise were alive in the net after backdown."

It's not likely that the most terrible of these incidents came to light at all. The National Marine Fisheries Service discovered (it seemed a bit surprised) that its observers were as welcome on the tuna boats as spiders at a wedding. At one time NMFS trained a group of observers but then could find no skippers willing to have them aboard, even though the law gave the agency power to put the observers aboard against the captain's will. The Service decided not to force the issue. In the background of one of the congressional discussions a fisherman muttered that the government "might get observers aboard the boats but they won't be coming back." When NMFS did ride out on some tuna boats—by chartering them and then recording what the fishing was like (on days fishermen knew they were being observed)—it discovered that each time the giant nets were set, an average of 51.9 porpoise were killed. That makes many a log entry ("thirteen porpoise killed. . . .strong current caused net to collapse and fold, trapped them under corks—some young got tired and just stopped swimming") seem like lucky days indeed.

How was it possible that every time a tuna boat cast a net, over fifty porpoises were likely to die?

Some of the log entries make it clearer. "School size before set: 8,000. . . .Porpoise captured: 5,333. . . .sixty-eight porpoises killed." Or: "School size before set: 4,000. . . .Porpoise captured: 4,000. . . .133 porpoise killed. . . .They were packed like sardines."

How realistic, how *typical*, were these reports made by the official observers on cruises where the captains must have been a bit more cautious about porpoise kills? Alix Jay, a young fisherman who worked on the tuna boats and came to regret it, went through a thick stack, several feet high, of reports on tuna fishing and picked out those which he said struck him as "typical of my own experiences as a tuna fisherman." And they went like this:

"Caught school of 3,000, too big for net that size. . . .505 mortalities. . . .Same school as yesterday—doesn't look as big. About 2,000 porpoises in net. . .326 mortalities."

And from various cruises: "Seven hundred and seventy dead: snouts caught trying to get out." Or: "Too many animals for a net that size; crowding was main problem. Porpoises panicked and ran into net. 505 dead." Or: "The porpoises weren't leaving, which led the captain to wish them to perdition, whereupon he ordered the crew into the net. Five minutes later he ordered them out again. 'We're wasting time.' Some unusual things I noticed were: a porpoise circled a dead porpoise for about five minutes. . . ." Or: "Mother got left pectoral caught in net on one of her dives. Baby son kept diving down with no rest until exhausted and drowned." Or: "Disaster due to rollup: 509 dead."

And all this, said Alix Jay, did not represent the worst cases. All this was simply typical. All in a day's fishing. Mostly, the reports were briskly factual, no exclamations, just the stark facts—and it was the starkness of those facts that spoke so loudly. Here and there, one of those reports on the porpoise-kill dwelt for a moment on how the kill had actually gone, moment to moment. Here is another report that Alix Jay could describe not as a worst case but as simply typical:

"Net collapsed in two places, trapping all porpoises and rolling them in net. Much blood and nine minutes later, we end, hauling net. A few porpoises still alive. Begin sacking up. Fourteen minutes later, some porpoises still alive, though I have watched them struggling for over twenty minutes. They have an amazing ability to grab just a breath of air and then remain submerged for one, two or three minutes. . . .Ten minutes later: still porpoises breathing. Final count: 187 caught, 124 dead. Hauling in of net is slow because of a pocket of dead porpoises next to the boat, which is entangled in the webbing. Much blood in water."

Even in this last extremity of their lives, up until that moment when the crush and the terror finally bested them, the porpoises remained the dextrous creatures Americans are familiar with from seeing them in marinelands and seaquariums. "I'm amazed," one observer took time to jot down during the heat of the massacres, "that even when trapped the porpoises swim in twos, threes, and fours as though synchronized as a ballet team, slowly and gracefully arching in and out of the water."

ABANDONING A CONCENTRATION CAMP

Congressmen, of course, did not have the advantage of knowing what the porpoise went through in these nightmare nettings. No congressman had suffocated before finding an escape route from a giant net that nothing in his experience had taught him to cope with. No congressman had been returned to the wild ocean, his body maimed, a fin cut, blood pouring from him, to be attacked by sharks.

By never focusing on the actualities of the terror, government agencies as well as the congressmen in touch with their activities felt justified in letting the tuna fishermen be granted a two-year exemption from the terms of the Marine Mammal Protection Act (passed in 1972) and further evade the Act's provisions for an additional two years.

The congressmen most directly involved were members of the House Subcommittee on Fisheries and Wildlife Conservation and the Environment. The name may sound benign, but it was right here that the hot-rodding effort originated all over again, in 1976, to overthrow a court order and once again let the tuna fishermen kill, kill, kill the friendly porpoise.

Listening to Walter Cronkite, Mr. and Mrs. America squirmed. A porpoise suffocates. Ah. Sad. But dimly and quickly—for the newscast rushed on to trouble in Rhodesia—the porpoise-loving but not very involved television viewer could have no accurate picture of the compounded horror represented in the figures he or she was hearing. Was it really possible over one-hundred thousand porpoises a year were still being killed? And before that, two-hundred thousand? And before that, three-hundred thousand? Good lord, how sad. But things were, at least, getting better. Weren't they?

Not necessarily. The government's figures on the kill-rate of the three vulnerable species—spotted, spinner, and whitebelly porpoises—were 313,000 in 1970, 197,000 in 1971; but the decline in this massacre to "insignificant levels approaching zero," the goal which Congress itself set, did not come about.

1974 was the year when *zero* was going to be just about right—when tuna fishermen would have adjusted their fishing techniques to allow porpoises to live. Whole flanks of government bureaucrats had done wondrous headstands on behalf of the tuna fishermen, always interpreting figures that were shocking in the extreme to mean that the fishermen should have more time. Yes, more time. . .and there was scarcely an expert in the whole fabric of the government's protection system who would interpret those figures to mean what many of us clearly knew: time was running out for the porpoise.

Senator Bob Packwood, the Oregon Republican, came before the subcommittee to expostulate with it when Zero Massacre year 1974 actually resulted in a tremendous upward leap in the porpoise-kills.

"The National Marine Fisheries Service allowed an extension for the compliance with Congress' goal, and what happened?" asked Packwood. "Between 1974 and 1975, the total kills climbed from 98,700 to a totally unacceptable level of 134,000. This was all allowed in the midst of the National Marine Fisheries' own statements that it did not know if this high degree of killing would allow the porpoise population to remain healthy and survive severe depletion which might threaten its very survival."

But what American in his right mind believes that the extinction of the porpoise could be accomplished almost in front of the eyes of Congress and the government and not be stopped? It sounded preposterous. America loves animals—and loves porpoises more than nearly any other. If the last century had tales of Paul Bunyan and his Blue Ox, the modern folk-tale was at its most fabulous in the sprightly undulations of Flipper, the porpoise star as much beloved in Japan and Europe as in the United States.

We have an image of ourselves as: a nation that cuddles soft furry animals—and

A purse seine net has entrapped both tuna and dolphins. The net starts to collapse due to a mechanical malfunction. The dolphin herd is alarmed and begins to panic.

The collapsed net is reshaped to give the animals still alive a few moments of free swimming, but they, too, eventually die because of the incompetence of the boat captain in handling this set.

Dead dolphins are removed from the net. White objects in the background are dead dolphins floating belly up.

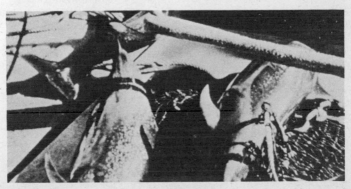

Dolphins not yet tossed back into the ocean lay on the boat's deck. This set wiped out an entire dolphin herd—900 to 1,500 animals. PHOTOS COURTESY SAVE THE DOLPHINS.

exults alongside the loping flanks of a hunting dog—and is stunned by the majesty of the lion, the elephant, the gorilla. Certainly we are amused—amused and touched—by the charming, brilliant porpoise.

It was said of Ivan Tors, the filmmaker and television producer whose stars included a bear named Gentle Ben as well as the world-famous Flipper, that when he stepped on a set he would always shake hands with his animal stars before he did with his actors because he "knew the animals better than he did the actors." In the 1960s, the porpoise-kill was actually headed for its zenith while "Flipper" was warming hearts by the tens of millions. Most people were unaware of massacre on the high seas and not all that interested in learning that, while a porpoise's natural life span may be twenty-five years, the porpoises taken into captivity and made into performers had a life expectancy, some investigators thought, of two years.

The porpoise, agile and strong enough to overpower a shark, had a buoyant cheerfulness and a gentleness toward humans that made it an alter ego for America itself. Many Americans deferred to it, claiming its brain size meant it might in some ways be more brilliant and developed than ourselves. Did the porpoise not embody many of those traits which we most admire? The sounds of noblesse oblige were, in the "Flipper" era, all around us. And this was, and is, an era of dark and troubled night for the porpoise—never, in a long history, has the porpoise been so plagued by humans as right now.

Only here and there did someone seem to sense what the ocean mammal was actually up against.

"Understanding the dolphin," wrote United Kingdom researcher Farooq Hussain, "proved to be far harder than anyone expected, and research has passed from those with broad interests and a love of animals to scientists with narrow interests and U.S. military money."

The wildest of the rumors eventually unleashed—that the United States was training kamikaze dolphins to blow up ships (acts that would also blow up the dolphins)—may have been untrue, but it was all the easier to believe since tuna fishermen readily sacrificed dolphins by the hundreds of thousands in order to achieve something far more tenuous than a battle victory. Would an official establishment that countenanced the sacrifice of hundreds of thousands of porpoises for a minor bump-up in the tuna harvest shrink from *any* use of porpoises for any goal at all? Not likely.

The general mindlessness of being affectionate but vague toward the porpoise, when not only its life but its life structure as a social animal was in dire peril, was eventually highlighted by a single dramatic act on the part of the man believed by his countrymen to know more about the porpoise than anyone else.

Dr. John Lilly, a neurophysiologist, pioneered an attempt to communicate with the dolphin. He became enchanted with subtleties he discovered in the nature of his captives. But he discovered that even researchers who cherished the dolphin were doing it wrong. "Conditioning" them with "rewards" for "doing tricks" had the net result, he thought, of making them "brainwashed and neurotic." He concluded that dolphins had the power to commit suicide—and were doing so, occasionally in groups, to end the pain of living in a restricted environment for exhibition or as the subjects of scientific studies. When Dr. Lilly, the most celebrated dolphin researcher of modern times, announced the abrupt cessation of his studies, he bleakly told the world: "I was running a concentration camp for my friends."

CONFUSION ON CAPITOL HILL

The Great Porpoise Debate, as actually waged in the hearing rooms of Congress, explained a great deal about the government approach to starting, passing—and then failing to enforce—animal legislation designed to correct historic abuses. Certainly the porpoise debate had a significance that goes well beyond even the major topic of porpoise survival. It's likely that only *Gulliver's Travels*, a lampoon of official bullying and buffoonery in the time of Jonathan Swift, offers such strange examples of officialdom deliberately enveloping itself in a deep fog.

Once you are into the problem of defining a porpoise as a tree or a person, there's trouble. Now and again, though, the fog lifted in those hearings. Christine Stevens, secretary of the Society for Animal Protective Legislation, related a personal experience recorded by an official government observer on a tuna boat.

" 'I went out there,' " she read from the observer's notes, " 'believing that the fishermen would do anything, even risk their life, to save porpoises. This was a complete fallacy on my part. First of all, there was only one rescue—.' "

Congressman Leggett, who knows how to interrupt an effective story before people start to get mushy, blurted, "What is the date of this document?" But Christine told her story, regardless.

"Secondly, the rescuer did not—he not only did not risk his life for the porpoise, he did very little to help them at all and I was surprised and a bit shocked when I saw him using a big gaff which he used throughout the entire trip to remove live porpoises from the background area [of the net]. Also, the net tender in this boat stayed tied to the back, not going to help porpoises until backdown was almost completed."

August Felando, general manager of the American Tuna Boat Association, chimed in immediately with the good news about gaffs. This was scarcely a gaff at all, it seemed.

"Captain Scafidi is here," said Mr. Felando, "and he has developed what we call now 'Scafidi Porpoise Grabber' and the gaff that we are talking about is used. . . generally speaking. . .like a crook, a sheep herder's crook, to assist the man in getting the porpoise out of the corkline. The porpoise-grabber that Mr. Scafidi has developed now is sort of a telescope-type handle that can reach in and get the porpoises that are not near the corkline to get them out. . . .We do not know what happened on that set; that might have been a perfectly good set. Maybe all the porpoises got out and back out. We do not know anything about it but just to illustrate the point, taking the use of the word 'gaff' by this observer and it is a different meaning in the tuna industry of that word—."

Christine objected that if the gaff or crook caused bleeding, and if the bleeding porpoise then attracted a shark, the porpoise would not consider himself rescued.

"I would not dispute that," said Mr. Felando, revealingly. "Sometimes if you do not push it right, you can cause an accident to the porpoise. But basically the device is used to assist the man rescuing porpoises."

Congressman Leggett had not been chairman of the Subcommittee on Fisheries and Wildlife Conservation and the Environment when it had considered the proposal eventually passed as the Marine Mammal Protection Act; but now he was in the driver's seat, trying to steamroll a bill he himself wrote with the main objective of letting the porpoise-kill go on in spite of the court ruling that four years' noncompliance was noncompliance enough.

"The reopening of the debate," said an API statement I issued, "demonstrates the full tragedy of not having an informed, ardent conservationist at the head of a subcommittee concerned with animal protection and environment protection." Dick Cavett put it differently for the benefit of politicians, who are supposedly tuned in to issues on which the voter takes a strong stand. "Based upon my personal discussions and the avalanche of mail that I receive every time I discuss the subject on television," said Cavett, "a significant segment of the public wants the porpoise saved, even at the cost of a few cents more per can of tuna-fish."

Confusing and delirious as they can be, the deliberations that attended the decisions on marine mammals' safety are deeply revealing. From an animal protectionist's standpoint, the following conversation thrashing out the respective merits of saving the seals and saving the porpoises — or letting them both go hang — raises pangs of many different kinds.*

Main participants here are Leggett and Carmen Blondin, assistant director of International Fisheries of the National Marine Fisheries Service. Leggett is pulling out information showing that the government needn't go all soft inside at the sound of the word *porpoise* because, after all, it has a long-term agreement with other nations under which fur seals of the Pribilof Islands are clubbed to death by United States government contract.

MR. LEGGETT: How many times do they [the fur seals of the Pribilofs] have to be hit in order to kill them?

MR. BLONDIN: If it is done properly, only once to stun them, followed immediately by severing the heart arteries. . . .

MR. LEGGETT: How do we get so excited about indicting South Africans for clubbing seals if we are engaged in a program when the United States is the biggest clubber of them all?

MR. BLONDIN: I think it is the technique.

MR. LEGGETT: The technique?

Now Blondin is assisted a bit by Robert Schoning, director of the National Marine Fisheries Service.

MR. SCHONING: . . .One of the recommendations was to bring trained Aleut clubbers to South Africa to teach the South Africans how to use the same type of club and procedure. It is my understanding that two Aleuts went there and showed the people how to do it. . . .As Mr. Blondin mentioned, the Aleuts in the Pribilof program have the greatest amount of killing but they do it with great skill.

MR. LEGGETT: That is terrific. Let me ask you this: Why do we get so excited about the taking of 80,000 or 90,000 porpoises as incident [to] taking food when we are party to international agreements that envision the taking of perhaps at least that many other kinds of mammals, to wit seals? The seals seem to be rather intelligent animals, balancing balls on their noses and things like that. . . .Why do not the environmental organizations come apart at the seams over the Pribilof Island and South African fur seal programs?**

MR. SCHONING: I do not mean to speak for the environmental community and I will not.

MR. LEGGETT: I am glad.

If Leggett sounds as though he's wandering aimlessly as he extracts these bizarre reflections on the virtues of killing the seal with a single blow of a club, he's not. Soon enough, he has Schoning informing him, "In scientific communities, conserve is defined as wise use of the resource. That is interpreted as meaning that you should take the harvestable surplus of a resource as long as you maintain it at the maximum level."

*The quoted passage is from "Hearings Before the Subcommittee on Fisheries and Wildlife Conservation and the Environment," October 21, 29, 30, December 9, 1975, U.S. Government Printing Office.
**It should be noted that humane groups worked hard to keep the pelts from South African seals out of the United States.

Animal protectionists know that it's possible for a species to outgrow its habitat. Deer do this and if the numbers grow unchecked, starvation may suddenly overtake a great proportion of a deer population. But the assertion that "conserving" means "wise use" (i.e., killing and selling) is a wonderful all-purpose defense for killing *any* kind of animal in *any* kind of numbers at *any* time. "War *is* peace" was the national slogan in George Orwell's book *1984*; similarly, nearly everyone killing large numbers of a particular animal would love to gain acceptance for the notion that "killing *is* conserving."

In the case of the seals of the Pribilofs, an agreement was made to let the United States kill off bachelor seals by clubbing on two Pribilof Islands (now they only do it on one) and those nations which had been shooting babies and nursing mothers as well as Pribilof males of all description would cease to shoot these same seals on the high seas where shooting can't be confined to the bachelors. This was (arguably, at least) an early attempt at environmental control on behalf of seals — and on behalf of the Pribilof islanders, who allegedly would be welfare cases for the United States government if there were no summer seal-kill. The first agreements go back to 1911 when it was believed the seals might be destroyed if killing on the high seas were not stopped. John Twiss, executive director of the Marine Mammal Commission, says the seal population has recovered from a low of two-hundred thousand in 1911 to a million and a half at present.

It was assuredly wise of the United States, in 1911 and after, to hold down the unrestricted killing of the Pribilof seals. The pelts of these bad-luck bachelors of the Pribilofs — seals who can't find even one lady while some of the bulls have as many as a hundred — wind up on the backs of fashionable ladies who read the ads in the top women's magazines and are unwilling to give up furs. There have been factors behind the Pribilof kill that were not strictly seal-altruism gestures by the government. Every skin goes to the Fouke Fur Company of South Carolina, possessor of a renowned "secret process" in making the pelts a lush luxury item. The original agreements are believed to owe a great deal to the founder of the company.

The old argument was that catastrophic killing on the high seas would result if the United States now begged out of sending a portion of the pelts to Canada and Japan (their reward for holding off the seahunt), but there is no reason to think the Japanese or Canadians or Russians would jump in to punish our country for suddenly ceasing the kill of the bachelor seal along with the others.

Russia, though it endangers the whale by disregarding international quotas, has been a model of good deportment toward the porpoise. It banned the killing of porpoises outright when the United States could not bring itself to do so. Canada faces angry millions trying to force a complete clamp-down on traffic in white furry baby seals — it hardly wants a new argument about nursing mama seals being killed at sea. Japan is unlikely to see the loss of a minor percentage of thirty-thousand pelts as a reason for reinstituting a long-dead sea roundup of elusive seals.

No harm would come from ending the Pribilof seal kill. And while that government-arranged clubbing goes on, it offers a backdoor approach to wrecking the provisions of the Marine Mammal Protection Act.

The Pribilof seal-kill — thanks to extensive lobbying by the sealskin processors — was the major exception to the Act. Leggett could see that here might be the wedge to assert a justification for the killing of porpoises, too. Hadn't the seal population grown enormously while the government killed and killed?

But it is a false analogy in all directions. The Pribilof seals are killed deliberately, by sex and age; the livers are consumed locally, the sex organs are sold in the Orient, the body of the animal is sometimes eaten by natives but usually becomes food for minks. Given all that, the killing does not constitute one of the great humanitarian efforts of our time—and humane groups have ceaselessly tried to end it—but it is nothing like what happens to the dolphin.

Christine Stevens told Leggett and fellow committee members: "The suffering undergone by the dolphins is enormously greater in both intensity and extent than that undergone by the Pribilof seals. The harassment alone, even for those who escape with their lives, is cruel, and this harassment involves repeated sets on the same animals. . . .None of the kill is quick, never is it done with as little suffering as a single blow to render an animal unconscious. And when dolphins are injured and half-killed, they are tossed overboard, not even humanely dispatched, when there is no hope for them!

The great porpoise kill was not an ages-old practice. It dated from the 1960s and existed as a strictly modern threat to a species that was never in any danger of vanishing until the tuna boats put tens of millions of dollars into a technology that not only made the old pole-and-line fishermen feel underprivileged but made porpoises into the slaves and victims of a system that is large, moneyed, and ruthless. Around the world, most tuna were *still* taken on pole and line. It was the United States, where the tuna fishermen believe divinely in their own right to fish as they please without harassment, that the porpoise proved—in practice— to have no rights at all.

ATTITUDES LEADING TO EXTINCTION

How do these marine messes—these inhumanities—come about? The same way they do on land.

Large issue or small—extinction or cruelty or thoughtlessness—the vast pressure that exerts itself to prevent any change for the better is a constant astonishment to anyone who works daily in this field.

The twentieth century pays lip service to humanitarian ideals as many other centuries did not. Thousand of college graduates tumble out each year, clutching their bachelors and their masters and their doctorates, and most of them know the language of humanitarianism. They engage in scientific programs involving animals and most of them show loving kindness to animals owned—to animals, you might say, of their personal acquaintance. But how many are slipshod when it comes to considering the effect of their actions—scientific actions, now!—on the animals they only know at a distance?

Jane Risk, the Animal Protection Institute's field director in Washington, D.C., suddenly called to the attention of the same subcommittee we've been studying here a plan for whale-tagging that seemed to have struck its originators as a crackerjack idea. In some cases, the tags were to be fitted "with four streamers, each seven feet long, which would help in recognizing the tagged whale at sea and on the flensing deck."

She's a cheerful and brightly candid lady, Jane Risk, but I can almost hear the moan in her voice as she went on to argue that whamming a whale with seven-foot streamers that reach the body as projectiles is scarcely a kindly work on behalf of their survival. If someone proposed to the originator of that whale-marking scheme that they be allowed to puncture his son with a set of four-inch high ribbons or to mark his dog in the same fashion so detached scientists could follow his travels around the neighborhood—well, he might have been a bit upset. But that scientist gives his child a name; and he gives his dog a name; and thereby he invests each with a sovereignty and is thoughtful of their rights.

The animals in danger of extinction are those which exist—splendid or unsplendid —with no name like Gump or Bill or Sport or Rex that has been conferred upon

56

The humpback whale became a mini-celebrity when Dr. Roger Payne recorded its strange wails for the LP **Songs of the Humpback Whale.** *The animal's unique vocalizations did not, however, keep it from the flensing decks.* **DRAWING BY LARRY FOSTER, GENERAL WHALE.**

This whale was conquered and marked with a flag (like a captured territory) and then dismembered at a California whaling station. The United States stopped whaling in 1971; other countries, including Russia and Japan, continue.

them by a human. Lacking names, they lack, for the unimaginative, a character. If the tuna fishermen had fifty dolphin trapped in a net but knew the differences in each creature—knew that this was Leonora and she was timid and this was Flash and he was a rip-around—it's most unlikely that they would continue with the kill, even if it meant dumping a substantial tuna-catch.

Because most of us can't, and don't, distinguish between individuals—the individual whale, the individual grizzly, the individual porpoise—we lose the power to identify with the animals' fate. This is especially true when there is a financial motivation that makes it comfortable for us to see the animal not as an individual but as a dispensable mass. The same principle operates in warfare when the enemy becomes merely "gooks," "gringos," "Japs," "Rebs." Winning a war is so all-important that participants blur identification of the individual in order to accomplish killing with the least injury to the conscience.

Tuna fishermen must have a conscience; but the primacy of money makes it possible to leave that conscience ashore. The quick accommodation that hundreds of tuna fishermen made to the new circumstances of the hunt—their willingness to stick it out through these disheartening porpoise massacres—indicts the human race at large. It was an accommodation to murder. It was not that the tuna fishermen were infinitely worse than the rest of society; the more terrible prospect was that they were showing what society can bring itself to accommodate.

If a choice were made of creatures whose qualities man himself should envy, there is the subtle contention of Loren Eiseley that the octopus is a superior creature. There are also primate specialists who would favor the gorilla above the chimpanzee. But who does not choose the porpoise? Whose list of the grandest of creatures would leave him out?

We could not have committed more terroristic warfare on the porpoise had we been spurred by demagogues crying, "Man, here is the chief of your rivals—slay him! Enslave him, he is clever! Use, trick, kill him—he is your rival, Man, and you must best him." Well, we did not even have the excuse that we saw the porpoise as a true rival. We let the killing go on not as a holy war but out of laxness. This is how extinction often comes about, particularly in modern times.

Hundreds of millions of years went into the making of the grizzly bear. In the last century and less, the king of the American forests has been reduced to a few hundred specimens. But the celebrated California grizzly, that stormy and all-conquering "golden bear" whose rush could not be stopped—where is he today? He exists on the state flag and as a football team. The last California grizzly to live was dead in 1923. Hunters killed them for meat, people poisoned them to be rid of them. The bear lost and lost absolutely. In San Francisco, at the Museum of Natural Science, the last California grizzly who ever lived still exists. Mounted. But he is not even on display. A taxidermist explained that "the expression isn't natural like we do it now." So the last of the golden bears is in a storehouse even in death; all that lives on are two glowing words, *golden* and *bear*.

We are not that much changed today from what we were in 1923. Yes, conservationists and animal protectionists abound; they do not, for the most part, hold sway in those legislative halls and regulatory agencies where the fate of species is at stake more often than we think.

The tuna fishermen's attitude was predictable. It derived from the intense nature of these fishing expeditions, where crew members are on shares and the more whopping the catch, the more whopping the shares. The goldrush is largely gone in this world; but the tuna-rush, on a good sailing, will yield what seems a bonanza to the fisherman who doesn't want to scrape by on eight or ten or twelve thousand dollars in an inflated economy. He is not looking to kill porpoises; he is looking to maximize the bonanza. His interest is as great as the skipper's, the skipper's as great as the company's. Tuna fishermen are not men in rowboats. Recent additions to the fleet have cost in the neighborhood of four-million dollars each. The huge purse-seine nets—they can be pouched and closed at the top like a women's draw-string purse—are a steep wall of webbing and they represent a huge overall investment for the tuna fleet at large. Working mostly around southern California and Puerto Rico, the fleet comes in with one-hundred million dollars worth of raw tuna in a given year ánd the year's catch—for a boat that costs three-million dollars—may total $1,400,000. The "ferocious competitiveness" frequently referred to as a characteristic of tuna fishermen certainly owes something to the bonanza aspect of the chase. The porpoise is caught up in the scramble by a fluke of nature—for reasons not truly understood, the yellowfin tuna swim in vast numbers below the easily spotted porpoise herds.

This has always been known. Seventeen centuries ago the Greek poet Oppian offered an opinion, popular with the Greeks, that would have been given short shrift by tuna fishermen. Killing of dolphins, suggested Oppian, was "an offense to the gods—as execrable as the murder of a human." The Greeks, too, fished "on porpoise." But, according to Pliny the Elder, Greek fishermen would share the catch with the dolphins as a sort of finder's fee; better than that—and it was Pliny's contention the dolphins waited around for this—the fishermen often returned next day to present the dolphins with something they especially liked: bread dipped in wine.

Fishermen may not have changed much at heart in the past seventeen centuries, but it seems likely that modern conditions put more hustle on them than they would have needed in Pliny's time. The tuna boats are the champion fishing craft of the modern world; the nets are a miracle in size and (to an extent) ingenious; small motorboats are an adjunct to the tuna fleet, and the death knell rang for over a million dolphin when, in the Sixties, it was discovered you could use these speedboats to direct the movements of the porpoise. The fast-skimming porpoise are usually flying onward but the boats herd them round, stop them in a single spot, and make a tuna-catch more certain because the net is juggled into position around the porpoise while the yellowfin follow their instinct to stay close by. This prevented many a "water haul," where the porpoise—hence, the tuna—would skip away before the net was fully deployed.

Killing off the dolphin was certain to eventually leave the tuna fleet without its guides. But the fishermen were always concerned with this year's catch, not the catch ten years hence.

Promises to perfect new equipment or techniques that would establish escape routes for the porpoise did not prove out. Government workers, docile enough in their proddings of the stubbornly forceful tuna fishermen, had little luck in selling the demand that speedboats be routinely positioned to help porpoise free themselves as tuna-catching maneuvers began.

Gerald Howard, southwest region director of the National Marine Fisheries Service, came back with the discomfiting word that only about once in twenty deployments of the net (five percent) were the speedboats used as they were supposed to be for porpoise safety. Another report suggested that in the heat of the chase this precaution was almost uniformly disregarded and where it wasn't—"in every case"—the boats were sent at the wrong time: *after* the porpoise were in trouble instead of before.

Reporting the tactics of captains who frustrated attempts to put observers on their boats—conceding that there couldn't be that much faith in the accuracy of the logs that the captains were bringing back—Howard nevertheless ended testimony at an "informal hearing" on the Marine Mammal Protection Act with a touch the tuna fishermen liked:

"If there is further reduction in the U.S. share of the yellowfin tuna caught on porpoises, there will be an increased incidental kill of porpoises by non-U.S. vessels over which no country exercises control."

That touch—from the government official, the government scientist, the government analyst—is, in the long run, the lesson to be learned from the Great Porpoise Debate. The porpoise had friends at the hearth, in front of the family television set; he had few friends in government.

Is killing a porpoise as much a crime as killing a human being? Is it even half as much a crime? A third? Nowhere does the evidence show that officials working on a day-to-day basis with this problem could even conceive of asking themselves this question. One government analyst was able to conclude that figures he assembled suggested that "the offshore Spotted Dolphin stock has responded to exploitation through increased reproduction." A fine discovery, indeed. Had the buffalo behaved in like fashion the Thundering Herd would have become a Clobbering Herd instead of being reduced to a straggly group of specimens. If exploitation had given the California grizzly a new burst of reproductive fervor, the golden bear would still be the wonder of the woods instead of being propped in a glass case at the University of California's Student Union building in Berkeley.

"If true," suggested this Resources Division analyst, "the increased reproduction would allow the population to withstand annual exploitation of 4.4 percent."

It was another way of getting to the argument that virtually all tuna fishermen and many a congressmen considered pertinent: How many porpoise can be killed off without plunging the porpoise into an intense downward cycle that means, for sure, the whole species will be gone?

That question can be considered from a number of angles:

How many Chicagoans can be wiped out, on an annual basis, before it won't seem like Chicago anymore?

How many residents of Whitefish, Montana, can be safely netted and destroyed before there will be no Whitefish?

Soulfully, in response to a request for setting forth what the researchers now knew about whether the dolphins were highly endangered or not, an ever-so-typical government official announced with pride that his Center would spend another $320,000 in 1976 to study the dolphin.

"We have come a long way in our research and have contributed much to our understanding of the interaction between tuna fishing and porpoise stocks," he proclaimed.

"At the same time there is, as everyone recognizes, a vast amount of work that still needs to be accomplished. This will, however, take more time and more resources."

But never, never did he come to grips with the question before him. What was the true state of the imperilment of the porpoise? To reach a conclusion—*to see the obvious*—might stop the research, save the money—why, it might even save the porpoise! And nobody could read the frequent proclamations of all those researchers and imagine that they were in any hurry to save the porpoise.

But no one needed exquisite government graphs, drawn at exquisite expense, just to duck around the question and keep the country from knowing that the endangerment of the porpoise was—on its face—both tremendous and monstrous.

A fleet of 135 fishing boats had managed, in a bit over ten years, to kill a million and a half porpoise. Nothing like it had ever happened to the porpoise before. The public, so slow to be roused to fever pitch, eventually became aware that the massacre was vast, evil and must be stopped. Congressmen charged with conserving the environment and its resources were far more witless than the public itself. And the government experts tended to be the worst offenders of all.

Why? Why should it be that way? Those "experts" were, to be sure, not pursuing their own financial interest. They must have thought it "good for the nation" to promote money-making in the fish business as somehow more important than the ultimate survival of the porpoise. But it was a strange blindness for, at best, the porpoise slaughter could only continue while there were still porpoises—and the massacre itself would have ended that. The federal court ruling, which fourteen organizations including API had brought about, took effect in late 1976. Somewhere along the line, the tuna fishermen seemed to have lost even Congressman Leggett. And so they were defeated.

For the time being, the porpoise massacre was over. Tuna fishermen were outraged. Some decided to follow through on that threat to desert to foreign flags.

The bottlenose dolphin is an endearing creature to millions, via "Flipper" and sea-quarium shows. But, since the 1960s, millions of his cousins—spotted, spinner, and whitebelly dolphins—have been killed "incidentally" to tunafishing operations. *COURTESY MARINE WORLD/AFRICA USA.*

Some went back to the old game of looking for allies in Congress. Some tried to confuse the public, once more, into seeing "fishing on porpoise" as just a little ol' harmless necessity. Even now, the diehards of the game seem not to realize that the porpoise killers came within an inch of being as notorious to inhabitants of the 21st century as the buffalo killers are to our own century.

If I could, I would say flatly, "We won." But we *can't* be sure—probably we won't know for several years yet—if Congress will hold the ground or will back up once more under new blandishments from the porpoise-killers. What we do know is: the fight is not over. The tuna fleets are sore losers. And our federal establishment is riddled in many places with "experts" who have a long, unholy record in upholding the maxim: Damn the porpoise, full speed with the net!

4

Who Cares About Animals?
Some Amateurs and Pros
Girding for Action

In an assembled meeting or on the street, with but few exceptions, it would be difficult to single out an individual who had an interest in animals. They look like "normal" people, and they are. Animal protectionists come in all shapes and sizes, from various backgrounds and geographic locations, in both sexes; there is no education, age, income, or employment factor that distinguishes them.

A survey of API's membership revealed a correlation between the respondents' replies and the general population: fifty-three percent were high-school graduates, twenty-five percent held bachelor degrees, and another ten percent had masters; agewise, thirty-five percent fell in the twenty to twenty-nine bracket, twenty percent were thirty to thirty-nine, another fifteen percent were forty to forty-nine, and thirteen percent placed in the next category; sixty-two percent earned $15,000 or less.

Protectionists are often dismissed, especially by hunters and trappers, as big-city dwellers who wouldn't know the front end of a cow from the rear end, but only thirty-one percent of the survey respondents lived in cities of two-hundred thousand or greater population; twenty-two percent lived in cities of less than fifty thousand, and twenty-one percent resided in rural areas. (These figures may even be somewhat slanted because of the Institute's practice of placing advertisements primarily in large-circulation, urban newspapers.)

Regionally, the Northeast and the West Coast appear most attuned to the problems of animals. Thirty-five percent of the Institute's members live in the northeastern tip of the United States, with another twenty-seven percent residing in California, Washington, Oregon, and Hawaii. A close third is the north central section with nineteen percent of the membership. The remaining nineteen percent are scattered throughout: the Southeast—six percent with one-third of that in Florida; the Midwest—three percent; the West—four percent; and the Southwest—six percent.*

*Northeast: Maine, Massachusetts, Rhode Island, Delaware, Vermont, New Hampshire, Connecticut, New Jersey, New York, Pennsylvania, Maryland, Virginia, Washington, D.C. North Central: Ohio, Indiana, Illinois, Minnesota, Michigan, Wisconsin. Southeast: West Virginia, Tennessee, Kentucky, Mississippi, Alabama, Georgia, Florida, Arkansas, Louisiana, North Carolina, South Carolina. Midwest: Missouri, Kansas, Nebraska, Iowa, South Dakota, North Dakota. Southwest: Texas, New Mexico, Arizona, Oklahoma. West: Alaska, Nevada, Utah, Colorado, Wyoming, Montana, Idaho. West Coast: Hawaii, Washington, Oregon, California.

Coyotes are the housekeepers of the West; they eat carrion and contribute to the balance of nature. Some Westerners, however, view them only as ravaging predators, and the coyotes who do cleanup work often get cleaned up on—as this horizonful of coyote (and bobcat) corpses attests. Guns, traps, poisons bring them down.

CREDITS: (top) U.S. DEPARTMENT OF THE INTERIOR, FISH AND WILDLIFE SERVICE, (bottom) RALPH CRANE, TIME-LIFE.

It's not easy to pinpoint the reasons for this distribution, but several factors are involved. The East, of course, was settled and industrialized first. Urbanization was a boost to the early humane movement for it was thus that the problems of animals became most visible. In the Northeast and the West Coast, especially California, there is also a financial element—as prosperity increases people can *afford* to look after problems other than their own. The three leading areas, with their access to large cities and to universities, have also been positioned to learn of new ideas and have demonstrated a more receptive attitude toward "movements." The Midwest, South, and West, with their farming and ranching activities, have been historically "closer to the land"; animals are often looked on as crops to be harvested, or useful adjuncts to harvesting those "crops," rather than feeling creatures.

The South has had the growth of humane awareness additionally confounded by the social problem of racism. Racial prejudices are not alien to the humane character—I once talked with a woman from Texas who felt blacks should not be allowed pets because (assuming poverty) of the inadequate diet to which the animals would be subjected. In truth, prejudices are not confined to the South. API has been sent, regularly and anonymously, printed tirades blaming Jews for all the evils of the world; and I can remember being taken to task by one irate member who assumed the Institute's management was a WASP stronghold.

Where the role of the sexes is concerned, the humane movement has traditionally been thought of as the ladies' bailiwick. Men were around—in fact, they occupied the positions of professional leadership—but it was women who made up the majority of organizations' memberships and who were most visible to the general public. The imbalance is not unreasonable. Women are not constrained about openly displaying compassion for an unfortunate creature. While compassion is certainly not lacking in the male psyche, admitting its existence in the form of a word or deed is too often regarded as unmanly. Also, women outlive men and, thus, in a certain age bracket, have more financial means. In recent years social forces have eroded the custom of a man being the figurehead while the woman does the work; today a large number of women successfully lead humane organizations.

Whether the humane leader is male or female, however, a mate's full support, vocal or otherwise, is invaluable. During my first visit with the woman president of the Clark County Humane Society in Billings, Montana, I met her husband. When I asked him if he was active in the affairs of the society, he replied, "No, one nut in the family is enough." He was, I subsequently learned, solidly behind his wife in every effort she undertook for the society.

Not only have men become more agreeable to working openly for animal welfare, but in the past ten years the movement has also attracted the well educated, the financially able, and those employed in the professions. The tendency can be traced to several forces. The ecology movement of the Sixties, though not aimed primarily at wildlife, certainly popularized the humane ideal; and fortunately, the back-to-nature movement, the idea of living in harmony and peace with one's environment, has stayed with us. The women's liberation movement has, as a natural outgrowth, or backlash (depending on one's point of view), encouraged men to be more open about hitherto "unmanly" feelings. The humane movement itself has expanded its vistas to include wildlife and exotic animals in addition to the traditional concerns of pets and food animals. All of these forces have worked to dispel the image of the humane worker as an esoteric, emotion-ridden, people-hating kook—an image dredged up largely by those unsympathetic to the cause and perpetuated through the use of disparaging labels.

The term "do-gooder" is synonymous with every movement whose objective is charitable or merciful and is automatically inherited by any group proposing change that will monetarily affect other individuals or groups. For a great number of years the line "little old ladies in tennis shoes" was a common label for those involved in animal protection work. During World War II the job of taking care of animals was left mainly to women. Tennis shoes were ankle high and worn by kids in school; but they were comfortable and practical for women on their feet long hours caring for animals. Now that everyone wears tennis shoes, the label is not so effective, but it did, at one time, project a negative image.

Times grow tougher for the grizzly. In 1976 a son of President Ford lamented how close the bears were to extinction. COURTESY U.S. DEPARTMENT OF THE INTERIOR.

"Humaniacs" was another term intended to be derogatory and hurled at animal protectionists. The impact was lost, however, when humanitarians themselves began using the word. Finally, as a result of efforts to save dogs from being sent to laboratories, opponents coined "dog-lover" to discredit humane workers, and the press popularized the term with the caption, "Dog-lovers win victory." "Dog-lover," "cat-lover," eventually melted into the all-inclusive "animal lover." Thus, what had been intended as a character assassination and discrediting verbal abuse, became a symbol of compassion and unity among all people who cared what happened to animals.

Contributing to (and resulting from) the traditionally negative image of protectionists is the accusation that those who care about animals are misanthropes. I don't claim angel wings for the movement; this criticism may occasionally be true, but, undoubtedly, a people-hating attitude is an impediment in humane work. Unfortunately or not, humans make the rules and it is humans who ultimately must be persuaded, or forced, to make those rules humane ones.

Usually, the antisocial accusation issues from an opponent. Often it resolves itself into the trite and downright stupid question, "Which would you save—the child or the dog?"—a remark that shouldn't be dignified with a reply. Simply because a person speaks out for animals does not automatically mean he or she considers animals more "important" than humans or is choosing to preserve animal life at the expense of human life. It does indicate the person's compassion has been extended to "dumb" creatures that may not have enough effective champions to ensure their survival.

And, humane work is not an exclusive interest. One of API's board members has for years been active in Big Brothers and Boy Scouts of America, another is a mainstay of the local Rotary Club. API employees' interests range from promoting planned parenthood and acting as candy stripers to managing swim meets and coaching little league baseball. The San Diego Mental Health Association presented its 1975 achievement award to one of our humane officers, a go-getter who also finds time for community theater and symphony projects. These individuals are not glaring exceptions. It's been my experience that those aware of animal suffering often become more receptive to the state of the human population.

A relevant observation here is that those who put forth this taunt aim to downgrade humane workers, for whatever reason, and rarely are themselves involved in charitable work of any kind. There is no shame in feeling for animals. The ratio of people agencies to animal agencies is a thousand to one, and the laws protecting people from other people or from animals rarely go unenforced. It's quite true that some people have told me, "The more I work with animals, the more I dislike people," but working for animals, in a real sense, is working for people, for when we do so we educate, and to educate is to civilize. Webster defines civilizing as bringing out of a condition of savagry or barbarism. These is no worthier contribution to mankind.

Earlier I spoke of angel wings. Like all movements and causes, the humane field has some participants who, although well intentioned, have given cause to be looked on askance. These are, fortunately, in the minority, but chief among them are the egoists who play on their protectionist posture for public attention and sympathy.

Such individuals are considered obstructive and embarrassing and are usually avoided by the organized humane movement. They can often be found at assemblies or meetings of humane groups, gaudily or poorly dressed to express self-sacrifice and monopolizing the platform with tales of self-accomplishment. They are not averse to making scenes; indeed, they often appear walking, talking spectacles.

I once had a woman approach me in the lobby of the Statler-Hilton Hotel in Los Angeles, dressed in a St. Francis of Assisi gown of burlap, complete with hood and attached cut-out paper birds. She fell on her knees directly in front of me, grabbing my coat and proclaiming aloud that we should all kneel in prayer to save the animals. I believe in prayer, but I also felt she was an inadequate substitute for St. Francis.

Is such behavior of any value to the humane cause? To a small extent, perhaps. Those already in the movement tend to be tolerant, primarily because the "spectacles" are, in a limited way, protecting animals—usually through local rescue or adoption programs. Also, these people may be motivators within their own circles of friends. However, much ground can be lost by setting these characters loose on the public at large as bona fide representatives of the animal welfare field. One can only imagine Madame Burlap-Gown in the hands of an unsympathetic news reporter or, for that matter, being drilled by a cynical legislative committeeman. Nor would any potential humane convert be encouraged by such antics—unless, of course, the newcomer was of like nature, and then the problem is compounded.

A clarification: I'm not saying don't ever be guided by emotions; but I do admonish anyone, in their work for animals, not to become a "figure of fun," to set up themselves and the cause they want to further as objects worthy of being ridiculed and, thence, dismissed.

You can count on almost every individual in the country professing himself an animal lover. Like motherhood and flag-waving, animals strike a responsive chord — as long as it's convenient. I have known rough, burly men who would take you apart if you so much as harmed a hair on their dogs' heads; yet those same men would shotgun the head off a rabbit sitting five feet away, in the name of sport.

This incongruity is one reason why animal-lovers are difficult to number. API's leadership takes a position of nondiscrimination in its protection programs, but advocates of one species are not always amenable to another, much less *all* others. There are those who love cats and hate dogs, those who hunt but see no sport in greyhound racing, those who trap but abhor bullfighting — all ideologically entrenched.

I was once invited to assist in the formation of a humane society in Henderson, Nevada. It turned out that the principals were members of a pigeon-fancy club who wanted to eliminate or incarcerate all cats in the community because of the animals' predation on pigeons. I was never asked to return. On a visit to her midwest home, an API staff member was dumbstruck when an aunt and uncle, both avid hunters, expressed incredulity at anyone enjoying rodeos; in the interests of family relations, perhaps her mute reaction was fortunate.

One Institute member wrote:

Dear Sir:
    You haven't heard from me lately because our sport of fox hunting around here has been lost due to all the trapping done in our area.
    We have a pack of 15 beautiful Walker foxhounds which are of no use to me now. We have had our dogs caught in traps, and so have our friends. We have never approved of trapping.
    I supported you in the past because I thought something could be done to stop this trapping before it was too late.
    Our sport of fox hunting has become a thing of the past due to trapping, so I do not care to support you any more.

The preponderance of humane workers in the United States are volunteers. They come from every crosswalk of life. They not only give of their time and energy but contribute substantially toward making the work possible. Because volunteers are usually engaged in providing their livelihood in another field, it is not always possible for them to participate on a full-time basis. Also, generally speaking, the volunteer is single-cause oriented, contributing time to an area of particular interest, such as dogs and cats, livestock, wildlife.

There is one kind of volunteer, especially, that can be a godsend — the celebrity. This is because a movie or television star has instant entry to the media and pulling power invaluable for local fund-raising events. Only when actress Mary Tyler Moore attended federal committee hearings on an antileghold-trap bill was the issue deemed worthy of national news coverage and thus disseminated to newspaper readers who previously had no idea of its existence. In addition, celebrities have loyal followings, people who believe — rationally or not — "the stars know best" on everything from orange juice to face soap. It's a good bet that fans of "The Mary Tyler Moore Show" sat up and took notice of the side she was on.

At the same time, a total dependence on personalities is self-defeating. Let's look at the news report in question, from the trap bill hearings.

WASHINGTON—"Behind every beautiful wild fur there is an ugly story," said Mary Tyler Moore. "Gobbledygook," said Rep. Don Young, R-Alaska, who had his hand in a steel trap at the time. . . ."It is a brutal, and bloody, and barbaric story. The animal is not killed (by a trap), it is tortured to death," said the actress. Young said trapping amounts to a regulated harvest of a "renewable resource. . .I'll defend to the death the right of Alaskans to trap."

Miss Moore and Congressman Young were, in effect, talking two different languages. Robert Redford and Barbra Streisand could have shown up as well, but if other humane spokesmen hadn't been able to testify that there are alternative traps, that few, if any, people depend on leghold traps for livelihood, and to add other applicable facts, then Mr. Young would have won the day hands down—at least in the minds of the committeemen.

Along with volunteers, the humane ranks contain professionals, employed on a career basis. It is helpful for professionals to have some working knowledge of the humane movement, but it is not always necessary or, for that matter, desirable. Professional workers have a somewhat more mechanical objective, that of using their skills to achieve objectives of an organization's program and activities, and it is these skills which should be scrutinized relative to hiring. A common shortcoming of humane organizations is their failure to recruit highly skilled professional help and to meet competitive wages.

In times of stress, one of my most frequently used expressions (which my co-workers are no doubt weary of), is, "We're not running a little boyscout game." It's true, humane groups are not formed for profit, but they must take in money and put out a service to survive. In this key sense, they are businesses, competing with all other businesses for economic survival. Hiring administrative personnel on the strength of their professed love for animals, without regard to their work skills, is suicide.

Wages are often a sticky business. Not only do humane organizations have trouble raising funds and thus hiring competent help, but if and when salaries are finally adjusted to be competitive, the criticism starts. Many people, often the more vocal ones, seem to think that working *for* a charity means working *on* charity, that the less employees are paid the more will go "to the cause." I disagree. The first criterion in any business is to hire skilled, creative workers; the facts of life prohibit these people from working for subsistence wages. If a clerk, a bookkeeper, or a public relations director is needed, several should be interviewed and the best candidate hired. Why should the animals settle for less? The humane effort is business and if we don't manage our organizations as well as or better than the opponents, we'll soon be *out* of business.

5

Two Who Cared Enough:
A Lady of Ohio and Film Actress
Kim Novak

Two exhilarating women — two ladies who can be unstoppable when man raises a hand against his fellow creatures — offers an object lesson in not bowing down to those who hold that animals don't count.

One of these is Helen Brach, who has aided humane organizations all over the world. The other is actress Kim Novak. Miss Novak was wondrously touching in "Picnic," providing an all-time portrait of the wistful yearner trying to hit that highway to happiness — to catch something beautiful out of life and hold onto it tightly.

When it comes to animals, both Helen Brach and Kim Novak have a serene ability for catching beauty and holding it tightly — or, rather, holding it softly. Their natural instincts are to care as ardently for animals as for humans. As Kim knows and as Helen knows, animals are worth learning from because they can be joyous "on one ounce of nothing." An animal *does* know how to catch the beauty implicit in living.

It is largely the advent of people — the messups that people cause in animal lives — that creates such modern anomalies as "the pet psychiatrist." Who imagined that with the invention of the snowmobile, idiot humans would chase deer and antelope until they dropped exhausted — sometimes dying — in the snow? Who would believe that, with his snowmobile under him, a boy who would probably not even be rated as neurotic by his friends would convert himself into a fox hunter, and eventually mangle the poor fox under the treads of his machine?

With incidents as cruel as that — more systematic than that, more stamped-for-approval-by-local-government than that — animals need champions. Just as ladies of the Middle Ages needed champions against the invaders.

But often these days it's the ladies who are champions of gallantry — it's fighting girls, fighting housewives, fighting grandmothers — who carry the cudgels against a marvelously indecent amalgam of animal mistreaters.

So here are personal impressions of Helen Brach and Kim Novak, whom I do not hesitate to call:

Two champions.

Helen Brach was raised in Ohio and has two homes there in the Tappan Lake region not so far from Cadiz, which became the center of an unearthly and altogether behind-the-scenes battle that has really been fought to establish that animals have rights too vital to them (and too vital to humans) to be put aside.

Petite and attractive, ladylike and reserved but capable of bursting out of that reserve, Helen knows in her bones what Herbert Spencer was solemnly warning about when he stated in 1851, "The behaviour of men to the animals, and their behaviour to each other, bear a constant relationship." Actually, as I guess I should confess, Spencer phrased that "to the lower animals." But I have taken out the word *lower*; it doesn't have quite the right feel at this later time. It wouldn't have the right feel for Helen Brach, who knows that we learn from animals and that animals often manage an exuberance that humans do not.

Still, there were some men around Cadiz, in positions of power, who would grumble at almost any indication that people *should* step nimbly to be kind to animals. One day Helen Brach found herself drawn into a confusingly complex struggle that should have ended before it started. And didn't.

It's a long, long road that leads from Cadiz, Ohio, to a chemical plant in Pennsylvania where — or so people came to believe — animals are used to test the effects of burning on live flesh.

Those who believe that such testing can legitimately be done would nevertheless be in no rush to contribute an animal of their own for the tests. The law in the United States has been generous to researchers, for it cannot know in advance what their problems are — nor what their successes might be. Thousands of researchers have been moderate and humane in their work. A good many have been needlessly cruel. Darkness pervades. Behind the walls of the laboratory, anticruelty laws effectively stop.

In a testing situation, depending on what the test is, a German shepherd has certain advantages. He's big. He's strong. He can endure. In the lab market, where dogs are needed for experiments and the "big dog" is at a premium, a German shepherd may be worth seventy-five to ninety dollars. Suppliers aren't likely to make the fate the animal faces a factor in their haggling. It's a Take the Money and Run situation.

An experiment can be ingenious and hold within it (sometimes in a very science-fictionish way) the portent of a different life for the humans it might affect. How exciting to read about the transfer of brain fluid from Rat No. 1 to Rat No. 2 to see if Rat No. 2 will now "remember" some of the things that were only learned by Rat No. 1. Such an experiment can go on with no interference whatever. The number of people who become concerned about laboratory rat losses is minimal. Still — the labs are cautious. When their experimental animals are not rats — when they are something else — researchers are well aware that the antivivisectionist campaigns of years past could flare again at any moment. Their own lab may be the specific target. Their need is for animals that can be routinely taken into testing programs — without recriminations.

But a man who discovers that he has lost his dog and who tracks it to a chemical plant where the rumors of flesh-burning are considerable: now *there's* a man who has recriminations.

I can't tell you what happens behind the doors of that chemical plant in Pennsylvania. We don't know. We know that one day a man who lived near Cadiz turned into a Humphrey Bogart-style detective, traced his dog to the local dog pound, found that the dog pound had unloaded it on a dog dealer, that the dog dealer had unloaded it in such a way that there it was in Pennsylvania behind closed doors. He retrieved the dog — a big, strong German shepherd — before any experimenting took place. But what troubled the people who learned about this was that hundreds and hundreds and hundreds of dogs had been delivered out of that dog pound to the dog dealer. And the dog dealer was operating in some thirty-three towns all across Ohio. The other towns must have contributed hundreds of dogs in each case, many of those dogs the big, strong, enduring type.

How many of them wound up in the lab in Pennsylvania, or labs like it, and how many of them were not just rambling wanderers—or the "wild dogs" on which Harrison County, Ohio (pop. 17,000), pays a bounty? How many were pets who got loose and might have been retrieved again had their owners had any skill as amateur detectives?

So far this is an Albert Payson Terhune story, and I should warn you in advance that it's an unfinished story with no satisfactory ending as yet. Terhune, you probably remember, was a lover of collies—of the gentleness with just-a-hint-of-wolf they displayed—and he wrote fanciful plots that nearly always climaxed with a pitiful and depraved dognapper being foiled just in time. They were fanciful stories mainly in the sense that, while dognappers assuredly exist, it's relatively rare for one of them to get foiled. Some of them set up networks and keep a sharp eye out for the seventy-five dollar dog. Enough dogs like that and you can have some excellent vacations in Jamaica.

The incident of the lost German shepherd brought about my close association with Mrs. Helen Brach. This lady of Ohio is much too determined and forceful to believe that you should sit quietly when dogs—possibly thousands—are being delivered without due process of law to unknown terrors.

Helen Brach, whose three dogs, including shaggy hair-over-her-eyes Lovey, all came from dog pounds, is the kind of mainstay without whom the animal protection movement could not be carried to far corners of the country. She knows that protecting animals is not a matter of rushing up to one vile individual and crying, "Scat!" She knows there can be long—seemingly endless—struggles with immovable officials doing their best to "not know" what they don't want to know.

Whoever comes in contact with Helen Brach learns something from her and they know they have met a force. What happened there near Cadiz is an indication of the complications and frustrations that occur when an effort is made to deal with the slowdowns and connivings of those who, as the country boys put it, are "just not gonna get off their duffs to save a dog."

I was a long time, at the beginning, in becoming acquainted with Helen Brach.

She had turned up simply as an unsolicited donor to the Animal Protection Institute. When substantial contributions are made over a period of time, you become curious about the donor. You wonder if the favorite causes of the organization are also the donor's causes, or if the donor is sparked by some deep-rooted sense of injustice about the status of animals close by. Confirmed supporters of animal causes don't send in money, normally, from a vacuum. They have eyes. They tend to be unusually alert to the same pitiful episodes that others, in their hometowns, will dismiss as "just part of life."

We fight on all fronts in API and at one time or another, when various missions seemed to be taking me close to her, I made arrangements for conferences with her in Chicago and again in Tappan, Ohio, and in Fort Lauderdale, Florida. The appointments kept falling through, and yet I was learning more about her.

She had joined API after seeing a newspaper ad—one of the ads we've used to speak directly to the American public about the gravest problems in the animal kingdom. She was, as it turned out, not contributing to API alone but to the animal protection movement all around the world, wherever it seemed to be doing effective work. I wrote her a note about a check that had come in. She had used the figure of five-hundred dollars but then, on the second line, had written five dollars. Returning it, I suggested, "If the intention was to contribute five-hundred dollars, we are genuinely pleased; and if it's for five dollars, we appreciate that, too."

Once we did meet in Chicago, her combination of vigor, soft-spokenness, clear plans, and absolute candor was just as uplifting as finding your way to a fresh, cool lake in springtime. But she was not only a lady who could be inspiring; she was a lady in deep anger, and Harrison County's brazen way of brushing off pet problems — not the people's way but the way of the dog pound and those directly controlling it — had put her into one of the profoundly determined moods of her lifetime.

As the name implied, her family had founded the Brach Candy Company. She was much better than well-to-do. She traveled, but she wouldn't have needed to be widely traveled to know that the public pound near Cadiz, in a remote location with horrible conditions and thoughtlessly brutal activities, bore no resemblance whatever to the "humane" organization that a publicly run pound is imagined to represent.

In one way Harrison County's Dog and Kennel Fund was not exactly the kind of dog and kennel fund you'd find elsewhere. It was thoughtful about sheep. A rancher who could show losses of sheep to wild dogs could collect reimbursement for his gnawed animals. The judge of the verifiability of the sheep losses was: the dog warden. Strangely, one of the supervisors on a board that proved bewilderingly obstinate about letting pound conditions be improved had a distinction: he seemed to be a leading local claimant in sheep damages, his claims amounting to over one-thousand dollars.

The deeper you looked, the odder it all seemed. The incident of the German shepherd hinted that the grievous misrunning of the dog pound (a situation that most communities are glad to fix up in a hurry when outside investigation is attracted) was perhaps no mischance.

Trying to check in all directions, Helen Brach sent a man to finagle his way behind the walls of the Pennsylvania chemical lab. Was fatal torture the usual end result of an experiment? But the labs are shrewd; at any rate, they appear to have picked up the same approach to impending trouble as a big city bar. Bouncers met her man and bounced him; they were, he thought, thuggish in the extreme. The implication of fried flesh became stronger. But right in the dog pound was evidence of inhumanity severe enough to jolt the sensibilities of anyone. Anyone, it seemed, aside from an implacable group of Harrison County overseers.

Those who have seen a wildly misrun pound will know what it was like there near Cadiz. The injured, the puppies, the big, the small, sick, lame, addled, all thrown together. Maggot-ridden food. Little or no water. An environment where a dog could come in looking like Tyrone Power but soon be a shambles, not seeming like a prize, ready for adoption. And too bad. In a pound, adoption is your ticket to life.

Strip mining and farming are the chief activities around Cadiz. Many of its citizens know what hard times are. They are closer, on the average, than many Americans to those hard-scrabble days when each small dab of money took some doing. And nobody in the family is excused from doing their share. Farm kids work. It can be exhilarating — but they work. A country dog has it all over the city dog in many ways. He isn't running afoul of the next-door neighbor every time he takes a sniff in a hallway. The country dog can bound where he wants to in glory. But he'd better be worth something. Watchdog, sheepherder, separator of cattle — the dog has a role, too. If he strays from the clutches of somebody who loves him — or never finds his true home and true vocation — the dropout canine of Cadiz will not find legions of folk looking in his eyes to see if he is a king of tender glances.

The reason there was a shortage of water at the dog pound was because nobody was willing to insist that a dog pound needed water. It had no pipes. From that alone, the rest of the story can be guessed.

Helen Brach decided that the town would have to have a new dog pound, and if its politicians were so stubborn they wouldn't appropriate the money, then she would fund it. She wanted no reward for this except that of seeing the pound run on humane principles, the animals kept in comfort and given a fair chance for adoption, painless euthanasia for those dogs who had to be killed rather than a surrender of them to a trail leading to labs whose secrets could not be penetrated.

Ohio law provides four ways to deal with impounded pets — adoption, returning to owner, supplying for research, or "humane disposition" — meaning that ending the life of the animal must be accomplished in the most humane, not the most profitable, system.

Amazingly, Helen Brach's last-ditch decision to build a pound — a proposal needing public sanction, for otherwise the empowered dog warden would still take the animals elsewhere — provoked belligerence rather than happy acceptance from the county supervisors. Yes, she would pay a staff. Yes, she would absorb many kinds of expenses.

The board was determined to sit on the proposal. Attempts to get action through the courts on behalf of the animals drew a profound silence from the local newspaper — which wrote nothing even when it was asked directly to do so — on the wrangle going forth. It was a *Jaws* story in reverse; rapaciously, the county proposed to swallow animals as they chose, digest them in defiance of established humane procedures, and be above question. An interim arrangement under which API paid for "humane disposition" broke down because the supervisors wanted to deal instead with the dog dealer, who was actually receiving payment from the county to take these dogs who knew where. The original dog warden, who I considered dim but pliant and cruel only because he didn't know how to be kind, needed replacing, and the supervisors replaced him. They had four applicants for the position of dog warden but somehow settled on Howard Fulton.

A study could be made, I suppose, of dog-wardens — the great, the not so great, and the very strange choices elected or appointed to fill that almost unfillable assignment as dog defender and dog destroyer all in one person. I've seen hard-looking dog wardens whose touch was so gentle and whose mastery of dog psychology so complete they could have dealt effortlessly with a doberman in the middle of its attack.

Fulton, though, was not your run-of-the-mill dog warden. How did he choose — how did anybody choose him — to be in the field? To those who had joined Helen Brach and API in trying to deal with Harrison County officialdom, he seemed like Bad News Arriving, and he was. "Aggressive. . .a know-it-all. . .They've told him that his orders are 'not to pay any attention to animal lovers.' " All these things were spoken. Fulton had been accused of shooting a neighbor's dog, a charge he denied. If he had taken some pains to demonstrate that all this talk was empty and foolish and that he cared about animals in a forthright way — well, there was a great desire to believe that someone in the power structure, however low or high, should at least get to the point of *claiming* that he cared about animals.

To Helen Brach and her friends it seemed clear that Fulton wanted it known by one and all: *he* was no fool for animals. Helen Brach knew you can't have an effective dog pound without someone at the head who at least aims to be civil about the need for helping animals. The rampant brutality that had started this wide-ranging battle had never ended; and if his wispish predecessor had been ticklish to deal with, Fulton was impossible. It was a condition of Mrs. Brach's putting up a one-hundred thousand dollar dog pound for Harrison County that only someone with respect for animals could be the director, and she stipulated this would not include Fulton.

An effort was made to compromise on the issue but no arrangement was finalized, and the county's on again off-again arrangement with the dog dealer was suddenly on

74

again. The argument had gone round in circles and the supervisors were determined that love for animals — even if accompanied by money — was not going to swerve them from their policy, which seemed to be: keep this dog dump a genuine dump — anything else is too good.

It may seem odd that an argument over humanitarian conditions in a local dog pound can set off political reverberations in all directions; but this is the nature of politics at the familiar I'll-scratch-your-back level. Betty Meder, a friend of Helen's whose husband wrote insurance for the county, discovered that suddenly the county was calling for new insurance bids. Teresa Luther, who, with Helen and Betty, had tried to influence the county toward humane relations with animals, suddenly found this was a controversial stance; there were threats of a boycott of her family's lumberyard.

Helen Brach has not succeeded in building Harrison County a dog pound that it needs and that she is highly desirous of providing. Yet this unfinished story *will* have an ending. It depends on a rising up to *make* the supervisors accept animal rights as a legitimate issue. One way or another, Harrison County must, and will, budge officialdom into reform.

The bitterness and bickering has left some supervisors muttering, "Those women aren't going to tell us how to run the county."

Which wasn't, and isn't, the issue. Nobody wanted to. Nobody even wanted to tell them how to run a dog pound; their hearts should have been telling them. But if their hearts weren't talkative on that subject, they could have made up for it by merely approximating the standards prevailing elsewhere (not always that high, but higher than the grotesque, mean menagerie near Cadiz).

A court eventually ruled that the county was acting illegally in handing its live dogs to the dog dealer. So the supervisors — who didn't want the courts to tell them how to run their dog pound any more than they wanted women to — rebelled and set up a system that somehow speaks for their whole way of doing business. They arranged for the dog dealer to come in and kill the dogs and haul them out dead.

No law protects the disposition of a *dead* dog.

What counts in all this is, I guess, that Helen Brach stayed shiny and determined and that she and her friends — with backbiting maneuvers aimed against them all the way — have still managed to shame the obstructionists into *slightly* better conditions. They have consoled themselves for not rectifying it entirely by always moving instantly to help an animal they know needs help. They are not persuaded that the smallnesses of politics can, in the long run, prevail against a determined detachment of animal righters.

Sorrowfully, now, I have to add a footnote. On February 21, 1977, Helen Brach was seen for the last time. Her mysterious disappearance from her home does not appear to have any relation to her work for animals — I'm sure it does not.

Where is Helen Brach? It became an encompassing mystery, unsolved at the time this book goes to publication. Not only for API but for animal protectionists throughout the world, it is an inexplicable and grievous loss. I have told here the story of a main concern in her home community where she did not hesitate to rile the local political powers in her search for justice for animals; but the wrangle in Ohio was a tiny corollary to her involvement in humane work everywhere.

Possessed of a fortune, she forcefully used it to repair the crimes committed daily against animals. It was a special irony that self-seeking persons blunted and side-stepped the good she could do for animals, there near her home. For the most part, though, she could not be stopped — she was urgently effective in many places in many times.

Where is Helen Brach? If she is alive — helping animals. It was her guiding, great obsession. If she is not alive — helping animals still. She put in motion campaigns and programs that will outlive us all. Only a few people manage to do so. There are those who do not see beyond their own family, their own business, their own cat. Helen Brach was not one of them.

SHE MARRIED A VET

When someone scans a list of the advisors of the Animal Protection Institute, they're not necessarily surprised to find that one lives in Nairobi, Kenya, and another in Kent, England, but they usually seem greatly startled to discover Kim Novak's name. And then they remember: Kim does surround herself with animals, doesn't she? And some recall that, at length and after a career that established her permanently as one of the most glamorous and memorable of movie stars, she married (it must have surprised Hollywood) a veterinarian.

Yes, Kim does surround herself with animals.

And one day she found herself in a typical difficulty for someone trying to harbor as many pets as possible, and shield them from the world, and deal lightly and lovingly with them.

The word "inhumane" has proved perfectly easy to misuse. It gets bandied around even by people who would gladly drive all the animals in the country to the other edge of the forest and then mow the forest down for a shopping center. When I read in a newspaper that Kim Novak had been accused by neighbors of keeping a horse under inhumane conditions, I wondered—knowing, from a distance, how much store she seemed to put in animals—if it could be true.

It's the kind of case that the Animal Protection Institute probes into—not because a movie star is involved but because, in a neighborhood squabble, it's easy for the battlers to lose all sight of the rights of the animals in the midst of their quarrels with each other. Kim—strangely, for someone having inhumanities to hide—had no objection to a thorough check by API.

It didn't take much investigating to discover that it was more a matter of whether the neighbors were going to be inhumane to Kim—and whether Kim's pygmy goat had been inhumane to a neighbor's prize roses—than anything else.

Whatever the slanted, haphazard, and altogether fragmentary accounts of her life-beyond-Hollywood have implied, Kim Novak has done a much better job of coming to terms with life than millions of people who live a stale existence, repeating familiar patterns, afraid to be themselves, afraid to be in the outdoors, afraid to establish some kinship with the life around them.

The truth about Kim seemed oddly, beautifully different from any portrait painted of her in the press.

She lived in Carmel and was truly the most extraordinary of all the Carmelites, an extraordinary bunch of people who tend to be either very rich or very seeking. Being a movie star had not made her extremely rich. But it had made her—or something had—a seeker. Kim had chosen her home for its wild, magnificent location on a cliff over the ocean. Her bedroom and a catwalk projected over a ninety-foot drop to a point where the waves, breaking on the shores of Carmel, were exactly the sort of waves that Hollywood cameramen love to get their lenses on. She could look down on her waves and do a slow dissolve into a life of thoughtfulness—of unfranticness—that many actresses seem to want and have difficulty in finding. Typical she was not. There could be ten thousand actresses turning up on the screen in dark raincoats with looks of fathomless mystery, and never another like Kim Novak.

On an acre or so of land, she found ample room, not only for herself and her flower-munching pygmy goat, Rosemary, and the close friends she enjoyed seeing, but also for a Great Dane, two or three cats (it was hard to tell how many for all

Actress Kim Novak attends an API Forum, where protectionist leaders consult. Meeting participants didn't know she had a secret under her hat—and it was curled in her hair.

the animals ran free), a little white dog of great presence, and an Arab colt that thrilled her with each graceful bound. There was at least one other inhabitant I hadn't discovered yet.

Kim radiated happiness and so did her animal charges. She realized I was there not on a spite mission but to take a measured look at charges that, the moment you stepped into her Dr. Doolittle acre, proved palpably untrue. All her animals had a history, some being connected with her movies—one cat, Piewacket, appeared in the film version of *Bell, Book, and Candle*. Perky Rosemary, the goat, was free to walk in and out of the house—Kim doesn't treat animals as they are treated in most American households, tempering love with the various Forbidden Zones where they are not allowed.

She was going to award the Arab colt, a gift from California Polytechnic Institute in San Luis Obispo, the same house rights Rosemary enjoyed. And that was unusual enough for the neighbors—just one family, except for the gentleman who was boggled by Rosemary's proclivity for eating roses—to decide they truly couldn't stand it. The "charge" against Kim they took to county authorities was really a cover for forcing her to accept their suggestion that she move away to Big Sur.

The modus operandi for this attack was the real estate covenant requiring protection of the flora and fauna of the area. The neighbor-family, well-to-do and certainly conventional to the extent that the idea of a goat in the house rocked them right down to the family silverware, felt they could not stand by and see an Arab colt having—my God—house rights in a Carmel home.

I've known a great many people who love animals so dearly and feel so keenly the extent to which humans have dispossessed them, that if they were living in the palace at Monaco they would assuredly tell the guards that when a pet wanted entry— *anywhere*—let it enter!

Kim had a beautiful home, beautifully kept, and the animals didn't change this. From her viewpoint, they enhanced their setting. Certainly they fitted the decor; Kim is an excellent artist and her paintings, some of them on the walls, are mostly of animals. Did the neighbor family have a right to think Kim had gone overboard in a way *they* wouldn't? Yes; and a good response for that might have been for the neighbors to do as they pleased and let Kim do as *she* pleased. They had resolved, instead, to plague her.

I wondered—and I do not know, even now—if there might be more to it than that. Kim Novak casts a mystic aura wherever she walks. I wondered if there were people in Carmel who would be only too happy to be the admired confidante of such a famous star—and would be unhappy, feel a bit insulted perhaps, if the famous star, for reasons of her own, found a pygmy goat and an Arab colt more fascinating than a great majority of people?

Nobody can say this is the case. But I trust there are a good many people in the world who, if Kim Novak turned up as *their* neighbor, would happily add their own pygmy goat and their own Arab colt and see if they couldn't develop camaraderie on such a basis. Share Kim's love for animals and you begin to share much of what she is about. And this applies to a great range of people besides Kim.

When I went to see the neighbors, the lady who was ever so adamant about pursuing charges on an official level, declared, "We do love Kim, but she's being childish."

Despite a large experience with inhumanity—which is practiced everywhere toward animals with the same casualness that a rainstorm has in taking leaves down the gutter—I was unable to discover what, in all of Kim's super-loving attitudes toward animals, could conceivably be construed as inhumane. Well, it was argued, there were wind eddies in this neighborhood of Carmel, eddies that could be cold. That colt—being in a place where the neighbors themselves would not have a colt—could get cold.

A false argument? Extremely.

I had gone to the neighbors with a profusion of compromising attitudes on Kim's part. She would be happy to build any kind of shelter for her animals the neighbors thought would be all right—so long as it was fine and comfortable. But she was not willing to have her animals driven from their home in the name of being kind to them. Nor was she willing to be driven herself from Carmel to Big Sur, not in the name of kindness or anything else. And this was not some vague impression that Kim held as to her neighbor's intentions, for I heard them saying to me: "We told her, 'Kim, you're unhappy, why don't you move to Big Sur where you'd have more room?' "

The other neighbor, who complained that he was forever being shorn of some prize roses by Rosemary, presented a most amazing offer when I visited him. And I suppose it shows it's possible to get as involved with roses as with animals. He declared that he had a terminal illness and said if I could find a way to take this plague of a goat out of his life he would consider leaving twenty-five thousand dollars in his will for the Animal Protection Institute. (This, as it happens, is not our style in acquiring contributions.) He was not hostile. Certainly not toward Kim. He did have a high desire to live a goat-free life.

When I went to county authorities with a clear enough statement that certainly there was no inhumanity toward animals on Kim Novak's part they were gracious in their attitude, super-gracious — and several expressed an anxiety to meet Kim Novak personally so all the details and ramifications of this could be discussed. (An indication, I think, that plenty of men had a renewable crush on that glowing lady they knew well from the screen.) The whole dispute actually came before the county commission as strictly a dispute about livestock and the local greenery and I made it clear that wind eddies were in no way imperiling her colt.

Kim Novak walked out cleared — and her animals were cleared too. Having made her point, she then, to keep peace in the neighborhood (but peace without being forced), sent the colt out in the valley with other Arab horses she owned.

This was my introduction — under circumstances that could have been strained but were actually a delight — to a celebrated and totally involved woman who has not hesitated to work in every way she can for animal rights.

Her involvement with animals is not faky or staged. It rises out of the purest of hearts — as I find it does with a great many people who are not celebrated at all. She at no time connected herself to our crusade on the basis of what a charity involvement could do for her (there have been stars callous enough to have this in mind when they have "fronted" for some organization). There was nothing the Animal Protection Institute could do for Kim Novak — except, maybe, not let the charge of inhumane be used against her when her attitude was the precise opposite. But there was a great deal that she could do for us.

In the atmosphere of animal-loving persons that this movement attracts, Kim Novak — as spectacular in her attitude as she is in her beauty — certainly represents the complete individualist at a highwater mark of total commitment to animal causes. She has given help whenever asked. She has "directed" in the true sense of urging us on toward causes where applied hard work can relieve the jeopardy in which countless animals constantly find themselves.

Once when we were holding our annual meeting near her home, we hoped but did not know if Kim would attend. And suddenly, wearing a long gown and driving a jeep — an arrival as rapturously playful as anything in her movies — she came to the session in Monterey, staying as late as the most dedicated. She was gracious and social, totally friendly without putting herself forward. The next day she switched to jeans but retained the hat she had worn with her gown.

Nobody, I suppose, except those who know Kim very well, guessed the secret of that hat. The members she was dealing with right and left certainly had no inkling. I would not have known it myself except for Kim's confiding in me.

Under her hat, in her hair, was that other treasured inhabitant of her menagerie — a pet garter snake. Her hair had become its den. It was very snug there and, to Kim, supremely inoffensive.

Back in the 1940s and later I began to meet many people who, distressed by all the disturbances of the world, man's inhumanity to man, man's inhumanity to animal, had all kinds of fine dreams for rectifying such problems. They were, in many cases, dreams either unfulfillable or unfulfilled.

But Kim Novak—you must know this—is different from the rest of mankind. After that episode in Carmel when she held her ground on behalf of the animals who had her love, she found a chance to go forward with a fulfillable dream. A Japanese interest bought her beautifully located home in Carmel and Kim built something better—built it from the ground up with her animals in mind. She took the architect right into her scheme for making that house a mix of animal world and human world.

Her fulfillable dream is the home she lives in, designed to accommodate Kim, her veterinarian husband, and her animals. She has a glass-encased living room where the animals of the house can always be seen, her ideal of a home that *in*cludes and doesn't *ex*clude.

Kim has cared enough to make that "caring about animals" the very fabric of her life. Her way needn't be someone else's way. Hers is extraordinary and she's an extraordinary individual. I happen to admire it. I think she stands as a symbol of another way, a caring way.

Humans must have had a fine manner, instinctively, for dealing with animals that once were all wild, for the domestication of dog and horse—and goats—has a long history. Some of that domestication probably came from humans looking at other species and wanting to share burdens with them—to get some service out of animals. But much of it came, I believe, out of a great, upsurging desire for sharing. Sharing the world because man and animal were born in it together.

Kim Novak has that spirit as much as anyone. When you see this spirit abroad in the world, it is like the world having another chance—another chance to see human beings in league with animals and not merely exploiting them.

6

When Byron's Falcon Had the Run of the House: Roots of the American Humane Movement

The England of the sixteenth and seventeenth centuries was a hell for animals. Bull-baiting, bear-baiting, cockfighting, and cockthrowing (throwing sticks at a tethered bird until it was killed) were the national pastimes. Oddly enough, however, it is to England that we must look for not only a clue to early American attitudes toward animals, but also for the underpinnings of this country's humanitarian movement.

In many European countries, a lack of feeling for animals has been attributed to: (1) the indifference of the Roman Catholic Church, epitomized by Thomas Aquinas's belief that the only purpose of kindness to "the brute creation" was to dispose man more kindly toward his fellow humans; and, (2) the theory of mathematician-scientist-philosopher René Descartes that animals were mere automatons that felt no pain because they could not "think."

In England, however, the general air of cruelty seems less a consequence of any institutionalized policy than of the lack of a countervailing idea. One must also keep in mind the historical perspective. The English people of the seventeenth century had seen the murder of a king, a civil war, rule by a commoner and his subsequent death brought about by counterrevolutionaries. Add to the national confusion the fact that the common human was sadly deficient in personal rights, and the absence of sympathy for animals becomes more credible.

It was not until the late 1600s that animal cruelty began to be viewed publicly with less than enthusiasm. Philosopher John Locke (1632-1704) wrote that "children should from the beginning be bred up in an abhorrence of killing and tormenting any living creature." Minister John Wesley (1703-91) and Bishop Joseph Butler (1692-1752) agreed that animals had souls. Artist William Hogarth (1697-1764) painted in 1742 *Four Stages*, portraying a link between cruelty to animals and criminal acts against man. Political thinker Jeremy Bentham (1718-1832) felt cruelty to animals should be a crime.

The first book devoted to the subject appeared in 1776 and was entitled *A Dissertation on the Duty of Mercy and Sin of Cruelty to Brute Animals*. Its author, Reverend Humphrey Primatt, wrote: "See that no brute of any kind,

Beginning falconers use a hawk, the American kestrel, which is not much bigger than a sparrow. But the kestrel is not really suitable for falconry—and the sport leads to nest-robbing in the wild, for the birds can be difficult to breed in captivity.
COURTESY SOCIETY FOR THE PRESERVATION OF BIRDS OF PREY.

Death of a hawk eagle. Man can find hardship and death in the wild, but this bird found it in the inhospitable environment of the city. No longer can pet stores sell raptors; this one died in the hands of its young owner.

whether intrusted to thy care, or coming in thy way, suffer thy neglect or abuse. Let no view of profit, no compliance with custom, or fear of ridicule of the world, ever tempt thee to the least act of cruelty or injustice to any creature whatsoever. But let this be your invariable rule, everywhere, and at all times, to do unto others as, in their condition, you would be done unto." Dr. Primatt's volume had a profound influence on those individuals who would later found the Royal Society for the Prevention of Cruelty to Animals.

A humanitarian movement of the late eighteenth century advanced the rights of man, and this new awareness extended to animals. But there arose no groundswell of popular support for the humane cause. The idea was kept alive by individuals, often literary figures such as William Cowper (1731-1800), Robert Burns (1759-96), and Samuel Coleridge (1772-1834), as well as prose writers and essayists. Some years later, in the early 1800s, poets Longfellow and Shelley made contributions.

I'm not a devotee of poetry but an anecdote about George Lord Byron caught my imagination. When Shelley and Byron were living in Italy, the former wrote his wife that Byron had ten horses, eight dogs, three monkeys, five cats, an eagle, a crow, and a falcon — all of which, except the horses, wandered freely about the villa. In a postscript, Shelley added five peacocks, two guinea hens, and an Egyptian crane to the list. "I wonder," he concluded, "who all these animals were before they were changed into these shapes."

In 1800 the first anticruelty bill was introduced in the English Parliament. It was intended to stop bull-baiting. Opponents argued that the sport inspired courage and improved the mind; the proposal failed. Nine years later a general anticruelty bill was introduced. Despite support by the Lord High Chancellor, it too was defeated. Not until 1822 was legislation successful. This measure pertained only to the larger domestic animals and was introduced in the House of Commons by Colonel Richard Martin, a Protestant from County Galway, Ireland. Two years later Colonel Martin and Reverend Arthur Broome, who had instigated a reprinting of Dr. Primatt's book, took the lead in organizing the Society for the Prevention of Cruelty to Animals, to function primarily as an enforcement mechanism for the Martin Act. The "Royal" prefix was added in 1840 at Queen Victoria's command.

If "Humanity Dick" Martin is the man who stands out in English humane history, in the United States the honor goes to Henry Bergh.

At first glance, there would appear to be little of the dedicated humanitarian in the youthful Bergh. He was born in New York City in 1813, the son of a prosperous shipbuilder of German descent. Christian Bergh sent his son to Columbia College to study law; Henry, however, was more interested in travel and the fashionable life and left in 1830 without graduating. He interrupted his travels in 1839 to marry Matilda Taylor, the daughter of an English architect and he and his wife set off for an extended period of travel in Europe and the Far East. It was in Seville, probably about 1843, that we first come across evidence of Bergh's humanitarian spirit; he and his wife were revolted by a bullfight at which twenty-five horses and eight bulls were destroyed. Bergh noted in his diary that one of the human participants, a picadore, was badly hurt, "but one's sympathies are not with the men, for they have reason, know their danger, are the inventors of this scene, and therefore richly merit death in any shape."

In 1863 President Lincoln appointed the New Yorker secretary of the American legation to Russia. In St. Petersburg, the diplomat quickly discovered that his splendidly uniformed driver could successfully cow Russian peasants found beating their carriage horses. Bergh commented on the incident, "At last I've found a way to utilize my gold lace, and about the best use I can make of it." To the dismay of his embassy colleagues, Bergh took advantage of the force of a uniform; he began going out of his way to find cases of such abuse.

The legation secretary left his diplomatic post in 1865; it's not clear why. According to one report, he found the climate too severe; another attributed his departure to ill health. The most colorful version paints the American Minister, Cassius Clay of Kentucky, as resenting Bergh's popularity and dismissing him. At any rate he went, and en route stopped in London to meet with the Earl of Harrowby, president of the RSPCA. It was here that whatever protectionist leanings Bergh felt must have been fortified, for upon reaching New York he set about paving the way for America's humane movement.

There was more than enough cruelty in New York to merit the undertaking. The move to urbanization had thrown humans and animals together in confusion. Herds of cattle and hogs were common sights on New York streets and slaughterhouse facilities were sprinkled about the city. Cockfights, dogfights, and ratting events (where the test of a dog's worth was how many rodents it could destroy) were the order of the day. The upper class indulged in pigeon shoots and coursing rabbits with greyhounds. And it was best not to inquire into the training methods of exhibitors of performing animals. (Bergh had run-ins with P. T. Barnum, but the latter eventually became an admirer.) Transport depended almost entirely on the horse. People were moved by "horse cars" drawn on rails. At their peak there were fifteen-hundred such conveyances pulled by twelve-thousand horses — animals that were usually overloaded and underfed, that were driven when lame, had their hooves eaten away by salt on winter streets, and often perished in fires because they were stabled in cellars or on second floors. The best lasted four or five years.

The problems protectionists face today are serious and constant. How much more so must have been the obstacles one hundred years ago, with no sources of inspiration or motivation other than Bergh's own. It is indeed incredible that he was not deterred by the public apathy (what he termed the "lifeless enemy"), the ridicule of unfriendly newspapers, the hatred and threats of those profiteering from animal suffering, the loss of personal friendship of those who could not or would not understand his motives.

Aside from his driving humanitarian spirit, Bergh had another major asset: contacts from his prosperous background and diplomatic service. Early endorsers of the humane ideal he espoused — whether from genuine belief or mere friendship — included philanthropists, a military general, a wealthy merchant, a diplomat, journalist Horace Greeley, poet William Cullen Bryant, Hamilton Fish (U.S. Secretary of State from 1869 to 1877), and New York mayor John T. Hoffman.

Many of these braved a winter storm to be present at Bergh's first public meeting on the subject of animal protection. The gathering was held February 8, 1866, at Clinton Hall and was well attended (the speaker had done his homework with the newspapers). The public heard a direct and convincing appeal: "This is a matter purely of conscience. It has no perplexing side issues. Politics have no more to do with it than astronomy, or the use of the globe. No, it is a moral question in all of its aspects; it addresses itself to that quality of our nature that cannot be disregarded by any people with safety to their dearest interest; it is a solemn recognition of the greatest attribute of the Almighty Ruler of the Universe, mercy, which if suspended in our own case but for a single instant, would overwhelm and destroy us."

Bergh's next order of business was the passage of an anticruelty statute. New York already had such a state law, passed in 1829, but it went unenforced. (Nor was this America's first instance of humane legislation: "The Body of Liberties," prepared by the Reverend Nathaniel Ward and adopted by the General Court of Massachusetts in 1641, forbid "Tirranny or Cruelties" toward animals usually kept for man's use.) Perhaps its quality of not being "the first" accounted for the bill's relatively easy progress. By April 19, 1866, it was New York law that: "Every

The U.S. Fish and Wildlife Service maintains a collection of battery, punt, and big guns used during the market hunting, preprotection days around the turn of the century. The battery gun on the left contains ten barrels that could be fired at birds by pulling one trigger. The punt gun in the center, capable of firing a huge quantity of shot, could down a great number of birds in a single blast. PHOTO BY REX GARY SCHMIDT, FISH AND WILDLIFE SERVICE.

Two Kansas City gunners display their day's kill. William T. Hornaday, who published this photo in his 1913 book, Our Vanishing Wildlife, *felt the shooters were not so much to blame as the system that allowed such slaughter.*

person who shall, by his act or neglect, maliciously kill, maim, wound, injure, torture, or cruelly beat any horse, mule, cow, cattle, sheep, or other animal, belonging to himself or another, shall, upon conviction, be adjudged guilty of a misdemeanor." The penalty for a misdemeanor at the time was imprisonment for not more than a year or a fine not to exceed $250, or both.

At about the same time as these provisions were enacted, Bergh secured a state charter for the formation of the American Society for the Prevention of Cruelty to Animals. Its founder hoped the society could eventually extend outside New York but this proved impractical. Most important, the charter granted police power to the group to actively enforce the new law. At an organizational meeting on April 23, Henry Bergh was elected president, an office he held until his death in 1888. Also at that meeting he collected $850 from the society's endorsers and officers, who then, practically speaking, retired from the scene. It was up to the president to put life into the ASPCA charter.

Bergh fulfilled the role admirably, functioning for twenty-two years as the guiding spirit and motivator of the society. His forte was law enforcement and the record of his exploits is a lively and inspirational tale for animal lovers. While serving as ASPCA head, Bergh saw over twelve-thousand cases of animal abuse prosecuted, with his side winning ninety percent of them. This is an impressive, almost incredible record, but it should be noted that the crusading New Yorker did himself serve as prosecuting attorney with the city's blessing.

By 1870 the legal load was becoming insupportable and Bergh accepted the volunteer services of Elbridge T. Gerry, a young attorney. Four years later Bergh and Gerry extended their concept of justice to include children as well as animals. Eight-year-old Mary Ellen Wilson had been regularly and severely abused by her foster parents. The case was reported, futilely, to several city institutions and, as a last resort, to Bergh. There were no child protection laws but the ASPCA president took on the case on the basis that: "The child is an animal. If there is no justice for it as a human being, it shall at least have the rights of the cur in the street. It shall not be abused." An offshoot of the case was the founding, in 1875, of the New York Society for the Prevention of Cruelty to Children. Elbridge Gerry, who had prosecuted Mary Ellen's case and obtained a year's prison term for her foster mother, served as its president from 1879 to 1901.

Child and animal protection were thus linked at the very beginning. Some humane societies, as in Ohio, collected child support payments from delinquent fathers, and records of the Indianapolis Humane Society detail expenditures for coal and grocery baskets for the poor and the aged, paid out as recently as the 1960s. A large part of the American Humane Association's program, even today, is concerned with child protection services. In the card catalogue of a metropolitan library there are two references under humane societies—"animals, treatment of" and "child welfare."

Henry Bergh was not the only humane-minded soul in the country, but he knew how and had the motivation to "get things done." The New York statute passed at his urging has been the basis for anticruelty legislation in all other states. The charter of the ASPCA was the first such document in the Western Hemisphere and has served as the pattern for almost all United States animal protection societies. Within five years of its granting, nineteen states saw the formation of similar organizations. Various SPCAs sprang up, all local and autonomous, usually requesting advice from Bergh: Pennsylvania (1867), Massachusetts (1868), San Francisco (1869).

Other organizations followed. In time, channels other than law enforcement were found to bring about relief and protection for animals. Shelters were created for housing, care, and humane destruction of small animals. The first was established by the Animal Rescue League of Philadelphia in 1874, and the idea was adapted throughout the United States to suit local conditions. Over the last century there have been hundreds of shelters of all sorts and of many names and functions. Many have prospered and expanded as times, conditions, and leadership have changed; many have long ceased to exist, for the same reasons.

Humanitarians came to recognize the value of public education and either incorporated such programs into existing societies' aims or formed organizations expressly for this purpose; the American Humane Education Society was founded in 1889. Rest farms were established for horses pensioned off by owners and overworked horses of the poor could get brief rest at little or no cost. The first animal

America's early settlers harbored superstitions about the magic of the bobcat—that its fur could be a wondrous remedy for cuts and wounds or that you could eat bobcat to cure a headache. In 1727 a bobcat bounty was offered in Massachusetts, and bobcats have been on the run since. No matter how hidden, someone—in this case (fortunately for the bobcat) a photographer—is always searching it out.

hospital was erected by the ASPCA in 1914 at a cost of two-hundred thousand dollars; another notable hospital originating from the turn of the century was Boston's Angell Memorial Hospital, operated by the Massachusetts SPCA. Free clinics appeared in Philadelphia, Buffalo, Pittsburgh, Chicago, Cleveland, San Francisco, and Los Angeles with the emphasis of their work on treatment of lame, injured, and diseased horses.

The National Association of Audubon Societies (the first society was organized in 1886) was typical of bird protection groups during the early humane movement. Such organizations were responsible principally for laws enacted to protect song and insectivorous birds in many states. Audubon was not intended then as an anti-cruelty society, nor does it function as one now. The organized movement against vivisection (surgical operations on animals in the name of medical research) began with the formation of the American Anti-Vivisection Society in Philadelphia in 1883. The society's efforts were initially aimed at regulating vivisection but were changed a few years later to a position of total abolition.

Henry Bergh was such a guiding light that his death would naturally have resulted in some dimming of the humane movement's force. Yet his demise, together with the disappearance of the horse from the urban scene, caused a tunnel-visioned stagnation in the movement, traces of which can still be seen today. As mechanization took over, animal cruelties were not so blatantly evident; most organizations had limited funds and became engrossed with dog and cat problems, catering to the interests of their urban supporters. It was not until the middle of this century that humanitarians saw fit to break new ground and turn their attention to humane slaughter, trapping, rodeos, hunting, laboratory animals—those out-of-sight cruelties which, nevertheless, had been present for decades.

7

War Dogs and the Winds of Protest: The Pentagon Reverses a Policy, Grudgingly

In war, particularly in modern war, there is no "typical way to die," but the facts are sometimes different from the way the folks at home imagine them.

Deaths in Vietnam are a case in point. On the average, the soldier who did not come back was not strafed by machine-gun fire as he loped down a village street, nor was he blasted from a helicopter by antiaircraft guns. He was not, on the average, the victim of sniper fire. His life was blown out in a great loneliness. And the telegram that carried news of his death to some family in Iowa or Nevada more often than not was inspired by a device whose deadliness was difficult to appreciate here in the States: the booby trap.

A defense was developed against booby traps: the war dog. Just one of these dogs was credited with detecting 159 booby traps in a single year. "That," said the dog's handler, "is 159 legs saved right there."

Skill at detecting a booby trap required training, but it was a type of training that could be given only to a dog, not a human. As Congressman John E. Moss of California was to tell his colleagues (on quite a different day and for reasons connected to the fate of these animals who performed life-saving feats) a dog has "forty times the smell, twenty times the hearing, and ten times the vision of a human soldier." On patrol, a war dog would identify a booby trap in advance and literally demonstrate its presence because the animal's incredibly sensitive ears would pick up the faint sound of wind passing through the wires of the mechanism.

The U.S. Army estimated that war dogs had lowered human casualties on patrol by an all but unbelievable sixty-five percent. Not every dog, of course, detected booby traps. They were trained as all-out battle helpers and—the Army being as alert to spell out its regulations for dogs as for soldiers—any dog pressed into service discovered it was his official mission not only to "alert to danger" but also to "receive the fire of the enemy."

This was scarcely a new idea. The Greeks had used dogs in warfare, too; the Romans drafted dogs for attack work, recognizing them as a definite Army unit; and the Spanish conquistadores who ravaged their way through lost kingdoms of Aztecs and Mayans were accompanied by lunging and powerful dogs that helped reinforce the notion that here indeed were gods on earth, equipped with a supernatural power to direct the forces of the animal world.

It took awhile to scout out possible uses of dogs in Vietnam, but even in

They died together. This photo was taken shortly before Lawrence Yochum and his dog, King, companions in combat, were killed in action on February 7, 1970, in Vietnam.

the rather technical field of modern warfare there remains an element of body-against-body combat; and far better to use the superior sensitivities of the German shepherd and the Labrador retriever—the dogs most suitable for Army work—than to throw away human lives in pesky countries on pesky missions in the countryside. All military commanders would agree to that; so would many animal lovers, putting human life first of all. There was no particular argument with the proclamation of Captain Richard Hale, ranger-trained infantryman who was the boss at Bien Hoa where the dogs were trained. "I don't know anyone who would say that a dog's life is worth more than that of a man," said Captain Hale.

The dogs, most of them a gift to the Army by United States citizens who wanted to aid the war effort, were sharp. They could be trained to their battle duties with amazing swiftness. Newspaperman George McArthur reported from Saigon that the military dogs "learn working Vietnamese commands in about three weeks. That's a far better record than that of most American soldiers." He added, "It may be a good thing since virtually all the dogs must stay behind while their handlers are gradually phased out of the Vietnam war."

This phase-out under which the American military proposed to leave the war dogs to a strange fate—in some cases, a fate even stranger than death on the battlefield, since dog happens to be a delicacy of the Vietnamese diet—was eventually to cause a remarkable uproar here in the United States.

The Army had not hesitated to paint the dogs as war heroes. But abandoning them during the American pullout certainly wasn't reminiscent of the more gallant practices of the American military. Cavalry horses who had done their duty were generally treated with admirable care right into old age. Many a plaque and statue had been raised to a horse that had done its bit for the country.

Was it really true that the American military was so ungallant as to abandon on foreign shores those same brave dogs who had done more than any general to lessen the deaths of soldiers on patrol? Was it?

That question, though many asked it, was naive in the extreme. Gallantry toward animals, as toward humans, certainly existed among individuals (it always has), but gallantry seemed to be passing out of the codebook of the high command. That was the most terrifying aspect of this unwanted and eventually unpopular war—there had been, in the era of "destroying cities in order to save them," an almost total freeze-out of moral evaluations of any kind.

Abandonment of the war dog was all of a piece with the rest of official policy. Wherein could the high commanders of American destiny bother themselves with such a trifle as the fate of a dog?

SURGICAL PRACTICE: A SPECIAL CONVENIENCE

Somewhat prior to the uproar over disposition of the dogs shipped to Vietnam, reports from Fort Bragg, North Carolina, provided a sobering glimpse of just how much persecution of these animals the Army, at its most ungallant, could tolerate.

The *Miami Herald* took up the reports, originally published more obscurely in *Veritas*, house organ of the Green Berets, of a "Green Beret canine shooting gallery" where dogs held at Fort Bragg were deliberately hit with battle-fire (wounded but not killed) so medics could race into the field and practice the art of surgery on freshly shot casualties. The *Herald* also noted the military's prompt reaction to the publication of that report: The Army, on the receiving end of two-thousand letters from "outraged animal lovers," did nothing to end the practice itself but issued a shush-up directive forbidding all future mention of the gallery "where Green Beret medics shoot dogs, then practice healing them. . . .Despite the outcry, the practice continues."

Specialists in shielding the military from complaints about such practices frequently have a great gift of eloquence, and I would rate a colonel who was acting director of International and Civil Affairs for the Department of the Army, as one of the niftiest of the breed.

Clarence E. Richard, managing director of the National Anti-Vivisection Society, tried to meet the issue head-on by demanding that Secretary of Defense Melvin Laird stop any practice that would involve staking out dogs for soldiers to deliberately gun down. Back popped a letter from the colonel, who "fully appreciated" Richard's "deep concern."

Yes, ahem. But there were other considerations, it seemed, that must be mentioned. In a long letter that couched the policy of the Army in unyieldingly humanitarian terms, the colonel tried to make it all perfectly clear. The special forces medical specialist was headed into a "primitive combat environment" and out there he would find himself required to treat "diseases, infections and injuries as well as wounds inflicted by 'punji' stakes, booby traps and gunshot. Consequently, the training for these medical specialists is of necessity designed to be detailed and thorough."

Only the very select individual, declared the colonel, would in time arrive at the final training phase where he would have ". . .a dog patient which remains his responsibility throughout the course. These animals are procured without cost to the Army from county, city and state-operated pounds. Animals that are accepted are taken only from those that would otherwise be disposed of by the pounds. They are housed in a kennel with a concrete floor, drains and a roof. Conditions are clean and sanitary. Each animal is under the specific care of a student but, as prescribed by Army policy, all the animals are under the general supervision and care of a qualified veterinarian as well. During the course of the medical training, the animals are kept under anesthesia during any time that pain might otherwise be experienced.

"Such training is considered essential to prepare the medical specialist for combat duty. . . .Please be assured that in every phase of each dog's important service, humane treatment of the animal is of principal concern to the Army. . . .Your suggestion that the Army should avail itself of the numerous cases of gunshot wounds which are received in hospitals throughout the country and in Viet Nam has merit. However, such a program of observation would not provide for the development of individual surgical skills which are required of medical specialists. This, together with the extensive complications in training management which would result from dispersing medical trainees in hospitals throughout the country and Viet Nam, precludes the adoption of this alternative. . . .I trust this information will reassure you that the program of medical training conducted at Fort Bragg is humane in every respect. . . ."

The letter made the whole process seem as antiseptic as a pailful of hospital sanitizing solution. What the colonel said was, assuredly, more gracious than replying, "We *gotta* do it—bug off!" It meant, however, the same thing.

Ever so deftly, the letter skipped all around the question of whether or not the Green Berets had a shooting gallery for dogs. It also very clearly showed they did.

The Army could be accused of many things toward the tail end of the Vietnam War, but it could not be accused—at home or abroad—of any overwhelming gallantry toward its dogs. The upper echelons seemed mainly to regret that a dog had but one life to give for his country.

Stubbornly, and against any facts that came to light, Army officials clung to the right to describe as "humane" almost any inhumanity that managed to surface.

REMORSE FROM THE BATTLEFRONTS

This high-level callousness was not shared by the troops; particularly it was not shared by those down-in-the-line soldiers who daily depended on the skills of the war dogs for their existence.

At headquarters level, Pentagon or Saigon, self-justification was the overriding policy. Headquarters could not even concede it should at least *look* for different ways to teach surgery than by maiming dogs. And headquarters invented ingenious reasons for sticking with a hard-nosed policy of abandoning the four-footed soldiers in Vietnam even after the practice had come under considerable public fire.

Let's go back to the beginning and study what flushed out the problem.

Soldiers did. The Army had humanitarians, all right, but they weren't in the complaint-answering division. They were out on patrol. From the front lines of Vietnam, the sorrow of soldiers who found that their dogs were to be left behind while they themselves came home, began to communicate itself to their families and to the Animal Protection Institute. We found ourselves in this particular fight almost alone, not because other humane organizations disagreed but because—after a quick testing of the waters—they concluded the Department of Defense couldn't be deflected. Too big.

API also had reason to feel dismayed, but staff members couldn't bring themselves to ignore the letters coming in. When word filtered in from the battlefront that there were threats of court-martial just because some soldiers were letting us know the fate in store for their dogs, it was a question of whether to be bullied into silence or to make even the mighty Department of Defense aware that animals, and the humans who rise in animals' defense, are not a mewling minority but a potent force.

As I sit here, reviewing the letters that led API to decide this was a cause it couldn't honorably desert, I'm struck by the forcefulness with which so-called ordinary people express themselves when they're truly touched, truly hurt, by man's inhumanity to animals.

There is the clangorous cry of the outraged schoolboy, Jerry Armantrout of

When the military prepared to abandon the dogs that had cut patrol casualties on the Vietnam front by sixty percent, a great national outcry developed. It started with the soldiers, was spearheaded back home by the Animal Protection Institute, was supported by school children writing to the Secretary of Defense and the President—and triumphed in a reversal of Pentagon policy.

La Porte, Indiana, who wrote melodramatically (but truthfully) to Melvin Laird: "For all the years of loyal service these dogs deliver, they are left behind to be mistreated or eaten. Think, Sir! EATEN!" And there was the quieter, heartfelt comment of Rosemarie Wawok, who asked Laird, "How can a high official sitting in a plush office possibly know how it feels to have only a dog to love?" And another young lady stormed at him, "If I were a dog, I probably wouldn't save *your* life!" The letters arrived, thousands of them, at newspapers, at API, at the Defense Department, and they reached a level of high-pitched incoherence—raging and frantic anger—but there were also, at the beginning, quiet and tormented letters received by API from Vietnam itself.

Mark Wrinkle wrote simply and sincerely, asking for help: "I am with the 43rd Scout Dog Platoon, located in Quang Tri, Viet Nam. . .I am writing with hopes that I can bring my dog Prince back to the United States with me.

"Prince is six years old, which is almost peak for working war dogs. He has been in Viet Nam for three of his six years. He has saved my life along with hundreds of other men. Soon he will be useless to the Army because of his old age and the Army will dispose of him. I feel the least I could do for him is give him a home.

"Prince is called 'The Old Man of the Platoon.' He has the friendliest disposition of all the dogs here. Aside from the fact that I'm sure Prince would never bite anyone, if he did, he would not hurt them, as his canine teeth are too worn down.

"I feel that, after a dog has saved countless numbers of lives and he becomes too old to work, the Army should do more for him than to send him down South to be put away and disposed of like trash. I feel the least the Army could do is offer the dog to the handler.

"My tour of duty ends in December and any and all help I can get will be greatly appreciated by myself along with everyone else in the platoon. . . .I will be awaiting anxiously for an answer as they are planning to send Prince down South soon."

By coincidence—or maybe not, since the temptation must be overwhelming to give the name "Prince" to a dog whose business is both fighting and life-saving—there was another dog named Prince who made it all the way from the warfront to Norfolk, Virginia, and was headed for a farm at Indianola, Iowa. *Was*—because suddenly it was discovered that this scout dog of Seal Team Two, once a police dog of Norfolk, had no right to such freedom.

Having declared that war dogs who went to Asia must stay in Asia, the military couldn't bear it that princely Prince—who had been publicly decorated and who wore two Purple Hearts for his service to his country—had almost gotten away. Prince, it was ruled, would have to be shipped right back to Vietnam.

John Svicarovich of the *Virginia-Pilot* headlined a story "U.S. Dog Hero To Be Exiled," and wrote darkly: "What is certain is the fact that Prince is being pulled back into the web of a policy which prohibits dogs used in tropical combat areas overseas from returning to this country." The Navy, which posted the orders to send Prince to the States, expressed all sorts of misgivings for having unwittingly violated a policy of the Air Force—which had jurisdiction over Prince and just couldn't make an exception even though Prince was already home. In fact, said John Svicarovich, "Prince was returned to Norfolk from Viet Nam three times and publicly decorated in ignorance of that policy."

One of Prince's handlers declared, "He's one of the smartest dogs I've ever seen, with unusual smelling and tracking ability. He's the only dog I've ever seen that could smell a man upwind, fifty to sixty yards away."

A lot of people were smelling something upwind from that nonsensical plan to whip Prince back to Asia again, his Purple Hearts dangling.

94

Incidents of this sort, illustrating the obstinancy and the pervasiveness of the official policy, emphasized more poignantly the letters from the warfront. The most significant of all of these was a message signed individually by an entire platoon, a message written as an open letter to America that attempted to deal comprehensively with the heavy-footed alibis being used to cover the crudities of the death-or-abandonment policy.

"Under present Army policy," wrote the soldiers, "not one of our hard-working and much-decorated canine friends will return to the U.S.A. alive. Instead, we will reward them for a job well done by sentencing them to mass euthanasia. A reason has been given for this brutal and unjust treatment. . . .Some dogs (not a majority) have contracted a disease called Idiopathic Hemorrhagic Syndrome or IHS. In lay terms, this simply means that the dogs bleed and the Army has not found out what causes it, hence the nickname 'bleeders' disease.' "

The platoon couldn't accept, for several reasons, what Army bosses were saying. ". . .Little, if anything, is being done to find a cause or cure for this disease in over three years of 'research'. . . .Present Army policy states that even when a dog has contracted this disease it is perfectly all right to work him until he drops dead or becomes too ill to function (in which case he will be destroyed). . . .Vietnamese mascot dogs are sent back to the U.S. frequently after short periods of quarantine and a few shots. . . ."

And the platoon dealt with the military's other official excuse, the dogs' status as killers: "Scout dogs and trackers, contrary to popular belief, have not been trained to attack or kill and in the vast majority of cases could quite easily be converted into wonderful and useful pets. Even many sentry dogs could be used by the Army and civilian police forces and thereby save thousands or even millions of dollars in training costs."

This letter—which API used as the basis for a newspaper advertising campaign calling attention to the plight of the war dogs—wound up with a declaration that the plea was just what Lawrence Yochum of Burney, California, would have wanted the platoon to do.

Because on February 13, 1970, Lawrence Yochum, "who was outstanding and assuredly a leader," and his inveterate companion in Vietnam, a war dog named King, had been killed in action. Together.

AN IMMOVABLE FORCE BEGINS TO MOVE

As a former Army officer I knew that if the heat is hot enough even the Army will try to cool down the kitchen. It was out on a formidable limb with "Idiopathic Hemorrhagic Syndrome" and the soldiers weren't the only ones suggesting a quarantine ought to handle that. API's broadside of publicity, advertisements, and letters had done its work. The first evidence of an Army turn-around surfaced when I telegrammed President Richard Nixon and sent out a flaming summary of complaints to Laird, who may not have appreciated a growing disposition on the part of schoolchildren to see him (from a dog's-eye view) as something of a war criminal.

Brigadier General Wilson M. Osteen of the Army Surgeon-General's Office answered API on behalf of the President and the Secretary of Defense. The General had drawn on kid gloves, declaring an intention to "save rather than destroy these valuable and faithful dogs." And he erased the alibi the military had been using as its chief plank in refusing to let the dogs come home.

That disease with the long name, he was able to report, had now had its "causative agent identified" at the Walter Reed Army Institute of Research. The cause was a tick and the same disease had been discovered in a lot of places—Puerto

Rico, the Near East, the Virgin Islands, even Florida. "Since this disease has extensive distribution in tropical climates," asserted the General, "there is no medical reason for not returning these animals to the Continental United States."

That left only one alibi.

If the military really wanted to hold its ground, it would have to refute the persuasive testimony of soldiers at the front with a scare campaign designed to show the dogs were murderous. It would have to prophesy that Jill, Jack, and Johnny would be wiped out on the way to first grade by these marauding war dogs, gone cuckoo when they returned to society.

EXILES RETURN

Tremendous winds of protest had, in this case, almost done their work. But that's not to say defenders of the status quo weren't sticking with their regulation books. One of the sadder but more telling documents to come out of this fight was the following assertion by Major Robert M. Sullivan of the Air Force's Directorate of Security police.

To Janice Petrowsky of Pompton Plains, New Jersey, Major Sullivan declared: "I would like to emphasize that your concern for the military working dogs transferred to the South Vietnamese is unwarranted. The standard of living and customs of foreign troops does not affect the methods in which these dogs are trained or maintained anymore than it affects other types of equipment or weapons such as ships, tanks or airplanes. Military working dogs are used by many countries of varied cultures. The methodology of dog handling, however, remains constant."

The assumption that would, I guess, drive many an animal protectionist wild was Major Sullivan's suggestion that dogs are fairly equated with "other types of equipment or weapons." Are they really? Does a ship complain at being left outside? Does a plane get that hurt look in its eyes at being exposed to the new and the unfamiliar? It is not necessary to have an evil view of the Vietnam forces with whom the dogs were to be left in order to view the abandonment as the callous act of detached and indifferent masters.

It was Major Sullivan who stated the official case for not returning the war dogs to American society for fear their murdering ways would scandalize us all.

"The dog," he said, "has been accustomed for years to the close, constant companionship of his handler. He has been trained to fear no human, to respond only to the commands of his handler and to attack on command or in defense of his handler or himself. After eight or ten years of this life, how could such a dog adapt to the sedentary existence of a house pet? How would it adjust to the confusion of a household? How could you be sure that the dog's natural protective instincts would not allow it to do great harm to children, visitors, or the milkman or postman? As you can see, such an existence would be most difficult for the dog or its owner." (Janice Petrowski, for one, could not see.) "It is our opinion, therefore, that military working dogs should be just that. When they become feeble, or incurably sick, and can no longer do the work for which they are trained, they should be euthanized. Believe me, this action is not taken lightly and every effort is made to keep our dogs healthy and working as long as possible."

This shaky planet is forever coming back to certain problems—certain overriding questions—such as the question of age. In some past civilizations it was common practice for old people to be put to death when they could no longer contribute to society. But nearly all civilizations, and all fragments of civilizations, have grown out of this practice. It was recognized for what it is: selfishness at a cosmic level, the new generations pushing out the old as "no longer useful, even to themselves."

We learned it for people. Most people learned it for dogs. On the average, American families find it feasible to cherish their dog through giddy youth into slumbering old age and at length see the pet die a natural death, not executed as summary punishment for no longer being able to play catch-ball with the kids in the street. Most of us, including most Army officers, are understanding with our family pets. How was it, then, that the military thought the only fitting end for a dog whose career was life-saving was prompt execution? Wherein was the dog less than the cavalry horse?

Major Sullivan said no, the dogs could never be released to society—families living with them would have to exist in quaking fear. But there were soldiers who knew the dogs better than Major Sullivan who said few dogs were actually killers.

Wasn't this a question to be settled on a dog-by-dog basis?

Many a soldier came out of World War II respectfully recounting the exploits of the dogs he had served with. A Guam fireman of the 21st Marines named George G. Flores recalled: "The Japanese would set up an ambush in a cave or in the jungle and the dogs would sense it. When the dogs started to hunch down and crawl in a certain direction, glancing over their shoulders at us, we would know that something was wrong. Most of the time, the enemy was ahead and we were then ready for him. . . .The dog would approach a cave very cautiously. If he went into the cave, we knew there was no one inside and we all breathed a lot easier. If he doubled back and ran, crouching close to the ground, we would get ready for trouble."

A standard defense of the military against the charge of callousness toward the war dogs was the reminder that all over the world, certainly on Guam, there were military cemeteries for dogs. This would have meant more if the same officers hadn't seemed so interested in banishing those dogs to the cemetery as swiftly as their war duties were over. When API sought a memorial at Arlington Cemetery—for dogs who had frequently won more decorations than many a colonel—the answer was "not enough space."

Even so, the winds of protest—letters from school kids, petitions from the front, the stalwart activity of a forceful congressman—soon routed all the military's quibbles. The congressman was John E. Moss and he had introduced, at API's request, a bill directing the return of the dogs to the United States and making it government policy to turn over the dogs to "a humane organization whose facilities permit them to care for such dog during the remainder of its life at no cost to the government."

We did not have to force action on the bill. Military officials, after a briefing in Moss's office, agreed to rewrite service regulations to reflect a change in policy regarding disposition of war dogs. At the end of this struggle, the animals were being returned to Lackland Air Force Base in Texas for reprocessing and retraining with a view toward use in civilian and other military law enforcement agencies.

It was not a total victory. The frequent plea that the Army release the no-longer-wanted war dog to one of its soldier-handlers who had gone back home, or to members of the public who wanted to adopt it, was not carried out. But the "no return" policy had been defeated by a wild public outcry that the Animal Protection Institute had organized after pleas from the war front.

If the Pentagon can be turned round on an issue, we have reason to believe other institutions behaving like warlords to their animal captives can also be bludgeoned with a bad press, until—from sheer embarrassment, if nothing else—they begin to act humanely.

Why didn't—and why doesn't—the military approach the question of the rehabilitation of the war dog on a dog-by-dog basis? No humane organization I'm aware of would favor killer-dogs stalking the inhabitants of the cities. But why did the Department of Defense imagine that all it had on its hands was a group of potentially psycho canines?

If the military wanted a "good example" of the proper way to deal with these exiles on their return, all they had to do was look at: themselves. For, as John Moss told the House of Representatives:

"During World War II, from 1942 to 1945, over 10,000 dogs were used by our military. When the conflict ended, and a dog was considered surplus to Army needs, the canine was immediately transferred to a reprocessing section for the purpose of rehabilitation for civilian life. Under the policy through which dogs had been secured for the Army, they were first offered to their original owners. In the event the original owner did not desire return of the dog, the animal was declared surplus to the needs of the Quartermaster and the Office of Surplus Property of the Treasury Department was notified of availability for sale to the public. The Treasury Department then announced availability of dogs for a purchase at a minimum cost and for handling and transportation. Requests from prospective purchasers were sent to Dogs for Defense, Inc., the non-profit civilian agency which had originally been set up to secure dogs for the Army. Each request was investigated to insure that the would-be purchaser was in a position to give the dog a good home. Reports on the prospective buyers were then forwarded to the Treasury Department where, if the report on a particular applicant was favorable, negotiations for sale were started."

I think the men in the troubled dog platoons of Vietnam would have bought all of it—except, perhaps, the routing of dogs through an "Office of Surplus Property."

When you're a hero of any description, it goes against the grain to be described in the official records simply as "property" and as "surplus." Heroes are not in surplus, not really. They never are, and we would do well to treat them kindly, even in the words we use to describe them.

8

Finding the Action That Fits
the Emotion:
A Personal Reflection

"Moving from Emotion to Action," the subtitle of this book, states what I consider the greatest need in the animal rights movement. It's not difficult to drum up sympathy and even fiery passion on behalf of animals. Passion abounds. Much more difficult—the crux of all social movements, I think—is using the energy generated by this sympathy and this passion to move systematically forward instead of remaining in one spot, stewing in our indignations.

When I was a very young boy, I stumbled on a principle of moving forward bit by bit that rescued me from considerable difficulties. If someone were to look for a subconscious reason as to why I have wanted so strongly to "set animals free," they would probably settle on the notion (I don't know how close to the truth it is) that there was a time when I—and all my family, really—needed to be set free. No one came along to do it.

We experienced the typical plight of the sharecropper family. I experienced the typical plight of the sharecropper child. Emerging from such a situation can be difficult, even impossible. Those who do break free must, I think, have either phenomenal luck or a special instinct that shows them how, step by step, one small movement at a time, they *can* pull themselves up and out. In truth, I never consciously formed this notion until later in life. It simply happened. And I can tell you how it started.

My family lived in the bayous of south central Louisiana, on a farm near the township of Marksville, and as a small boy I spoke only French. (I later discovered this was a remarkable experience for a boy in America.) My father sharecropped, a system where you always seemed a little further behind this year than last. At times he would go off on a raccoon hunt, killing the mother perhaps but occasionally bringing me a baby raccoon I could raise. I could certainly speak better to raccoons than to those people who spoke only English.

The raccoons would stay with me until they disappeared into the forest again. Because, I suppose, a small boy in a big bayou has a great deal of affection to lavish, the raccoons liked me and I could handle them; but others could not. My father would grow terribly aggravated when a raccoon became trapped in a tree and he could not coax it down. I felt proud because my raccoons were so definitely mine and because I could get them out of their troubles. It seemed to me a talent worth having.

I wish it had been that simple to do something about the troubles of my family. My father had ardently wished the same thing.

In this part of Louisiana, a sharecropper was likely to work a six- to ten-acre plot of ground. He would try for one bale of cotton per acre but God had to be cooperative for him to achieve it. The boll weevil did his worst. And it had to be a very good year indeed to plant the thought that maybe—just maybe—you'd have a tiny bit of money left over, after paying the company store, that could be used for a move and a new life. All staples came from the company store, and it was the common condition of sharecroppers that they owed more to the store than the crop was going to bring in.

One year my father was jubilant because he'd taken over six bales of cotton, of which our share was three. Settlement day was eagerly awaited but it ended sadly—we still owed more than the cotton was worth. The landowner tried to soothe smashed hopes with some gifts—my father received cotton work gloves, my mother a sunbonnet, and my sisters and myself peppermint candysticks. My mother was crying. It meant we must, again, stay another year. Lard, salt, salt pork, flour, cornmeal, baking powder—those were the provisions; our life was not unlike that of the raccoon babies I adopted, with the exception that my parents had to work like demons—there was no one to rescue us from predicaments, and there certainly was no forest escape to a lusher, easier life.

When we did get away, it was under sad circumstances. My father fell terribly ill and wound up in a New Orleans charity hospital for eighteen months. He had ulcers and other stomach problems and he needed surgery. My mother, my three sisters, and I careened from pillar to post. We stayed with uncles and aunts and a grandmother; but these relatives were sharecroppers, too, and there were limits to how much there was to give.

In 1930, after the Crash, we moved to the outskirts of Alexandria, Louisiana. My father, no longer strong enough for sharecropping, entered a state farming program for fifty cents a day plus a fifty-cent-a-day loan. Altogether, he received $150 in this way; ten years later, there was a demand for payment and, because of interest, the amount due was an enormous sum.

Readers will understand, by this, why some of those blues songs originate in the bayous.

In this worst of times, I was having a marvelous life. Elementary school forced me to learn English, and my French background actually became an asset—I was bilingual in a nation where it wasn't all that common.

Many adults, caught in the emotions and indignations of being denied what they want in life, sputter to a stop. Denied the chance to get what they want in a single leap, they frequently fall back, defeated. A child is different. He doesn't realize all the possibilities of life. He grasps what he can see around him. My grades at school were poor because I was often absent to help family finances by cutting and selling wood. My father was a hard man and the discipline was severe—severe to the point of insanity—but I loved him dearly. Our family was Catholic, sometimes receiving Catholic charity, and that involved rigidities too. Not an easy life, and yet—

I had begun to shine shoes on the street to earn spending money. I also had an early morning paper route—a walking paper route because I couldn't afford a bicycle. When I heard that a bike was available, I went round to the gentleman owning it, whom we all considered "an aristocrat," and told him I had seventy-five cents down payment and could make payments of a quarter a week. Bikes then had balloon tires but my purchase was definitely out of date; it had the skinniest tires in town.

This acquisition was not, however, as big a step forward as the deal I struck with Mr. Pye, a dairy owner. It was customary for me to shine his shoes on Saturday for five cents, although sometimes he just needed a brushup worth only two cents. I liked his business, though. Milk was delivered by horse-drawn cart and I loved to ride the carts with their dogwood insulators. Watching the dairy-packing, I speculated that if I had a box for eskimo pies I could strap on, then I could become a sort of dealer.

Mr. Pye set me up with a box and eskimo pies at forty cents a dozen, which I could sell for sixty cents a dozen. A nickel bought half a pound of dry ice to keep the merchandise frozen. In an hour's time, I sold out my first load, came back for a dozen and a half more, then for another dozen and a half, all in one day. I was dizzy with success.

When I came home with my pocket full of change, my mother couldn't believe I had earned so much money honestly and my father was dogged if I had. I blurted out my story and he seized me by the arm and carted me off to confront Mr. Pye with this tall tale. And when he learned it was all true, my dad, because he had a strict sense of fairness, seriously and sincerely apologized.

My dairy orders did so well that Mr. Pye supplied a special box that I equipped with a bell. I had invented the Good Humor Man, or rather the Good Humor Urchin, and didn't know it. I suppose other boys, somewhere, struck on the same discovery; but to me it was a revelation and something I could use all my life.

Somewhere along the way there *is* a breakout route.

I rang my bell so hard, summoning potential customers, that it cracked. Like the Liberty Bell, it was, indeed, the sign of a liberation. My mother still has it.

Ice cream happened to be the product for the territory, and my income, often greater than my father's, was a big help to the family. The following summer I rigged up a huge box on a pushcart propelled by bicycle wheels. The idea was planted by a trip to New Orleans, a prize won in a paper-route contest, where I spotted a three-wheel bicycle, pushcart-perfect. By the third summer, Mr. Pye had recognized my enterprise as a lucrative business and he outfitted several men with pushcarts. My business was thus watered down — too much competition for the same market.

Now I looked around: Camp Beauregard, packed with soldier boys, loomed as a whole new market. I tested the water and sold fifty dozen ice cream pies in no time. I called back and said, "Mr. Pye, I've sold out."

"You've sold fifty dozen? We don't have any more."

"I could sell one-hundred dozen."

Mr. Pye and his dairymen worked all night making ice cream pies, all of which were sold out in half a day to the soldiers. Selling two-hundred dozen eskimo pies at Camp Beauregard was no problem. My father joined me at it — twenty dollars could be made in one day — and for the rest of the summer we worked Camp Beauregard. In 1936, however, the camp concessionaire maneuvered for a piece of the action — he put a limit on what could be sold and took fifteen percent of the profits.

We needed a new idea and I had a brainstorm.

"Mr. Pye," I said, "we ought to make it easy to buy ice cream by having a drive-in place."

Unfortunately, Mr. Pye thought this was a foolish idea, and I did not have the money to undertake the venture myself. Millions of dollars were later made by Dairy Queens, based on just such a notion. Whenever I see a Dairy Queen, I'm reminded of the old days with Mr. Pye.

In fact, though, life pulls you along, and there are other avenues to pursue if you can once get out of the bayou. When I was sixteen I tried to join the Navy but was rejected by them as too young. So I went to the Army recruiters and lied about my age. At five-feet-two inches tall, I didn't make a very convincing eighteen-year-old; but this was 1939 — World War II was coming and the recruiters weren't standing on detail. A blank on the enlistment form asked for the year of my birth. I made a swift mental calculation and declared I'd been born in 1925.

"You mean '21, don't you?" said the recruiter. I had gone the wrong way with the two years. He knew it and I knew it, but he let me in.

I suppose it was that early fun I'd had with the raccoons that made me relieve tediums of Army life with a menagerie I gradually established while living off the base. I raised animals, strictly for pleasure, and also played veterinarian to the pets of a large number of soldiers. But these soldiers would get transferred and have to abandon their pets; naturally, quite a few got dumped on me.

I married at eighteen and my wife must have wondered at the kind of household I kept. At one point we had twenty-eight cats and nine "regular dogs," but the dog population could easily swell to fifteen with the birth of pups.

In much the same way that my life hedgehopped from selling one ice cream bar to selling a ton of them, my life with animals has also hedgehopped, since that day, from seeing what can be done for animals by one family in one home, to seeing what can be done for them on a worldwide basis.

This is an American system that I did not invent: snowballing. It worked for Carnegie. It worked, in a lesser way, for Mr. Pye. It worked for a boy out of the bayous. I'm sure it can work for the animal rights movement.

We cannot merely sit down to weep over conditions. We have to view animal crusades — crusades that *can* be won — as areas requiring a unique methodology for success. In each crusade, there are successive steps that have to be taken.

You must have an achievable objective — whether it's a local movement to get a reduced-cost spay clinic or an international campaign to stop the clubbing of harp seal pups. You cannot succeed on talk alone. I couldn't have sold the first eskimo pie without a box and I couldn't have sold the ten thousandth without the bicycle-pushcart. A campaign for animals needs a base of funding — a platform to start from. You need to see new opportunities in the midst of defeat; otherwise, the first setback will drive you home again, resolved that man is simply a brute and that animals will eternally suffer and that's all there is to it.

Now, making some progress in the humane movement is infernally complex compared to selling eskimo pies, but I think success in it only comes on that step-by-step route. Many setbacks of the crusade have occurred because someone imagined correcting injustice would be as simple as standing tall for the space of one single, beautiful speech — and thereby reforming the world. Reforming the world, where the evils are often old and absolute and cry out for attention, is a huge, painstaking process.

But it's possible.

It's possible for someone who is forever driving away, like a battering ram that will eventually burst through, at the sins of the System. The System of America's Wild West grew up to be supremely careless of the wild horse, and the wild horse had almost nothing going for it — except that, in time, there grew up a counterbalance, a counterbalance that has at its base one woman — Velma Johnston, known as "Wild Horse Annie." In the next chapter, which relates the progress of Wild Horse Annie to a victory at the highest level, you'll see what is meant by that phrase "Moving from Emotion to Action."

No one felt the plight of the wild horse more emotionally than Velma Johnston. But there were others who felt the same without knowing how to stir things up. Using

The author and a friend.

her emotion only as the spur, Wild Horse Annie Johnston moved on to that extraordinary succession of maneuvers and confrontations which confounded her enemies and finally brought millions of Americans to recognize that the wild horse *does* have a place in this country.

9

On the Trail with Wild Horse Annie:
How To Work Wonders Beyond
the Old Corral

A fair share of hate mail arrives at the headquarters of WHOA! (Wild Horse Organized Assistance) in Reno, Nevada, but they don't get that many flags.

The most memorable one arrived in a packet postmarked November 30, 1973, originating from Idaho Falls, Idaho—a replica of the "Don't Tread On Me" flag American colonists once used to flail the redcoats with their sense of independence.

The flag with the snake on it.

Nothing could be more American, but the message that came with it was meant to speak like a rattler's tongue. Vigilante stuff.

"We will unitedly maintain our basic God-given rights," said Annie's hidden defamers. "Down with intervening layers of lawmaking bureaucracy!" This odd message was signed: "The Vigilante Committee of 10,000."

Ten thousand vigilantes against one frail-looking woman does not sound like good odds, but it would be unwise to put your money against Annie.

For Annie Johnston is a withstander. She has withstood a thousand threats and she has withstood something even worse—the slowness of society to react when something precious is being destroyed.

By 1973, this lady, whose real name is Velma B. Johnston but who is known the world around as Wild Horse Annie, had won more than her share of battles. But it didn't mean that all those slit-eyed folk who considered her an interfering, cussed lady had decided to bug out on the whole struggle. That Idaho postmark was understandable. Annie had been her hard-driving self about what had happened up in Idaho. Near the town of Howe, in 1973, seven horses were found dead at the base of a cliff. As their fate and the fate of forty-six other wild horses was explored, shock waves vibrated across the nation.

The killings, heartlessly carried out, showed an element of sadism that could curdle the blood of even those who prefer to look the other way.

This massacre was to become a test of the law protecting wild horses and wild burros—a law that came about only because Annie had ceaselessly fought to give status to the creatures of the open range. The legislation was intended to outlaw the very kind of horror that had happened. But westerners who had accomplished that roundup of fifty-three horses—killing some in shivery fashion—were "apparently attempting to rid the range of the horses before the new wild horse protective regulations were implemented."

From early January through late February of 1973, ranchers had hunted down the horses; the official report indicated that thirty-four of the fifty-three captured horses eventually wound up at a pet-food plant in Nebraska. A suckling colt and two others died. Six horses were apparently kept alive and ended up on various ranches. Three were shot. And the seven found at cliff-bottom gave plentiful hints as to what the roundup had been like.

When Annie first began to crusade on behalf of saving the wild horses and wild burros of the western ranges, she had to harden herself to the horrors she was frequently forced to look upon. But the Idaho massacre, as it came to be called—coming so late, at a time when this kind of slaughter was supposed to be officially over—was so shatteringly brutal that Annie grows pale even now when she flashes the slides that project the graphic evidence of how those roundups of wild horses have sometimes been pursued.

API's *Mainstream* magazine reported: "Hog rings were placed in the horses' nostrils, clamping them partially shut. . . .This was advised by a veterinarian and was done to restrict breathing and make the animals easier to control. During the weeks of pursuit, many mares aborted foals they were carrying. . . .Round-up participants testified to this, saying they saw the bloodied areas around the mares' tails. Previously undisclosed information in the report revealed the use of chain saws to cut the legs off three horses that were helplessly caught in crevices in the rocks of the 'trap.' Unable to free the caught animals, the ranchers cut the horses' throats and sawed off the legs in order to dispose of the bodies over the cliff."

The facts did not come out smoothly or easily.

At the outset, an effort was made to cast a cougar as the villain in the piece. In this scenario—which would have made the ranchers incidental to a crackpot tragedy engineered by Mother Nature—the horses had supposedly become so frightened of a cougar that they bolted in panic over the cliff. But cougars who deal in hog rings and chain saws are rare, and one of the participants was clear enough in testifying that the facts were quite different.

"In the process of laying him[the horse] down [to put rings in his nostrils] we broke his leg. When we turned him up, he floundered and fell over the cliff." A second horse, a mare, fell from the cliff but somehow landed alive. Not that she would recover. "We just left her. We quit," the rancher said. He came back to the horse a few days later—now she *was* dead.

Commented *Mainstream*: "Other testimony indicated the horses had been previously run with helicopters on two occasions—a probable violation of the 1959 law forbidding the use of aircraft or other motorized vehicles for the capturing or killing of unbranded wild horses. The helicopter pilot, if he could run the animals out of the rocky terrain into land where they could be captured, was to receive ten dollars per head. Snowmobiles were also used at one point in the pursuit."

Sometimes it's difficult for decisions taken at the top to filter down. The Bureau of Land Management had taken charge of the protection and well-being of wild horses shielded by the law Wild Horse Annie had fought for. But out in Idaho a local BLM official, who had worked for twenty years under a different policy had managed not to understand—or not to implement—BLM's specific directive on how the new law was to be enforced.

"He insisted," said *Mainstream*, "he knew the horses belonged to private parties while admitting these parties had never claimed ownership. Further, despite the buildup of horses in the region as ranchers released unbranded animals, he had taken no trespass actions against the offenders."

The Idaho Massacre was far from the first but it was also not the last time that determined westerners decided to defy what many of them were anxious to see as just Annie and a bunch of busybodies, spoiling a good thing. The situation was vastly confused by the fact that some free-roaming horses truly are wild while others are horses that ranchers claim to have let loose to graze on federal land.

Hog rings were stapled in the nostrils of this horse—one of those killed in the "Idaho massacre."

Until 1934, almost anything was permissible on the open range, and overgrazing was rampant. In that year, however, Congress passed the Taylor Grazing Act, which required permits for the grazing of owned animals—these could be domestic livestock as well as horses. The permits sought to control the number of animals on public land, with the amount of available forage determining the number of permits issued.

"Although domestic livestock limits were enforced occasionally," says Annie, "there was never any watchfulness maintained on the release of domestic horses. Since few, if any, states require that horses be branded, it was an easy matter to resort to a ruse." With the silent acquiescence of lawmakers of the various areas populated with wild horses, ranchers could claim not only their own but much more than their own. The wrangler could point unbranded stock onto the government land and come back a few months later to "get his stock." Sometimes he would capture and shoot everything in sight—released horses, genuine wild horses, and who was to say whose was really whose?

To make sense of this confusion, Congress had eventually followed the lead Annie suggested; so the new law read: "All unauthorized and unbranded horses and burros on the public lands, except those introduced onto public lands on or after December 15, 1971 by accident, negligence, or willful disregard of ownership, are presumed for the purpose of management to be wild, free-roaming horses or burros."

The idea was fine—and it was working. But greed and antagonism still run high in horse country. And those sawed-off legs showed there were still some wranglers not at all squeamish in their pursuit of income from the horsemeat market.

A Wild Horse Annie was needed to bring the law into being. Without her, chances are, there would have been no WHOA! and therefore no stop to the kind of roundups that were swiftly depleting the country of the last of its wild horses. But the coming of the law, as the Idaho incident and other events since have proved, was merely a stage in the saving of the wild horse. Annie herself understands this better than anyone.

She is not about to whoa.

AN AMERICAN ORIGINAL

Nothing in her appearance forewarns you that Annie is as apt as John Wayne to have odd adventures out there in the sagebrush.

Her life should have tamed down by now, but not so long ago—years after the time when her husband sometimes had a rifle along as a pacifier because of the unruly types they dealt with—Annie was in a predictable kind of scrape. She had gone off with a film crew into the barren country where horses lope in the far distance. It was spring but freezing cold. The helicopter landed, dropped off Annie and the filmmakers, and rose in the air again; it was to be gone only an hour or so, skittering back after additional equipment. As quickly as it was out of sight, though, the helicopter had fuel pump trouble and had to land.

The pilot gave a try at radioing for help. His receiving mike proved to be dead and he couldn't tell if the messages he was sending were getting through. His own plight was bad enough, but he knew the five people he'd just let off were in far worse shape.

Out in the wilds, unprovisioned, they were in no condition to be on their own. They were dressed lightly because the plan was to shoot a quick scene, get in the helicopter, and fly out again. They were so far from even a one-shack outpost that there wasn't a chance of walking to shelter. And not a soul in the world but the helicopter pilot knew where they were.

As the afternoon wore on, Annie and the filmmakers began to recognize their predicament. They built a windbreak and burnt sage-brush in an effort to repel the oncoming cold. Just before dark, rescue came—the pilot's outgoing signals had brought help. Annie had racked up one more escape. To her, it was nothing—she'd never bother to tell it as one of those hair-raising stories that others bring back from their adventures. "Oh, that's routine!"—she has said it many times and means it.

Strange predicaments *have* been routine for her, though she scarcely looks the part of an embattled lady whose adventures from childhood onward are inextricably intertwined with a sense of purposefulness. Annie doesn't adventure for its own sake. It's always been for a cause. She has been businesswoman as well as battler, and it is her nature to proceed compassionately and never with any vindictiveness, even toward those who raise their howls of retribution in her direction.

She is an American original, honor-bright and as unembellished as Quaker oats.

She's had polio and is in constant pain as a result of the early ills.

She says she's held together "by hairspray and a girdle."

Polio, which struck when she was a child, put her in a body cast for a long, torturing period; and the primitive treatment then available couldn't save her from suffering spinal damage. But she grew up to have a whole array of skills. Even now, she chooses to design and make her own clothes, and a friend confides, "Annie's a crack shot" (she doesn't prove it by shooting animals). The husband who sparked with determination, just as Annie does, died of emphysema and she was a widow. This didn't stop her, either. Annie is a *withstander*. It may, however, be an inherited trait.

Her mother, eighty-two years old in 1976, has all the vim of WHOA! workers half her age. Annie is the product of an old pioneering family and, like parents and grandparents before her, she goes at every task like she's building that first cabin in the wilderness. It's a famly trait — in some ways, a Nevada trait.

Those who joined with WHOA! don't have the luxury of fighting all their battles purely on paper. They go to the aid of the horses when the horses most need help. Annie and co-workers know what it is like to forge into the mountains when blizzards are raging, trying to find and save the last remnants of the often well-camouflaged herds that survive in the stormy outlands.

Life with Annie is a postgraduate course in coping with elements. Dawn Lappin, a co-worker of Annie's, remembers a day when WHOA! was determined to save a band of eight-hundred wild horses trapped by a blizzard in the mountains of northern Nevada. With Indians as guides, they made a great circle, searching for horses in a raging blizzard and a twenty-below-zero temperature.

"We'd seen piles of horses, as we circled, that hadn't made it," said Dawn. "Saw their corpses, jumbled against the snow fences, disappearing into the banks of snow. And you'd see the colts standing by their dead mothers, unwilling to leave them." They were taking hay to the survivors — if they could find them. At last the rescuers saw the same sort of sight that Annie herself has thrilled to. "Almost like a dream, the horses were coming over the snowy ridge. It was real and not real —

"We'd seen piles of horses, as we circled, that hadn't made it," said Dawn. "Saw their corpses, jumbled against the snow fences, disappearing into banks of snow. And you'd see the colts standing by their dead mothers, unwilling to leave them." They were taking hay to the survivors — if they could find them. At last the rescuers saw the same sort of sight that Annie herself has thrilled to. "Almost like a dream, the horses were coming over the snowy ridge. It was real and not real — unbelievable. Through the blizzard now, you could see not the clear images of the horses but just their outline. And it was so beautiful and like a dream — the horses in the snow, alive! — and when we moved off a bit, when the horses felt they were safe from humans — they would come down off the ridge and go where we had been. And then the Indians went back and collected all the colts that had been with their dead mothers."

Dawn Lappin and many others are complete converts of Wild Horse Annie Johnston, one of those wondrous women whose influence is actually so motivating that others vow, "Well — I could be like that, too."

The wild horses are in peril from man and nature both, and Annie tries to make WHOA! their defender from both. The quality that has given WHOA! so much giddyup is Annie's essential unstoppability. Her successes with Congress, instead of causing her to rest and let others take the campaign the rest of the way, merely spur her to further action. She's a director of the Animal Protection Institute, has acted helpfully toward every group or fact-finding mission that could use her help, and when something like the Idaho Massacre occurs, it's Annie who insists that officialdom can't just throw a blanket over the whole affair and forget it.

Unprincipled slaughter in the wilds does find its way into the newspapers, when discovered, but the discoveries are only an occasional interference with what used to be the everyday reality of casual massacre. The system of converting wild horses into

Wild Horse Annie (left) poses with her biographer, Marguerite Henry, author of Mustang: Wild Spirit of the West.

pet food didn't vary much from the way it was being carried out when Annie first realized what a huge and scandalous practice was afoot.

This is a description of what it was like in a typical abattoir: "A crowded carload of horses would come in with the cowboys very proud of themselves. The horses would be jammed together, squashed tight as they drove in. There would be a steam-driven chain hoist ready. The dropman would hit a horse right between the eyes with a four or five-pound sledge-hammer. That was to stun it. Then a loop chain, like a hangman's noose, would go over the back leg. The animal was jerked in the air about four feet off the ground. Then they would take a kill knife, slit the throat, a gallon of blood would spill into a trough—and then the horse was dead. A good skinner could dress out the horse in a few minutes—maybe ninety seconds from life to death and on your way to the canning. If the price was fifteen to eighteen cents a pound and the horse weighed about twelve-hundred pounds, the fellow who let the horse in for it felt pretty good. That's what he was after—a fast buck."

It was a brush with the grisly aspects of the traffic in wild horses that started a serious young woman named Velma Johnston into a crusade that has had no end.

At the time, about a quarter of a century ago, she was living on the Double Lazy Heart Ranch east of Reno—but there was certainly nothing lazy-hearted about

Annie. Polio behind her, she was as full of sizzle as a bee. And one day she was driving down a highway when she saw blood seeping from the back of a truck ahead. Almost anybody else might have had a grim speculation or two—and kept going. Not Annie.

She hied the driver over, investigated the load with him and discovered that a colt had been trampled to death by other horses in the back of the overcrowded truck. All were wild horses—and all were headed for the pet-food plant. She drove to the plant and found out what was happening to the horses of the Nevada range; and she made a promise to herself, that day, that somehow she would see it stopped. Her life was unalterably changed as a result.

The story of that life is remarkably told in the biographical *Mustang—Wild Spirit of the West*, a chronicle of the wild horse, the wild West, and Wild Horse Annie herself that has won the Western Heritage Award of the National Cowboy Hall of Fame. Written by Marguerite Henry, the book follows Annie's increasingly triumphant path (she was very nervous at first—and very determined) up through the point where she convinced skeptical congressmen it was within their province, and certainly their duty, to bring justice to the open range. Uneasy as she was at her initial appearance before these august personages, she had rhetorical powers from the beginning. They were based on clarity and seriousness, not on war whoops. They immediately brought the thoughtful to her side. A handsome young congressman named John Lindsay saluted her roundly for the grace of her first appearance.

Wild Horse Annie has been to the White House and she has successfully pursued her crusade to the Supreme Court. But she has stayed level-headed throughout, keeping always at the front of her mind a sense both of where the crusade started and where, ultimately, it must go.

When it comes to figuring out what's going haywire in the new West, we need to know a bit more than movies like *The Misfits*—which used the wild horse roundups for atmosphere—can ever tell us. In a way, the movies tell us wrong. True, the men who accomplish the roundups *are* misfits (the word was well-chosen and it's the greatest insight the film gives us); but there are no cowpokes on these hunts who have the enigmatic charms of Clark Gable or Montgomery Clift. As a Nevadan who has watched them at it says, "Some of the things these guys perpetrate are just pathetic. They're not western characters. *They're just a scrubby bunch*. Not in a thousand years would you get them to understand consequences. They're a rough bunch and they're thinking about money. They're *not* good people."

TACTICS OF A WINNING CRUSADER

That flag which was sent to Annie in an effort to frighten her into silence was immediately tacked to her wall. She cannot be intimidated, and that attribute is a part of the secret that has made her a great living force in the animal protection movement.

Many years ago I read about her in *Reader's Digest* and, because I hoped to make some strides in the same direction, or at any rate do what I could, I summoned up my bravery when going through Reno and called her for an appointment.

The graciousness that she turns on everyone was turned on me in full. It had to be a life-long friendship. Though she probably is threatened almost as often as the President of the United States (violent calls still come in about once or twice a month), the threateners themselves would be disarmed if they were exposed to the force of her personality. No faking anywhere. No facts ever twisted to suit her arguments. As Dawn says, "She is honor bound."

Elusive wild horses of the West are usually spotted only in the glimmering distance.
But the land they are allotted can be a sun-baked bombing range or those high
retreats where blizzards hit hardest.

The honor-bound person is a rarity in this life and it gives Annie much of her strength. But she was not an executive secretary and a chief accountant for nothing. She understands follow-up, and anyone joining the animal crusades would be well advised to consider the meticulousness with which she answers letters and initiates them; pursues the facts until she has them; marshalls photographs and documents to prove a case.

At one point when I thought she could use it, I put the entire staff of the Animal Protection Institute at her service so she could have manpower to draw on as needed. As a director of our organization, her balanced judgment gives us insights extending to many areas beyond the fate of the wild horse and the wild burro.

When she was asked to describe some of the factors that weigh in the successful management of an animal rights organization (WHOA! has ten thousand members now, some as far away as France and Germany) she immediately harked back to first principles:

"It is a normal reaction of most people, when hearing of unpleasantness that has not actually touched their life, to pretend it isn't there. 'Maybe it will go away,' we say. With me, it was the certain knowledge that wild horses were hunted down by aircraft throughout the West—that they were captured and hauled away for slaughter—and seeing these mutilated, bleeding horses—that caused me to take action. Through questioning, I established that the truckload I discovered at the outset was not unusual. It was happening.

"And then this had touched my life and I could no longer pretend it wasn't there."

How did she move from sympathy into action? "I knew that I had to have facts," she said, "so I went about learning all I could. About habitat—numbers—volume of traffic in equine flesh—who the commercial mustangers were—what the areas of operation were. Pictures were difficult to obtain because the operators knew that an informed public would be an enraged public."

This is the central truth of the animal protection movement—when injustice and cruelty are regularly practiced, an informed public *is* an enraged public. Yet that process of informing, believably and broadly, can be elusive even if those involved have a firm grasp on their facts.

"I sought out irrefutable proofs in the form of eyewitness stories," said Wild Horse Annie. "I collected old-timers' testimony as to how many wild horses were in certain areas when these operations began and how many were left after the 'harvests.'

"One of the most shocking discoveries I made was that our own governmental agencies not only condoned but encouraged the operations. It cleared the open ranges for the benefit of cattle and sheep operators who used them for their own profit-producing animals.

"The most time-consuming aspect was the education of the public as to what was going on behind the scenes: the atrocities, the very real danger of annihilation of a species. It was made doubly difficult because information outlets were not readily available. The news media were reluctant to become involved. Livestock operators and producers of the commercial products from slaughtered horses were a formidable force for them to oppose. To say nothing of the governmental agencies that wanted the practice continued."

In the beginning years, her quest proceeded entirely by direct contact—letters she could write, editors she could meet, appeals she could make at meetings, hearings she could go to. As she wrote and wrote, and spoke and spoke, the outlets widened. She was sought after.

Dawn notes that Annie has none of the airs of the living legend, encourages no one to make a fuss about her, and yet "we can seem to be going along quietly and then, jeeminey, everybody's there." Reporters and cameras flick away, for Annie's legend travels on before her. Dawn herself now serves in a program that Annie helped bring about—putting captured wild horses not into dog food or rodeos but into the arms of families who want to adopt them. Dawn is Adoption Director in a process that carefully winnows applicants for the "free horses" (they're not really free because upkeep is the most basic cost in horse ownership). Through 1978 some seven thousand wild horses may be placed with families reaching out for them. To be adopted, the animals must first be captured. But the style of capturing has changed from pre-protection days.

The aerial hunts, made notorious by Annie's exposure of the damage they caused, could throw horses into a panic. The object was to drive them toward traps, traps occasionally more dire than even the hunters had in mind. Panicked, the horses could bolt the wrong way and dive off cliffs. The pilot maneuvering them had far from perfect control—there were canyon sides to watch out for. "You had to be a pretty good bush pilot to go in those box canyons," says WHOA! board member Gordon Harris, "or you'd wind up on the rocks instead of rounding up horses."

Under the program worked out with the federal government's Bureau of Land Management, current roundups are accomplished by playing a waiting game. The horses come to water eventually and a camouflaged corral in the watering area will secure them without endangering them.

Captured wild horses usually have a ragged appearance (the movie vision of trumpeting stallions can be more rapturous than real), but they often shape up handsomely when maintained under good conditions. API has a follow-up program for the adoption system which was conceived as comparable to an orphanage's later checkup to see that the "good parents" are as good as they looked.

They don't have the glamor of wild horses, but Wild Horse Annie fights for the rights of wild burros, too—in fact, for a democracy of the open range.

"I dislike seeing the horses captured," says Dawn, "but I'd rather see them adopted than dead. Some of these horses are starving and you recognize that adoption is better."

Says Annie: "I believe we are progressing as reasonably as can be expected in a world of changing values and considering the fact that encroachment by man is constantly shrinking the living space of creatures in the wild, dependent upon the land for survival.

"My goals have not changed, but in many ways there will have to be other considerations that were not paramount when I began twenty-five years ago. . .how to keep numbers within the carrying capacity of the ranges to maintain healthy wild horse and burro bands since the former rich bounties of the land are constantly raped to meet the immediate demands of the burgeoning human population. . .how to combat the political pressures that are increasingly forcing changes in every level of our lives."

HOW MUCH DO WE OWE THE HORSE?

Well, how much do we owe Henry Ford?

If you could stand back and see America from the perspective of many generations, you'd probably notice immediately that the horse has shaped our lives as surely as the motorcar — and for centuries longer — yet no creature has been horsed around the way the horse has.

The most gaudily horrifying moment in modern fiction comes in *The Godfather* when a valuable racehorse is decapitated and delivered to the bedroom of a sinner against godfatherism. Chilling. Redeemed by the fact that it is fiction rather than fact. But is it so much more chilling than this? In the nineteenth century, when they were used to pull streetcars, twenty-five thousand streetcar horses died annually — their lives cut short by the heaviness of their labors — and the most desperate trick of the streetcar owners was to compensate for animals going lame by bringing the lame ones on duty only at night when their condition was less noticeable.

Tracing the origins of the "wild horse" is an interesting study in itself. There is an offhand assumption that the tribes of wild horses came down from the days of the Indian wars. But the origins of any particular horse are more difficult to prove than one supposes.

The horse actually came twice to America. For a million years — until the advent of what writer Francis Haines called "a selective catastrophe" — there were both horses and camels on the American continent. And they remained until some fifteen thousand years ago. But when the Spanish came, the Indians had no horses, and to many an Indian the horses seemed more godlike than a Cortez or a DeSoto. The history of the West in the nineteenth century is a history of how the Indian stood off the superior firepower and the superior numbers of the white man for long decades — through superior horsemanship.

And yet the horse came gently, gently — in the beginning — to the land of the plains Indians.

The Nez Percé, said Haines, have passed down a story of the first horse the tribe acquired through trade — "a gentle white mare, from the Shoshone in the Boise Valley. Day after day the curious Nez Percé gathered from all around to watch the mare crop grass near the village. They learned how a horse acted: how it fed, how it exercised, how it rested. In a few weeks, the mare dropped a foal and the crowds increased. Soon other villages sent south for horses of their own, to be treasured as curiosities and pets. At The Dalles, Oregon, some two hundred miles down river from the Nez Percé, the first few horses were led around at festivals and were shown at the big dances. . . ." Though centuries passed before the Indian learned to adopt the horse as his own, this adoption program, once started, proceeded like wildfire. Within fifteen years of the time a tribe obtained its first horse, it was apt to have a strong herd.

That mighty Sioux nation which created the thunder of the Indians' most imposing, most desperate stand against the white man, streamed to the sunrise in a golden haze of horses. Yet only a few years before the Sioux became the greatest light cavalry on the continent, there was not a horse in the whole Sioux nation. They were a woodsy people living in the swamps of Minnesota, eating mostly wild rice and traveling by canoe.

George Catlin, the great artist of the West, thought the horse gave the Comanches (a tribe he considered "heavy and ungraceful") a touch of lightning. Catlin called the Comanches "one of the most unattractive and slovenly-looking races of Indians that I have ever seen; but the moment they mount their horses, they seem at once metamorphoses, and surprise the spectator with the ease and elegance of their movements. A Comanche on his feet is out of his element, and comparatively almost as awkward as a monkey on the ground, without a limb or a branch to cling to; but the moment he lays his hand upon his horse, his *face*, even, becomes handsome, and he gracefully flies away like a different being."

The cowboy who succeeded the Indian as the trail boss of the West kept, as often as not, a whole string of cow-ponies. He could have a cutting horse, a roping horse, a night horse, a "girlin" horse (for courting), and broncs he rode to town. The famed Conestoga wagon had its matching engine—the Conestoga horse.

In that age any horses escaping to rimrock were not necessarily the unlucky ones. Many of the state humane laws begin with admonitions against the over-working of animals—for they grew out of a nineteenth century so hard on horses that most died by the age of four or five and could be fairly described as overworked, overburdened, underfed, and ill-treated.

An age that has so readily embraced plastic surgery may understand a nineteenth century that, as *Mainstream* reported, was full of "fashionable cruelties." "For appearances, tailbones were broken and reset, tails docked, winter coats clipped close (removing the animal's natural cold-weather protection), and bits were used which were capable of fracturing jaws."

No, the America that came to worship Man O' War, Whirlaway, and Secretariat, has tried many attitudes on the horse—but solicitousness has rarely been one of them. Little girls treat horses well. Smart farmers house them well. But the lesson of what we owe the horse is hard-learned, easily forgotten.

And so came Annie. We needed her.

As identified as she now is with the wild horse, Velma Johnston does not take the attitude that the wild horse has more right on the range than other animals. She takes the position that there are equal rights on the range and that these apply to cows as to horses and to sheep as to cows and to horses branded and unbranded, somebody's and nobody's.

"No one herbivore should be considered over another," she says. "Every single animal that's out there has a right."

In the area where Annie lives, it is easy for the rancher or wrangler to convince himself that a belief that makes him a little money is a sanctified belief. There are even those who will say it is ranchers' propaganda that coyotes kill off sheep. ("That's a trick sheepowners use. They can write it off through the tax-laws by claiming, 'Ten percent of my sheep lost to coyotes.' Coyotes eat rabbit, not sheep. The only sheep they ever eat is a sick one.") But many a Nevada car or pickup sports a bumper-sticker that says: "Eat Nevada Lamb. Coyotes Do." Or: "Eat Nevada Beef. Coyotes Do."

The discovery that wild horses meant money from pet-food processors or rodeos made it much easier for those who might otherwise have ignored their presence to decide that the wild horses were grazing down their range and constituted an insupportable nuisance.

But Annie made the whole world aware that the horses were not a nuisance but a glory to be preserved.

Those horses of the hills are not home free and it is not WHOA!'s expectation that they ever will be—not entirely. But WHOA!'s people have hopes and they have brought about a number of important new procedures—protections that formerly did not exist.

Annie doesn't quit working—for many reasons. There are the horses of a refuge in southern Nevada whose nightly prayer could be, "Now I lay me down to sleep—too bad this refuge is a federal bombing range." On Independence Day of the bicentennial year—and the date was assuredly oversymbolic—fifty three wild horses were found dead on the military base at Dugway, Utah. When Wild Horse Annie tried to find out why, knowing that sheep had died there previously and that biological warfare was more than a remote possibility, there were suggestions from officials that the explanation, in the case of the horses, might be: intensive heat, the water situation, other stresses. A hard theory to buy.

The horses have found a way of living in these terrible heat-patches—at the headquarters of WHOA! nobody accepted the notion that the horses had suddenly run out of any resistance against the heat. So the Dugway mystery exists—and still needs to be solved. If only as a way of protecting the horses in the future.

While WHOA! goes on with the adoption procedures for wild horses and has found a receptive public (actor Burt Reynolds took two), Annie has an eye on that future time when the federal government will have a more profound vision of what is needed to ensure the long-term survival of the wild horses.

She is a realist, able to find and accept real solutions to these very real problems; nevertheless, she doesn't spring to the support of proposals that *sound* good but hold within them the seeds for ultimate destruction. On refuges, she says: "My position is that we do not want refuges exclusively, because they would be at the expense of the free-roaming wild horses located outside of them. . . .Senator Laxalt has tried to get us to agree to establishment of a one-million-acre refuge, to include the bombing range as well, which would accommodate a population of 4,000. But, and here is the clincher, all other horses at large in Nevada, and there are estimated to be 25,000 altogether, would be eliminated. We oppose it bitterly because the price of 21,000 horses for the security of 4,000 is too high."

The wild horse needs the territories that give size and range to his roaming. Annie knows well the beauty of an independent horse who arches his neck, proudly travels fifteen miles for water and proudly dashes miles away again in moments.

Always frank, she recognizes that tempting bait in the form of a refuge system may beguile parts of the public into thinking the habitat problem of the wild horse has been answered when it hasn't. With her own keen mind to put such schemes into proportion, it's not likely that the public will stay beguiled—they have learned that the most utterly honest appraisal of what *actually* benefits the wild horse will come from Annie herself.

WHOA! goes on, then—with a great record, but with many turns ahead where it has to be watchful. And the wild horse still rears itself in certain remaining outposts of the not-so-wild West.

Annie and her followers are forever struck with that vision of horses only half-seen, coming over a snowy ridge—horses dreamlike in a world well outside our own. These horses are survivors and that means a lot to her. Wild Horse Annie had her own survival fight when, as a small girl, she outlasted polio. She is the withstander who can outlast almost anything. She can even outlast the snaillike habits of Justice, often so slow in arriving.

10

Fragmentation:
Splits, Huffs, and a Hope
for the Future

Today, there is mass confusion among the public and, to a great extent, within the humane movement itself, about who does what and why. Each organization is autonomous, whether it is chartered as an anticruelty society with multiple purposes or as a dog shelter with a cute name. Leadership is equally wide-ranging — from prominent citizens to obscure animal lovers inheriting the gavel by virtue of owning thirty cats or dogs.

In 1877 the first national humane organization was formed and christened the International Humane Society. The following year the name was changed to the American Humane Association. AHA was an outgrowth of the early stirrings of the humane movement generated by men like Henry Bergh and George Angell. To it can be applied the adjective *traditional* with a clean conscience. Not only is the Association an organization of long standing, but its concerns have been those assigned, in the mind of the general public, to the realm of "the humane society." Early endeavors followed paths forged by contemporary humanitarians and included protecting children, enforcing humane laws, and enhancing the lives of horses and food animals. A century after its founding, the Denver-based organization functions as an association of local shelter-operating societies, and the emphasis is on pets.

This shift in priorities reflected societal changes wrought by technological advances. By the turn of the century, the horse was no longer the chief means of transport, and early societies founded because of the animal's pitiful circumstances found themselves with less work. As impetus and motivation decreased — and humane work lost some of its status — a number of local groups were entrusted to paid managers. In these cases, endowments that had been built up by early good works eliminated the need for memberships and volunteer workers; in others, strong volunteer leaders did most of the work and refused memberships to all but a few well-selected friends. For a time, these societies rode on the coat-tails of previously-achieved successes. Some gained financial strength, some simply existed, some fell by the wayside.

All the while, the country's population of surplus dogs and cats was growing. Where the local society was strong, it contracted with the city or county government to police for strays and to house, care, and humanely destroy those which could not be placed in homes. Where there were weak or uninfluential societies, or none at all,

*API volunteer humane officers Ed Church and Barbara Check. The animal protec-
tion movement draws no sex barriers.*

city and county governments took on the job. Dogs and cats had been the domain
of humane organizations for decades, but it wasn't until the mid-twentieth century
that stress was placed on the great number of *surplus* animals. Following World War
II and the human population boom, the matter of controlling stray dogs—or, for
that matter, owned animals generally—became the key issue of humane societies
throughout the country. By the early 1950s public pounds and shelters were killing
such numbers of dogs and cats that when the nation was swept with a frenzy for
medical research, its perpetrators looked to these facilities for cheap sources of
experimental animals.

At about the same time, several staff members of AHA, convinced that the
Association's operation was marked by tunnel vision, began agitating for programs
to deal with laboratory animals, livestock transport and slaughter, and humane
education in the schools. For such policy changes to occur, the Board of Directors
had to be persuaded; however, since AHA's Board consisted (and still consists)
partially of directors and managers of shelter-operating societies, such advocacy was
risky.

119

The employees were eventually fired — an action that resulted in their formation of the second national humane organization, the National Humane Society, incorporated in Delaware in 1954. Later, via an AHA-secured injunction, the name was changed to the Humane Society of the United States. The late Fred Myers, previously editor of AHA's *National Humane Review*, is credited with founding HSUS. He was assisted in its operation by Helen E. Jones and Larry Andrews, formerly education director and field services director, respectively, for the Association. Some years later, Miss Jones left to form the National Catholic Society for Animal Welfare (now Society for Animal Rights), and Mr. Andrews departed and founded the National Humanitarian League.

Also spawned from the ranks of HSUS were Humane Information Services, Fund for Animals, and the Animal Protection Institute of America. And apart from this family-tree development, there are others — Animal Welfare Institute, Defenders of Wildlife, Friends of Animals. Most sprang up during the responsive, imaginative period of the late 1950s through the '60s.

Many of these organizations, obviously, were bred from others; fragmentation within the humane movement seems inherent. Aside from the fact that disunity eventually erupts in every cause or movement, the reasons for splintering in this field range from the ridiculous to the sublime. Most frequently, the catalyst is a clash between strong personalities over policies or methods of accomplishing a society's stated purposes.

Such disputes are, of course, closely related to the attitude of an organization's leadership. Most groups, I've observed, stick with problem-solving approaches used during earlier periods. Where leadership is vested in one or two dynamic individuals, the situation is obstructive enough; where a board of directors is involved, the added inertia is sufficient to fatally frustrate any advocate of change.

Most groups tend to keep the same directors year after year. This may be the result, as well as the cause, of resistance to new ideas; less invidiously (excluding ego and paranoia as factors), directors may be comfortable in their positions, feeling no need for new blood. It's quite possible, at the same time, that new or additional leadership *cannot* be obtained, as in the case of a financially troubled or highly controversial organization. Such conditions are natural obstacles to enlisting support from community leaders, and directors — even those desirous of stepping down — are forced to continue.

Executive directors, who manage day-to-day affairs of organizations, work for the boards of directors. While such administrators may have a firmer grasp of operational deficiencies and potential as-yet-untried solutions than do directors, it is these latter who have the votes and must be persuaded to the appropriate view before significant changes can occur. Depending on the executive's tenure, past performance, and methods of politicking, alterations are possible. Often, however, the very size of boards — they range up to twenty-five members — can be defeating.

This, then, is how static, noninnovative leadership ultimately sets the stage for new groups and ideas, for updated and redirected approaches, for progress in helping animals. In founding API, my vision was based on the simple necessity of breaking out of the forest so as to see the trees. I was employed by a regional board of directors that was, in turn, controlled by a national board. By the time new ideas, approaches, techniques made the rounds for approval, they were lost in the shuffle, died of neglect, or were disapproved as unworkable or too radical.

Just as large boards can frustrate humane administrators, so, too, can the present number of humane organizations perplex the uninitiated. Aside from inquiries about animal abuse, the question I'm repeatedly asked is, "Why don't you all get together?" — implying, perhaps not illogically, that much more could be accomplished for animals if there was one organization where there are now ten or twenty.

API's executive vice president, Charlene Heinen. She was one of the new wave of young people who have taken the humane cause to heart and made animal protection and environmental concerns life goals.

Could it?

Forgetting, for a moment, the mechanical difficulties of "getting together," the vision of a single agency directing all humane work is not without its horrors. The most obvious outcome would be the unavoidable establishment of a huge bureaucracy, complete with red tape, conservatism, and inflexibility of operation. Competing groups not only guard against staid policies, but they also allow a degree of specialization functionally impractical, in terms of efficiency, within a single agency.

Even if the goal of complete unity were deemed desirable, the very real problems of achieving a giant merger are practically insurmountable. It's rather like balancing the federal budget: were we starting from square one, a balance is a desirable and an attainable goal; with a ready-made deficit of billions of dollars, chain effects of fiscal and monetary actions incredibly complicate the picture.

The realities of the existing organizational structure — and idiosyncrasies of human nature — preclude the idea of union. Single-cause societies — shelters, spay programs, wolf protectors, beaver defenders — are, by charter, required to limit themselves to specific areas. Even nonspecific humane groups have different emphases — rodeos, spaying, wildlife — or varying operational techniques — law enforcement, humane education, consulting services. Couple with this the dominance of individual leaders (paid and volunteer), the wishes of large contributors who must be appeased, and the bad blood held over from past splinterings, and the immediate obstacles to unity are all too evident.

Each humane group is necessarily imbued with the task of survival, a consideration that also operates on a personal level where employees are concerned. "Looking after number one" is by no means an unexpected or an unworthy philosophy, but when humane workers equate steps toward united operation with a threat to their livelihood, the result is an undermining, negative—if not hostile—attitude.

Not long ago I met with Cleveland Amory, president of the Fund for Animals, in Chicago for the purpose of working out a merger of our organizations, a step we felt would be mutually beneficial. We discussed mechanical procedures, selected an appropriate name, and agreed on leadership roles: Mr. Amory would continue as president of the newly formed organization and I, because of my administrative background, would be second-in-command with responsibility for program and personnel. But we had failed to reckon with the feelings of Fund's executive personnel—most of whom were present—regarding such an arrangement. Their reaction was such that, within twelve hours of our initial conference, Mr. Amory and I could only conclude that any merger plans must be suspended for the time being. In post-discussion, the sentiment was expressed that the only way mergers of nationals could ever occur was by purchase or acquisition of one organization by another, rather than by cooperative action.

Humane groups are classified as charities, but there is nothing especially charitable about their dealings with each other; competition in the humane field is just as real, and can be as fierce, as in the profit-making realm. This fact of life often shocks those who feel groups doing "nice" things should *be* nice—it did me. Having entered humane work directly from military service, I knew very little of the movement's history, politics, economics, or organizational structure and naively believed: humanitarians were gathered in a solid unit with headquarters in Washington, D.C.; the central authority could immediately crush any act of cruelty brought to its attention; and, those involved in animal welfare work were the nicest kind of people.

My baptism of fire took place on one of my first assignments, in Salt Lake City, where I'd gone in answer to a frantic plea for help from the president of the Animal Rescue League. The League was operating a shelter with a policy of no euthanasia and the facility was pitifully overcrowded. There was no money to buy food for the animals or pay bills—water and electricity had been shut off—sewage had backed up, and the Board of Health had ordered the place closed. I visited the shelter, consisting of a converted poultry shed housing 240 dogs and a detached garage for 135 cats, and found the filth, stench, and pandemonium unbelievable.

In a call to HSUS headquarters, I learned there were two other organizations in town, the Salt Lake City Humane Society and the Utah Humane Society—both had money and would probably be helpful. Wishful thinking. Actually, the three groups had been warring for some time. The president of the first called the League's shelter a "den of iniquity"; the head of the other was sympathetic but reported her funds were committed exclusively for humane education purposes.

Pressed for a decision on disposition of the animals, I told League officials any animals left after forty-eight hours would have to be put to sleep. Homes were eventually found for some of the animals, but not nearly enough. After witnessing the euthanasia ordeal, I retreated to my hotel room, cried uncontrollably, and the next day called a meeting of the three societies (it took place in a park because none wished to meet on another's "territory"). With the help of Hal and Beverly Gardiner, the three organizations were merged into an HSUS chapter, pooled their funds, and after eighteen months had built one of the most modern animal shelters in the country. At this writing, the Utah Humane Society is bustling with activity, doing a great service for animals and the community it helps.

The reality of warring humane groups, with "nice" people on all sides, was an eye-opener, but it was only the warmup. One of the societies had been affiliated

122

with the American Humane Association, another favored HSUS, and while negotiating with the various principals I was exposed to the slander that Fred Myers was a communist and HSUS was a communist-front organization. I had just left military service and my last assignment had dealt with production, assembly, and testing of atomic and hydrogen warheads—a position requiring top-secret clearance and a loyalty oath. Had I been duped? While I couldn't conceive the logic of a communist-front organization being interested in or connected with animals, the allegation could not be ignored, for, if nothing else, communist sympathizers and employees of such groups could lose their pensions.

Earlier in my military career I'd served as chief of intelligence at the Army Language School in Monterey, California; remembering intelligence procedures, I telephoned the Pentagon and determined that HSUS was not on the Un-American Activities Committee's list. My next step was to call Fred Myers himself, who informed me the charge was a tactic used by his former organization to discredit him and his splinter society. I'd been treated to a further example of humane groups' competitive spirit. The basis for the rumor was Myers's joining, as a young newspaper reporter in 1934, the Newspaper Writers Guild. He left the Guild shortly after its formation, but in later years it was infiltrated by communists and eventually cited as a front organization. There was, according to my boss, another tidbit used by his evil-wishers. In 1944, he and sixty other Americans, including the Secretary of State, had traveled to Russia to receive the Russian Red Star. The decoration was in recognition of work on behalf of the Russian Relief Society, which had provided food and clothing for the poor and homeless in that country's war-devastated areas.

It was impossible for Myers to take legal action against such character assassination, for nothing suable was ever put in writing; the only terms used on paper were such insinuating ones as "colorful" and "traveler."

The basis for such below-the-belt tactics, personal vendettas aside, is a group's fear that members and funds will be diverted by other organizations, especially newly formed ones. This kind of thinking implies a fixed population of "compassionate thinkers" from which humane organizations must draw support: increasing one group's share decreases another's. Frankly, I don't buy that. Each society must continually locate members and tap new funding sources, and the market consists of 215 million Americans, of which only a fraction are aware of animal problems. An API survey revealed that only a small percentage of the organization's members also supported what could be termed competitors; this is probably the case generally. Each humane organization has particular techniques of publicity and member acquisition, and each stresses particular areas of animal abuse (many people have special interests), considerations that argue against substantial membership overlap.

I think everyone acquainted with humane work would agree that there is not enough support for the rights of animals. These creatures desperately need all the help they can get, from as many people as it's possible to muster. If this can be achieved through formation of additional humane organizations, I say the more the merrier.

Building the Animal Protection Institute into the leading humane organization of its type took seven years. I never had to resort to name-calling or innuendo, even though retaliation could many times have proved momentarily gratifying. In fact, my admonishment to API employees is, "If you can't say something good, don't say anything."

This policy is not as goody-two-shoes as it sounds; it's common sense, for interorganizational abuse is a single-edged sword that cuts the wrong way. People are not stupid. When they give money to a society, they do so on the basis of

123

what they want to see accomplished, often bolstered by their knowledge of the group's past achievements. If an organization's members are satisfied with its program, criticism by an official of another group will only reflect unfavorably on the criticizer and his organization and contribute to an image of pettiness and jealousy and to the suspicion that the latter group can't stand on its own merits. (There's also a Catch 22 at work: The longer a person supports a society, the more loyal he is, simply because of a human inability to believe one could have been "taken in.")

Recently, the head of a local shelter-operating society decided to form a national organization. He had, previously, become familiar with API operations, had proved extremely cooperative, and had even been considered for employment. Now he wrote advising me he intended approaching one of the Institute's substantial contributors for financial backing, a letter that arrived while I was away from the office and thus went unanswered. His first epistle to the API member was, indeed, all it could have been. The writer was complimentary toward me (for whom he had "considerable respect") and for my organization but noted that his program was "not at all similar." Since the recipient of his request was not interested in the plan outlined—my comments were not solicited—there was no response. His second query, six weeks later, was more transparent:

Dear M_____:

We are nearing completion of our San Francisco Low Cost Spay and Neuter and Animal Welfare Hospital program, our building has already been purchased, and we are looking towards a January 1976 opening. The Denver, Houston, San Diego and Chicago programs are in various stages of development and we are anticipating opening two additional facilities in 1976. A dynamic and dramatic beginning for a small organization, one that really lacks adequate funding.

I know of your involvement with API, and frankly M_____, I can't understand why. There are many groups such as ours, ours is the only group that is National in scope, that are [sic] providing real animal protection services and not just giving lip service and sending out flashy materials.

We need your help M_____, and I would be more than happy to meet with you, at your convenience, in order to thoroughly explain our programs and our desires. Can you help us? I'm eagerly anticipating your answer.

Needless to say, perhaps, such a message successfully squelched any chance of funding from the recipient, for the current project or any future one.

A second factor in public sniping is the "tarring brush" syndrome. The general public really doesn't know, and cares very little, about the difference in animal welfare groups; the tendency is to lump all as one and the same. Thus, the spokesman who lambasts all organizations but his own is tossing out bombs that are going to backfire when it comes down to obtaining public support.

Lest I present a totally bleak picture, however, let me point out here that, although competition is a reality, cooperation between humane organizations also exists. What is said about whom, depends on the subject of conversation. For example, Group A might be tolerable and Group B's employees actually fun to work with, while Group C, whose leader is a "glory hog," utterly impossible. Attitudes of one society toward another can depend on: past associations and person-alities of leaders (denigrations can be and have been handed down by a group's old-timers to all new employees—it's part of "learning the ropes"); any official policies regarding cooperation; status or financial position (practical ability to go it alone).

The attitudes of present managers, chiefly, determine if and how closely one organization works with others. Generally, the more progressive administrators view cooperation as desirable for the united front it projects and for the large numbers of followers that can thus be directed toward a specific action. The boycott of products made in Japan is much more newsworthy if eighteen societies oppose that country's killing whales rather than just one or two groups. In legislative committee hearings, congressmen can only be favorably impressed with a humane coalition that has coordinated various testimonies to avoid gaps and redundancies.

Realistically, joint actions are also a very real method of sharing expenses, especially in situations involving lawsuits. At one point in 1976 API was a participant in legal action to stop the aerial gunning of wolves in Alaska, revise the regulations for the incidental killing of dolphins by United States tuna fishermen, change the hunting hours for the shooting of waterfowl, stop a fur company from importing sealskins from South Africa, and reschedule the hunting season on migratory waterfowl. Most would have been financially impossible had not other organizations been sharing the bills.

Hopefully, humane leaders are moving toward a more enlightened attitude regarding unity. Nine years ago, however, founding a national organization was as popular with the "system" as a hair in a bowl of soup. API was incorporated in California in April 1968, and its beginnings could not have been stormier.

In early 1968 I had held the position of executive director of the HSUS California Branch for almost five years, during which time the state program had been both progressive and successful. Membership had risen seven-hundred percent. Funding was on a sound basis, and a high level of activities was being maintained. My direction was based on the belief that humanitarians had to stop talking only to each other—the public had to be gotten involved as well. Under California law, individuals could be commissioned state humane officers, empowered to enforce humane laws. The branch had made wide use of this provision and had also initiated television announcements publicizing HSUS programs.

In 1963, the Society's founder and president, Fred Myers, had died. Though he had publicly indicated his desire for me to succeed him, the board of directors had, instead, installed an interim, volunteer president. It wasn't until five years later that the position was officially filled. The new president was Mel Morse, then executive director of the Marin County (California) Humane Society; earlier, Morse had worked for AHA and had been, ironically, the person who fired Fred Myers in 1954. The president of the board of the Marin County society, Fred Kerr, was also a member of the HSUS national and California branch boards.

Knowing Morse's attitude to past programs of the California branch, I began to suspect the handwriting was on the wall. It was common knowledge that he considered volunteer humane officers more trouble than they were worth, and he'd labeled television publicity as "gimmickry." My suspicions were confirmed when he informed me that the California branch was a case of "the tail wagging the dog" and would have to cut back on its activities.

After a great deal of deliberation, and a consultation with Dr. Hugh Hamilton, president of the branch board, I regretfully submitted my resignation, giving six weeks' notice. Shortly thereafter, I notified California members of my decision and included the news that I'd accepted a position with the Animal Protection Institute "because I believe my skills in humane work can be better used to help more animals," effecting "new approaches to solving old problems." The letter invited memberships in API and three-hundred recipients responded.

I was not around for six weeks. Within two, my replacement—Mel Morse's brother, Bertram—turned up to relieve me, and soon I was served with notice of a lawsuit filed by HSUS against API, its founder, and twenty John Does. There were numerous charges, including theft of the Society's mailing list, mismanagement, and misappropriation of funds. Damages of $250,000 were sought, and a temporary injunction was obtained forbidding API's contacting any of its members who were also members of the Society.

During API's embryonic stage, there were few problems except those the litigation caused, but these were dismaying enough. The legal proceedings consumed a considerable amount of time and the meager resources available. In addition, all project efforts were dogged by rumors and slanders emanating from the organized humane movement. Everywhere I went I was asked about, or treated to distorted versions of, the lawsuit against API. Friends fell off like flies. The pressure was so intense and insidious that it was hopeless to undertake any field activity without a preliminary conference to set the record straight and clear the air.

The Institute was supported at inception by a five-thousand dollar low-interest loan from the Society for Animal Rights (even one friend can be a life-saver!), but it certainly didn't have funds to spare. Rather than spending more money on legal fees to counter the injunction, the membership was not contacted. It was obvious to all concerned that the strategy was to "kill the baby," to stifle API's efforts by drying up its present and potential funds. Fortunately, members were not the sole source of income.

Part of the Institute's program was assisting local humane societies in reorganizational efforts, a project called HEARTS—Humane Education and Research Team Services. HEARTS was composed of three to five staff members who went on site, conducted a survey of the society's activities, and made recommendations to its board of directors. Essentially, the team was employed under contract on a fee basis, remuneration being based on the contracting society's means and, of course, the time involved. One such service performed by the HEARTS team was on behalf of the Indianapolis Humane Society; it employed a five-man team for three months for ten-thousand dollars. The Society's board of directors later attested to the success of the HEARTS program.

Dear Mr. Mouras:

It has been my privilege to serve as an Officer of the Indianapolis Humane Society during the period July 15 through October 14, 1968.

During this time, I have witnessed as complete a job of revamping as any Humane Society could ever expect to undergo. You and the members of your consultant team not only made the following recommendations, but implemented many of them:

1. Recruit and train an executive director, a shelter manager and other necessary shelter personnel.
2. Direct the shelter, law enforcement, education, membership, publicity and fund raising activities of the IHS.
3. Recommend policies and procedures to govern the operations of the IHS and implement approved policies and procedures.
4. Plan, initiate and conduct a membership drive.
5. Plan, initiate and conduct a fund raising drive.
6. Plan and implement an extensive publicity campaign to promote and complement all programs and to generate the interest and support of the community.
7. Plan and implement a women's guild to support the efforts of the IHS.

The consultant team of the Animal Protection Institute displayed an exceptionally high degree of professionalism. A recital of the usual competencies must seem anti-climactic by comparison with the above listed accomplishments.

The API cannot be commended too highly for the humanitarian work they have done for the animals and people of Indianapolis.

Sincerely yours,

Guenther K. Wehrhan
President

Thus the Indianapolis Humane Society contract provided sustaining funds. At the same time, however, it removed the principal staff for a three-month period, which inhibited the ambitious program initially instituted by API. During the next two years API barely existed. Its fiscal policy was one of deficit spending, and bankruptcy was averted by the sheer determination and tenacity of its three directors.

Although financially disastrous, API was enormously successful in conducting two other phases of its program. One was the establishment of a Los Angeles Area Committee specifically for spearheading a drive for a public spay clinic in the metropolis. The Committee eventually disbanded prior to the formation of the clinic, but it was successful in mobilizing the efforts of local organizations that ultimately carried the campaign to its successful conclusion. The first public spay clinic in the United States opened its doors in Los Angeles in February 1971.

The second highly successful phase of API's program was the production of "How to Care" public service announcements (PSA's) for television. Three PSA's were produced and distributed to all television stations in the country. The spots were sixty-second, color-on-sound films dealing with the basics of horse care, dog care, and cat care. They were run at no cost by the stations as a service to the viewing public and were aired over a period of two years.

When the PSA's were first shown, API was inundated with mail, far more than had been expected or prepared for. The horse-care spot invited inquiries for additional information on owning a horse, and there were one-hundred and sixty thousand viewers, minimum, who took up the offer. The Institute did its level best to answer all of the three-hundred thousand pieces of mail received, but it was a costly proposition. Rarely was a contribution enclosed; if we were lucky, a letter contained a stamp for sending the material. Responding necessitated, of course, considerable expense for printing and postage — labor costs were avoided by use of volunteers. Some were provided by the Sacramento Volunteer Bureau, but most were recruited by the Mouras children from among their high school friends. Tens of thousands of pet-care responses were prepared and mailed during evening and weekend sessions by these youngsters.

In using television public service announcements, we learned two valuable lessons: first, with API's limited capabilities, the PSA should not contain a message to write for information; second, such announcements provided great exposure of the Institute's work to the general public. This public recognition had the quality of establishing credibility, and if API had had the resources considerable help for animals could have been obtained by a follow-up campaign. As it was, we had to be satisfied that we'd reached over forty million people with multiple messages of how to care for animals.

Running simultaneously with the television announcements were radio PSA's. These were produced on thin, plastic disks from the soundtrack of the television spots. Such a process provided for an extremely long shelf life and inquiries were received up to five years after the original mailing to seventeen-hundred radio stations.

Meanwhile, the litigation proceeded at a snail's pace. I had countersued early in the game for recovery of seventy-five hundred dollars from the HSUS pension

127

fund. The entire matter was settled out of court, after two years, with a token payment to me. The Animal Protection Institute had weathered those precarious times and had painstakingly expanded its membership from three hundred to thirteen hundred.

The hard feelings also survived. Five years after those turbulent beginnings, I made a move to bury the hatchet with HSUS, at the suggestion of a friend of both groups. The feeler was "officially" rebuffed.

Mr. John Hoyt, President
Humane Society of
  the United States
1604 K Street, N.W.
Washington, D.C. 20006

Dear Mr. Hoyt:

At the suggestion of many friends I write you in hopes of establishing avenues of communication between our organizations. I believe that you and I share this need.

While I have only observed your work for HSUS from a distance, I am impressed that you are doing an excellent job. Mutual friends believe in your leadership qualities and in you as an individual. I share our friends' views.

To my way of thinking, a meeting with you would be meaningful and mutually beneficial. I am aware of the subtleties and do not wish to place you in a difficult or delicate position. However, if you find it would be helpful to the cause we serve, I would be pleased to help bring about such a meeting at some convenient time.

In the meanwhile, greetings and best wishes, and I wish you success in all your efforts.

Most sincerely,

Belton P. Mouras
President

Mr. Belton P. Mouras, President
Animal Protection Institute of America
5894 South Land Park Drive
Sacramento, California 95822

Dear Mr. Mouras:

Please forgive my delay in responding to your letter of March 8 which arrived just as I was leaving Washington for a trip to Buffalo and Detroit. I appreciate hearing from you, as I had suggested to Col. Bernie Beck that I felt it would be more useful for us to correspond directly than to have him attempt to arrange a meeting together for us.

As you are well aware, there are many grievances that exist between you and The Humane Society of the United States, most of which I know only second hand. However, several persons still associated with The HSUS know these first hand and, consequently, are most reluctant that I should engage The HSUS in any association with you personally or the Animal Protection Institute as an organization. At this point, I shall respect their judgment, as I do not make it a practice to disregard the advice and judgment of my associates. Thus, in my capacity as president of The HSUS, I must decline your invitation to attempt "to establish avenues of communication between our organizations."

However, I would be most willing to meet with you on a "person to person" basis. Because of my great respect for Bernie Beck, who has expressed his hope that a meeting between us might be of mutual benefit, and because of my reluctance to close doors to anyone, I would welcome such an opportunity. Such a meeting should be quite personal in nature with no implications for the organizations we represent. Perhaps out of a meeting such as this can come the basis of communication between our respective organizations some time in the future.

Please let me know if this kind of personal meeting is of interest to you.

Sincerely yours,

John A. Hoyt
President

Taking a leaf from Abraham Lincoln's book, all humane organizations will not cooperate all the time. Differing philosophies of leaders, preoccupation with various issues, financial and geographical limitations, members' interests—all combine to ensure that animal abuse is assaulted from many directions with a wide range of weapons.

Such diversity is often refreshing and valuable. However, a cooperative spirit has surfaced and bloomed in the past few years, aided by the addition of a "new guard" of professional protectionists and by a surge of public interest in the cause of animals. It's a spirit that can only work to the benefit of the humane movement as a whole.

11

Many Names for Many Games: Deciding Who Stands for What

"We protectionists love animals."

"No, we conservationists love animals."

What's this argument about? Hunting. The logic of it all and the definition of love may become difficult to follow, but the lines are sharply drawn, and it is more than a semantic argument. It is a battle that is slowly moving into the courts and the legislatures. And it is the major issue that divides—sharply and seemingly irreparably—animal-oriented organizations into two camps.

Protectionists want to allow wild animals—*game animals* is the term used for those hunted—to live in their natural state and surroundings without unnecessary interference from man. Conservationists want the animals "managed" to produce a "harvestable surplus" each year. *Harvest*, you've probably guessed, has become the euphemism for *shoot*.

On the one side are the hunter-supported "conservation" groups like Ducks Unlimited, Inc., and the National Wildlife Federation. This coalition has a diverse group of bedfellows including the National Rifle Association (whose incorporated purposes are to defend the instruments of killing and promote conservation), big-money trophy and safari clubs, and, surprisingly, the American Humane Association.

The other side is composed of groups like API, the Fund for Animals, Society for Animal Rights, Friends of Animals, and a good many smaller organizations on both the state and national levels. There are also many nonhunters who feel strongly about the hunting issue because of incidents with hunters—damage of property, shooting of animals, and trespassing are common ones—or because they are amateur photographers, naturalists, hikers, or outdoor enthusiasts. This growing segment is often referred to in the literature of the battle as "nonconsumptive users of wildlife."

The battle itself has become a heated one. The nonhunters have poked fun at the immaturity of hunters, questioned their sexual prowess, and even suggested that they improve the thrill of the chase by draping themselves in fawn color and pursuing each other during the hunting season. In return, the hunters have slung mud and misrepresentations. They have attempted to discredit the leaders of humane groups, have perused our literature for "antigun, antihunt" statements, have published various interpretations of our financial statements, and have asked governmental regulatory agencies to "investigate" us.

The cheetah is the swiftest animal in the jungle, but speed doesn't keep it from being endangered. The birth of three different cheetah litters on an American wildlife compound, Lion Country Safari, was thus a bonanza.

Probably their most successful ploy has been to associate the issues of gun control and hunting. The NRA, for example, issued a letter that was later published saying API was "antikill, antihunt, antitrap, and antigun." This last adjective was the clincher, for gun control is a highly emotional issue. By associating antihunting groups with gun control, the NRA has succeeded to some extent in solidifying a block of progun people—some who hunt and some who do not—in opposition to humane arguments. In fact, API has no position on gun control, has never issued a public statement on gun control, and in all likelihood never will.

Adding to the paranoia are hunting magazines like *Field & Stream, Outdoor Life, Petersen's Hunting,* and *Fur-Fish-Game,* which turn a tidy profit telling hunters where to find 'em and how to shoot 'em or catch 'em.

These publications, which never quite disclose how much of their corporate profits they contribute to genuine conservation, produce a steady flow of "exposés" on the antihunting groups. One wonders if perhaps these magazines that have, over the years, promoted predator-calling, African trophy-head safaris, bighorn sheep shooting (including the "Grand Slam" trophy kill of one of each species of bighorn), and an unending barrage of animal killing, do not indeed "protest too much." Surely some doubts about the sanity of it all must enter the reader's head.

The public's changing attitudes toward hunting are an offshoot of the environmental movement of the late sixties and early seventies, although many humane groups espoused the concepts quietly, if not vocally, for many years previous. The feeling now is that the world's resources, including wildlife, are no longer to be played with. The deer carcass draped over a car fender is not a symbol of manhood or an object of admiration. (Some hunting publications have even told readers that public sentiment against this type of display is so strong that dead animals should be transported out of public sight.) Trophy heads on a wall are now viewed more with sympathy for the animal than with esteem for the killer's conquest.

The day is long past when hunting in this country must be done for food. The accoutrements of the chase — gun, transportation, protective clothing, walkie-talkies — have brought the price per pound of hunted meat to a ridiculously high figure. The excuses are blown and hunters have to face the fact that in many instances the public questions the need for continuation of this type of behavior toward animals. There is a new attitude that says "we're all in this together — let's start acting like it."

Other influences are opening fire on hunting. There has, in general, been a recent reawakening to, and an interest in, natural science. A holistic approach, looking at all interactions, to our entire environment has brought about an understanding of animals as part of an ecosystem. The wolf, for example, is no longer seen as a vicious predator; his pack structure has been carefully studied and his role in maintaining the balance and health of herbivore species is recognized. Television, capable of bringing wildlife into everyone's living room, has been most influential, and the number of wildlife specials and their popularity are on the ascendancy.

As people join in the hunting controversy, even environmental organizations are being called upon to take a stand. These groups are concerned with the total environment, of which animals are a part. Some condone hunting of current game species but oppose expanding to new species; others say they do not oppose hunting but do not address the humane aspects of it. Changes in these large organizations — like Sierra Club, Wilderness Society — are being generated on the chapter level, where more and more nonhunters and antihunters are active members.

If you feel strongly about the hunting question, ask for a well-defined position on it from any group you're considering joining or contributing to. Don't be misled by cute wildlife stamps and offerings of wildlife prints, glasses, or needlepoint kits. Don't be double-talked by the jargon of the battle. A frequently used, issue-avoiding statement is that the gun and the trap are "tools" of wildlife management. Well, the electric chair is a "tool" of civilized society — if you happen to believe in capital punishment. If you do not, you would probably consider it barbaric. Ask for specific answers, not academic definitions.

The basic premise supporting hunting is that every species naturally produces a surplus and that some of this surplus can and should be taken by man. In the natural system certain parameters influence the reproduction and survival rate of animal species. These limitations include food, water, shelter, predation, climate, and competition. By controlling these factors — providing nesting areas, removing predators, planting food, removing food of competing species — wildlife managers can ensure that a "harvestable surplus" of desirable animals is ready for hunters in the fall. For some species, like deer, this works well; for others, like quail and mourning doves, which experience a natural die-off in their populations, hunting could be terminated.

One of the primary problems in the whole arrangement is that the managers are paid by the hunting community. In effect, their livelihood depends upon pleasing the hunter and providing him with a reasonable success ratio. In practically all states, conservation or fish and game departments are supported by revenues from the sale of hunting and fishing licenses and excise taxes collected from the sale of firearms and ammunition. This latter tax, set up by the Pittman-Robertson Act of 1937, is collected by the federal government and then redistributed to the states on the basis of the number of hunters within a state.

Such a funding system provides hunters with ideological ammunition, the argument that they pay for what they kill, while it leaves nonhunters practically voiceless, in spite of the fact that hunters kill animals belonging to *all* the people (if to any).

This funding system creates real problems: game managers, reluctant to antagonize their source of funds, permit hunts in questionable circumstances. In Pennsylvania, for example, the black bear is in trouble because of excessive hunting, road kills, and urban development. The number, physical size, and age of the bears killed each hunting season have been declining, and a wildlife researcher said in 1975 that it would take at least three years of no hunting to bring the bear population up to such a level that there would be one cub born for every bear killed. Still, despite the evidence, the Game Commission allows one-day "seasons." In 1974, around 130,000 persons hunted bear, taking 223 animals; in 1976, 550 bears were killed.

In Alaska, polar bears were shot by hunters brought to the icepack in small aircraft. The bears had little chance of escape and hunters took a tremendous toll. Despite the lack of sportsmanship in this type of shooting, Alaska's game managers allowed it to go on until public outrage at all aerial hunting caused federal prohibitive legislation to be passed.

Predators are not the only victims. In a number of warmer-climate states the mourning dove season opens before nesting is completed. The hunter's bullet packs a double whammy—when the parent bird is killed, the nestlings are left to starve.

API and most antihunting groups support measures to provide alternate sources of funds—preferably a tax on a commodity used by all the people—for conservation work so *all* the people will have a say in the fate of wildlife.

A basic criticism of hunting—aside from the ethical question of whether an animal's life should be taken because a hunter enjoys taking it—is the capability of the individuals carrying the guns and shooting at the animals. No marksmanship test is required before purchase of a hunting license. No eyesight examination is given. The applicant need not prove he can identify his target (something only a small percentage of waterfowl hunters can do) or whether he fully understands what animal—male or female, for instance—may be shot. There are no laws requiring that wounded animals be trailed or that hunters control their consumption of alcohol while hunting. The pain game animals experience is overlooked to perpetuate the system. The only pain considered reportable is that experienced when one hunter shoots another.

Humane organizations are forcing a reevaluation of hunting, a rethinking we believe holds great promise but one that will need the informed backing of this country's citizens. Changes have already been wrought: some state governments have appropriated general funds for wildlife work; others have alternate-funding proposals under consideration. Our goals may have to be long-range, but they are not unrealistic. Nonhunters will eventually be represented.

In spite of the irreconcilable positions of prohunters and antihunters, the hunting question has proved an obstacle to working relationships between protectionist and conservation groups in only a few instances. The great majority of humane groups' activities deal with nonhunting issues, areas where conservationists can join in a firm proanimal stand without contradicting their distinguishing concept of animal *use*. Likewise, humane and environmental groups have found each other compatible. Saving the environment naturally focuses attention on the animals living there, and, vice versa, one cannot protect animals unless their habitat is preserved. Thus, goals often mesh.

The coalition of humane and environmental groups is most forceful in the area of legal actions, as mentioned in the previous chapter. But, undoubtedly, the most positive demonstration of the power humane and environmental groups can exert by joining forces is the save-the-whales campaign. The boycott of consumer products from Japan and Russia has expanded from the United States to other countries; it has brought a reduction in the killing, including smaller quotas set by the International Whaling Commission, and it may eventually bring a complete end to the slaughter. API was one of the initial groups calling for the boycott, in the fall of 1973. While the move was thought rash by many, it gradually spread to all humane and environmental groups. The whale battle had to be fought, as is so often the case, on economic grounds; moral suasion couldn't turn the trick.

Just as there is a great variety of causes in the humane and environmental arena, there is a great variety of groups organized to fight for these causes. Crusaders exist on the national, state, county, city, and community levels. Some extend their program and staff to work for all animals, some work only for specific species like whales or seals, some operate shelters for pets, and some work only in their local communities to change laws and educate residents.

Nationally, there are six large United States humane organizations. These are the Animal Protection Institute, the Fund for Animals, Friends of Animals, the Humane Society of the United States, the Society for Animal Rights, and the Animal Welfare Institute. All have a national membership, follow legislation and monitor enforcement of existing laws, and maintain offices or contacts in Washington, D.C. The activities of these groups encompass all animals — pets, livestock, wildlife, and exotic animals. A seventh national group, Defenders of Wildlife, operates similarly but confines its work to wildlife.

Within this framework there are smaller, specific organizations, each concerned with a particular animal. Some of the animals are local in terms of range, but battles for their welfare generally reach from state governments to Congress. Committee for the Preservation of the Tule Elk, Friends of the Sea Otter, Society for the Preservation of Birds of Prey, Wild Horse Organized Assistance, General Whale, Project Jonah, and Save the Dolphins are some of the most widely recognized specialized groups.

Like national organizations, smaller groups and committees maintain mailing lists or memberships. They are often headed by a single, devoted individual (many times a volunteer), are influential, and command considerable public respect.

State-level humane groups are usually federations of shelter-operating societies. Sometimes, too, they are committees formed for specific purposes, such as to outlaw the use of the steel-jaw, leghold trap or to oppose the introduction of greyhound racing. When specific goals are accomplished — a bill is made law, for example — these disband.

In a few states, SPCAs have state-wide recognition and influence. The Pennsylvania SPCA, for example, has a number of shelters throughout the state. The Associated Humane Societies of New Jersey, while having its main shelter in Newark, operates throughout a large section of the state. The Massachusetts SPCA and the American SPCA in New York both extend their activities beyond their immediate areas (because of its name, the ASPCA is often confused with national societies).

Most of the large SPCAs, many of which have substantial financial holdings, are associated with the American Humane Association. AHA is composed primarily of shelter-operating organizations; it has a mailing list of about one thousand locals and advises them on various aspects of shelter operation.

Finally, at the community level and serving pet owners with specific problems, are small citizen groups that sponsor spay and neuter programs, run lost-dog registries, serve as watchdogs for city pound operations, and represent the pet-owning segment of the community at city council and governmental meetings. All of these groups serve animals, and probably the ones providing a most-needed service are

The comeback. A poodle on the thin edge of death—almost starved, palpitating with neglect—was nursed back to normal by the Florida Injured Wildlife Sanctuary. Although the Sanctuary is primarily concerned with treating injured wildlife, its staff had no red-tape rules to prevent rescuing a dog that clearly wouldn't have lived without help.

those which assist low-income pet owners in having their animals spayed or neutered.

In some instances these groups or committees are providing a community service that should be covered by the shelter-operating society but is not. Although it may be difficult for anyone concerned with animal welfare to comprehend, some large shelters with city animal-control contracts make no attempt to curb the pet overpopulation problem. In fact, they wish to see it perpetuated so they will be kept "in business."

This was brought home to me in the early sixties when I persuaded a California state assemblyman to sponsor a bill to require public animal shelters and shelters operated under contract with municipalities to have female dogs and cats spayed before sale or adoption. Prior to public hearing before committee, there was virtually no opposition to the bill. In fact, it was considered a shoo-in. But before our very eyes, at the hearing, no less than eleven paid directors of shelter-operating societies showed up and gave testimony opposing the bill. We were literally dumbfounded. The excuses used were precisely those humane workers generally attribute to "uneducated pet owners" — "spaying is too expensive," "children should see the miracle of birth," "let them have one litter first." Needless to say, the chairman tabled the bill. The opponents, the "Elite Eleven," came from old and prestigious societies, with San Francisco and Los Angeles well represented.

At the community level, one can also find unique shelters run by dedicated, hard-working, and determined individuals. These facilities may be limited to certain animals, such as cats. For wild animals, some cities have sanctuaries where animals can be rehabilitated and rescue groups are ready to cope with emergencies such as oil spills. Another community-level service in an ever-growing number of cities is the publicly funded spay and neuter clinic. Promoted by nearly all humane groups, these clinics use the money that would ordinarily be put into destroying animals into preventing their birth in the first place — a far more sensible approach.

12

Techniques of Human Education: Or, How To Plague the Bullies

Nothing of value happens in the animal protection field without the knowledge and support of numbers of people. The trade term for the process of disseminating information toward this end is *humane education*, i.e., communicating with the public.

It can be a horrendous problem, not unlike that faced by educators: every teaching day they must get and hold students' attention, must tailor their messages to be neither over the head nor mundane for a variety of recipients.

Rule 1 in communicating is *get the facts*. This will involve research. Look for books, articles in periodicals (especially environmental and humane journals), contact protectionist organizations and individuals who may be regarded as authorities. Also — and this is important in any controversial situation — identify active or likely opponents and familiarize yourself with their arguments.

There is an advantage to knowing the enemy aside from the obvious one of thus combatting him more effectively — you may find ground for cooperation.

In the early sixties, shortly after President Eisenhower signed into law the federal Humane Slaughter Act, campaigns were organized to get legislation passed on the state level (the Act applied only to meat and meat products sold in interstate commerce or used in federal institutions). Ranchers and farmers were fierce in their resistance to any state laws molded after the federal one; they feared they would not be able to kill an individual head on their own property without installation of expensive humane slaughtering equipment.

It wasn't until I attended a cattlemen association's meeting and talked to individuals socially that I learned the facts. Farmers and ranchers were in favor of humane slaughter, but they held that stunning with gunshot prior to slaughter — as they were doing and their fathers had done before them — was a humane method. This was an astonishing revelation, for the federal law and the proposed state laws approved gunshot as humane. We in the humane movement had failed to communicate. We were poor teachers, indeed.

Rule 2 in communicating is *get the facts out*. Dissemination can take several forms: personal letters, printed literature, advertisements, press releases, letters to editors, radio and television publicity, personal appearances, petition drives, demonstrations. None of these methods demand highly advanced skills. Organization, dedication, and some basic knowledge can work wonders.

Rare forms of life are preserved in the Pacific's Galapagos Islands. API organized a Galapagos trip so that members could see what Darwin saw and wondered at.

Personal Letters

A letter is probably the most effective means of communication; it is quick and inexpensive and can elicit the desired reaction if a few simple guidelines are followed. You already know the subject (Rule 1) so it's easy to *be specific*. State what the problem is, what should be done about it, and why. Most letters about what should or shouldn't happen are based on feelings of right and wrong—a legitimate basis—but maudlin messages are easily ignored by neutral or unsympathetic receivers.

As much as possible, *be concise*. If you must go beyond three or four paragraphs, use a brief cover letter and expand on the subject in an attachment. Don't deal with several topics in a letter. One could receive immediate action, but if another requires research or policy study the entire matter is needlessly held up or, perhaps, lost in the intraoffice shuffle.

Make your message legible. No letter is effective if it's unreadable or conveys a slovenly impression of the sender. If you can type well and have access to a typewriter, use it; if not, write clearly on standard-size stationery. Type-written missives are more eye-catching, as are letters on company or business letterhead or printed personal stationery.

Other attention-getting devices are sending your messages via certified or special delivery mail, or by telegram. For flat rates, Western Union has "public opinion telegrams"—fifteen words plus name and address—and one-hundred word "mail-grams"—transmitted electronically to Washington where they are put in an envelope and mailed for next-day delivery. Such methods convey a sense of urgency as well as the profound interest of the sender.

Perhaps most importantly, *mind your manners*. Don't brag, berate, or threaten. An overbearing attitude can scuttle any letter, even one offering potentially helpful criticism, for it's easy to rationalize such a message as a "crank letter" and discard it.

Can associations and businesses be moved by an individual's communication? The popular view is that one person is helpless against such forces. This is not, however, the case.

Not long ago a national corporation operating wildlife parks received newspaper publicity alleging mistreatment of some of the animals. When the public relations director called me to investigate the charges he was jumping through hoops of hysteria because thirty-five people had written letters of criticism. This multi-million-dollar company seemed prostrated at the potential damage to its business.

Some situations exist because of ignorance. When API National Advisor Marj King noticed mechanical ferrets* being advertised in *Prairie Farmer*, she warned the midwest publication the devices were illegal in Indiana. The reply was favorable.

Mrs. King,

Thanks for your information on mechanical ferrets. I did not know they were illegal in Indiana, and still don't know their status in Illinois and the other Prairie Farmer states.

However, this type of ad will not be accepted by us in the future. (It was too late to pull it from our December issue, which was just mailed this week.)

Once again, thanks for your help.

Yours truly,

Jeff Weber
Classified Advertising Manager

---

*Mechanical ferrets are coiled-spring instruments cranked into holes and dens. Sometimes this chases the animal out; if not, the operator can wind the coil in the animal's fur and pull it out.

Other cases may not be illegal but an objection on ethical considerations can do the trick.

Manager
The Bookstore
University of Washington
4326 University Way Northeast
Seattle, Washington 98105

Dear Sir:

It has been called to our attention that you are offering for sale in the Bookstore caps and other articles made of genuine coyote fur. I would like to take the liberty of pointing out to you, in the event that you were unaware of it, the extremely cruel method by which such furs are obtained.

The enclosed brochure, ad and poster will describe for you the steel-jaw leghold trap and its action. Leghold trapping accounts for virtually all of the wild animal skins taken in this country, and it is almost certain that the skins you are marketing in the Bookstore were taken in this manner.

There is legislation pending in both houses of the U.S. Congress to eliminate the use of the leghold trap. It would seem that, in an institution devoted to the civilization and humanization of young people, articles obtained by barbaric torture devices would be inappropriate.

We sincerely hope you will consider removing the coyote-fur articles from sale in the Bookstore. Thank you for your kind attention.

FOR THE ANIMAL PROTECTION INSTITUTE OF AMERICA, INC.

Most sincerely,

Belton P. Mouras
President

The store's merchandise manager replied, "We have no way of knowing whether the animals slain for these hats were obtained by use of the leghold trap or by more humane methods"; but he agreed to remove the hats from the bookstore shelves.

Often, a condition that moves you enough to compose and send a personal letter, will have also motivated other individuals.

Executive Offices
Sears, Roebuck and Co.
303 East Ohio Street
Chicago, Ill. 60611

Gentlemen:

As an animal welfare organization, we officially protest the sale of steel leg-hold traps in your retail and catalog operations.

The cruelty involved in such traps is such that legislation has been introduced in Washington, D.C., to ban the interstate shipment of furs and skins obtained in such a manner. We feel that a national retail operation of your stature should not be a party to animal suffering.

We would appreciate your comments on this subject.

FOR THE ANIMAL PROTECTION INSTITUTE OF AMERICA, INC.

Most sincerely,

Belton P. Mouras
President

Mr. Belton P. Mouras, President
Animal Protection Institute of America
5894 South Land Park Drive
Sacramento, California 95822

Dear Mr. Mouras:

For some months, Sears, Roebuck and Co. has been reviewing its position relating to the sale of steel leg-hold animal traps.

Since you contacted us in this matter, you will be interested to learn that we will no longer sell these devices through our retail or catalog operations.

As we are always interested in our customers' comments, we want you to know that we appreciate the time you took to write.

Sincerely,

Hubert Burnham, Jr.
Director, National Issues
Sears, Roebuck and Co.

H. C. Hiebel
Buyer, Pet Department
F. W. Woolworth Co.
Executive Office
Woolworth Building
New York, New York 10007

Dear Mr. Hiebel:

We have received a complaint from the Central Missouri Humane Society regarding the pet department in your Columbia, Missouri, Woolco Store. Specifically, we understand that store is beginning to deal in exotic pets such as boas, monkeys, jaguar kittens and even an anteater. We are wondering if this is a new policy for all Woolcos.

The Central Missouri Humane Society reports they have had calls from frantic mothers whose children have had nightmares after seeing store employees feed live rodents to the boa. In addition, one of the monkeys came through the post-mortem laboratory at the University's veterinary school. It was dead from parasites.

Columbia is a college town and provides a considerable market for these types of novelty pets. At the same time, I am sure you, as a buyer, are familiar with some of the problems resulting from dealing in exotics. The animals are often captured under conditions that are far from humane. The parent animals may have been killed to obtain the infant as it has more appeal to the prospective buyer, who generally has no knowledge of how to provide adequate care for the unusual animal. It has been our experience that the whole area of exotic pets is one that has caused extensive abuse and suffering to animals. It has also caused decimation to many foreign species, particularly those from South America.

We have certainly appreciated your assistance in the past and look forward to your reply regarding the Columbia situation.

FOR THE ANIMAL PROTECTION INSTITUTE OF AMERICA, INC.

Most sincerely,

Belton P. Mouras
President

Mr. Belton P. Mouras, President
Animal Protection Institute
5894 South Land Park Drive
P.O. Box 22505
Sacramento, California 95822

Dear Mr. Mouras:

We received a letter on May 19, from Nancy J. Brooker of the Central Missouri Humane Society in regards to our Columbia Missouri Woolco store telling us that this store was selling large pets such as you mention in your letter.

First, we want you to know that it is definitely against the Woolworth Co. policy to sell any large animals. We contacted the store at once and stopped the sale of exotic pets. We also contacted the firm that sold these animals to the store and told them that the F.W. Woolworth Co. will cancel their complete listing if they ever sell animals of this sort to any of our stores again, and we will not honor their invoice. Also a letter was issued from this office to all stores notifying them to remove from sale at once any animals such as monkeys, boas, etc.

Each store has an exact listing of the pets they are permitted to sell.

We as a company are not interested in getting into the large or exotic animal business in any way, neither in Woolworth nor Woolco.

Our stores are only to sell fish, birds, hamsters and the like as we have for many years.

We are sorry that this had to happen; however, we do thank you for bringing this to our attention so that we can put a stop to this type of operation at once.

Thank you for being so understanding; for the record, we sent a prompt reply to Ms. Brooker's letter informing her of our policy.

Sincerely,

H.C. Hiebel
Buyer, Pet Dept.
F.W. Woolworth Co.

Maybe it's human nature. Most people like to feel they're doing a good job, not offending the people with whom they do business. In my own situation as head of API, a single letter, right or wrong, from a disgruntled member can negate a hundred letters of praise with respect to attention awarded each.

Where large volumes of mail are a daily occurrence, letters, even brief ones, are not always read. This is particularly true with national legislators, whose mail count can range from a few hundred to ten-thousand-plus a week. This doesn't mean, however, that opinions go unnoticed. Letters are separated as to their stand on an issue and a measurement is made of the numbers of people for and against.

Legislators are aware that mail is not always an accurate indication of public opinion: it's the more educated, socially aware, and politically active they hear from. But correspondence is respected because it is this same segment of the public that is most likely to be the voting segment.

Writing congressmen is not so different from communicating with the business community, though the former may inspire a sense of awe — or frustration. Don't hesitate to write. Congressmen expect and welcome letters as a means of keeping in touch with constituents. At the other end of the spectrum, don't feel justified in trying intimidation because your legislator (theoretically, at least) represents you. Abuse is an instant turn-off.

Because of the volume of legislators' mail and because animal welfare measures often receive low priority, it's most important to be accurate and specific. If the recipient or his or her aides must do research to understand your request, chances are they won't make the effort. When writing about a bill, identify it by number and include its major provision(s); if possible, name the sponsor(s). Over twenty-thousand proposals are introduced in a single congressional session and it's probable legislators never hear about many of them.

Don't put away your pen after one letter, either. Each person has two senators and a representative, and they may require several letters each before an issue is settled. And, keep in mind the value of thank-you's.

Sincerity and originality pay dividends. Form postcards and letters, and messages containing standard or recurring phrases, though noted, do not have the impact of spontaneous communication showing the writer has thought out his or her position. Form letters are more likely to receive form replies or none at all.

At the same time, there's one multiple letter any constituent should be happy to get — that indicating a tremendous amount of mail and public concern about an issue.

Dear Friend:

I have the petition you signed concerning HR 66, a bill which would discourage the use of painful devices in the trapping of animals and birds.

I am co-sponsoring this legislation since I am in accord with its humanitarian sentiments. I do not believe the use of steel leghold traps and other painful trapping devices should be permitted nor do I approve of the indiscriminate killing of animals solely to obtain their pelts for the luxury fur market.

Unfortunately the volume of petitions I have received necessitates this less than personal response. I hope you will understand and accept my appreciation for taking the time to advise me of your feelings on this matter.

Sincerely,

Edward I. Koch
House of Representatives

A common policy of legislators is to avoid committing themselves to constituents. There's a valid reason: bills can be amended beyond recognition, requiring a position reversal or, at least, further consideration. It's also possible a bill will be killed in, or never considered by, committee; if the measure is controversial, a legislator would lose nothing by remaining neutral. Or, the issue may be viewed as too complex to explain to the constituent.

We've been discussing elected representatives but the same general rules apply to heads of federal departments. Unlike the former, these bureaucrats are appointed; however, the appointer is usually the President, who *is* elected, and a ruckus over any agency's action can shake his foundation of public support.

In 1974, in cooperation with the National Parks and Conservation Association, API published a report on budget cuts made by the Office of Management and Budget that would drastically reduce wildlife programs. Ironically, OMB was refusing to spend money that had already been appropriated by Congress. No funds were to be spent for acquisition of wetlands for waterfowl; an Endangered Species Office request for $5.2 million to acquire habitat was reduced to only $1.3 million; and a Forest Service wildlife management program needing approximately a million and a half dollars was to get a mere $209,000.

When API publicized the cutbacks in its magazine, members were asked to protest to OMB. The agency received so many letters a staff member called our Sacramento headquarters to say the actions were being reconsidered.

A similar demonstration of public concern was elicited by humane groups when the Presidential ban on the use of poisons in predator control was under attack. The ban, established by an executive order signed by President Richard Nixon in 1972, forbade the shipment in interstate commerce of 1080, strychnine, thallium, and cyanide for use in predator control. Woolgrowers in particular were continually pressuring governmental agencies to have the order rescinded. When one such effort appeared near success in early 1973, humane and conservation groups sent out an emergency alert to their members. Within two days the Department of Interior received two-thousand letters supporting a continued, enforceable ban on the use of poisons.

Thanks to continued vigilance on the part of humane organizations, the executive order remained intact until President Gerald Ford modified it in 1975 to allow the use of cyanide.

Humane Education Literature

Pamphlets, brochures and flyers are the basic communication tools of the humane business. They are an important part of reaching the public, including school-age children, and should never be ignored.

API vice president Susan Lock holds a club and a gaff, instruments used by the harp seal hunters.

Publications serve to create an impression of a group as a working entity long before an individual either visits the shelter or meets someone connected with such a society. They can also influence the extent to which financial support is given, particularly in cases where the donor never sees the organization's physical facilities.

The composition and production of pamphlets and other such items should be carefully planned and executed. Their purpose is to get the message read and remembered, and here, too, the cluttered, single-spaced, typewritten sheet is out of date. If the reading of a publication looks like a major chore, chances are it will be read only by the hard-core supporter of your cause. The individuals you really want to reach, however, are those new to the humane cause. To attract their attention, you have to entice them to read your position.

144

In putting together a brochure, there are a number of points to consider.

First, decide on the message. Consider budget and priorities. Do not put out an expensive pamphlet, for example, on the problems of giving baby chicks and rabbits as Easter gifts when a wider service could be performed within your community by a pamphlet on state laws protecting animals. Give priority to whatever topic will do the greatest good for the greatest number of animals — unless, of course, your financial resources are unlimited and allow for detailed diversification.

Second, stick to the theme or main point. If the subject is whales, do not confuse the reader with a paragraph about seals. Substantiate your information with sources and backup figures whenever your position may be open to question. Always try to illustrate your stand by giving examples.

Third, use uncluttered graphics and clear photos to make the piece readable. Choose eye-pleasing type. Old English typeface, for example, may look elegant on a wedding invitation, but it is impossible to read in paragraph blocks. Clarity is important, both in the type and in the artwork.

Fourth, emphasize your most important points with boldface type, subheads, screening, a second color, or a different typeface. When doing this, think of a person scanning your finished product rather than reading it thoroughly word for word. You want this person to retain and understand the message even though he or she may not delve into the details.

Fifth, do not date your message unless you plan to print in small quantities that can be revised at every reprinting. There is always a financial advantage to printing in large amounts and, in the long run, the savings can be considerable. If your publication is on shelter operations, the pet population problem, or some other long standing issue, write the copy so it will be valid for several years. Another trick is to design the piece so corrections or updating would only have to be done on one side. Depending upon the method of printing you use, this can save the cost of at least one new printing plate every time you reorder.

Sixth, make certain your group's name, address, and any identifying symbols are clearly and noticeably on the publication. In some instances, you will want to include a coupon for becoming a member or contributing to a campaign. Emphasize the clip-out marks around the coupon and arrange the layout so a picture or sketch appears on the backside. Thus, the message will not be destroyed if the coupon is removed.

Finally, whenever possible, put your message on some item that will be retained for easy reference. The Animal Protection Institute has had special success with pet care charts and bookmarks. These give the basics of pet care and can be used indefinitely. Bookmarks are inexpensive to print and are always welcomed by schools and libraries.

Talk to a printer after you have thought out your brochure, and get bids from several of them. Many times a good printer can make suggestions for inexpensively improving a piece. Colored ink on colored stock, for example, makes a brochure more eye-catching. Tints and screens can be used at little or no extra cost to make portions of a message stand out. Use of a sketch instead of a photograph can sometimes cut costs. Also, photographs without contrast will not reproduce well and checking with a printer beforehand can save a costly mistake.

Distribution of the finished product can be handled in a number of ways. Use of a group's membership provides the best continual outlet. Ask members to place the materials in their businesses, have their children take copies to school, pass on a copy to a friend. This latter suggestion will quickly double the number of people who know about your work.

School systems and teachers are generally responsive to free information, especially if the message can be incorporated into a subject or unit already being taught. Packets can be mailed to individual schools, or, in larger cities, to a central district distributing center, where they are then delivered to the schools.

Libraries are always an outlet for materials, and, in addition to keeping materials on display, some maintain animal welfare reference files. College bookstores and book co-ops are other possible distribution outlets.

Traveling exhibits or booths at shopping centers are effective, and teachers' conferences and conventions are also ideal places to set up exhibits.

Finally, an expensive but efficient way of distributing your message is through the purchase of a direct-mail list. List brokers can supply lists of pet owners in a given locality, individuals donating to ecological efforts, persons buying pet supplies by mail, or names and addressed of people meeting just about any criteria you wish.

Lists are rented on a cost-per-1,000-names basis. The expense of using this method — cost of list, printing, postage, stuffing, and handling — can be high, but if the issue is important or urgent this system can work. Direct-mail list buying should definitely be considered by any group undertaking a major fund-raising drive.

Advertisements

Advertising humane issues is a concept pioneered by API. And, while it has brought considerable flack from opposition groups, it has also brought humane messages, in many instances for the first time, to millions of people.

A shining example is the Institute's ad stating the cruelties of the steel-jaw, leghold trap. The horrors of trapping have concerned humane groups for years, but the information remained with a small circle of people knowledgeable about humane work or with members of a humane group. The problem had never been brought before the general public, and it is the public that applies the pressure to eventually force a great reform.

The experience of an API staff member illustrates the beneficial effects of such advertising. Jane Risk, the Institute's Washington, D.C., director of information services, visited senators' offices asking support for the newly introduced antitrap bill. Several legislative assistants pulled copies of the trap ad, clipped from newspapers, from their correspondence files; constituents had sent the ad with the urgent plea, "Do something!"

Advertisements can be constructed to be multipurpose. They can educate, protest, oppose, inform, alert, and appeal for support. The stereotyped idea of advertisements being only a medium for the selling of a consumer product is outdated. Today, humane groups must compete in the marketplace of ideas. We cannot be only in the business of warehousing, killing, or placing animals; although these activities alleviate the immediate pain and suffering of an individual animal, they divert from the real issue. Our target must be the attitude of the person initially responsible for that animal. Call it moral suasion, humane education, or whatever title you like, protectionists must be in the business of changing people's concepts about animals.

Like any effort at change — civil rights, women's liberation, human rights — we must continually try to drive home our ideas, and to do so we first have to get the public's attention. The age of the mimeograph is over, and we must learn to professionally use the means available for reaching the public.

Following are some guidelines for putting together a humane ad.

(1) Use attention-getting photos. An appealing animal or a child with an animal are two old standbys. Another approach is to use an animal in distress, giving the ad a sense of urgency. Impact can be heightened by the illusion of eye contact, having the animal or child look directly at the reader. Sometimes the suggestion of a threat makes the point. One Canadian group ran advertisements featuring a vertical photo of a scalpel; at issue, as the copy under the picture explained, was

This photo of a raccoon that died an agonizing death became the symbol of the antitrap movement. Many an apologist for trapping claimed this was a fake photo. It wasn't. COURTESY MONTEREY COUNTY (CA) SPCA.

the city's plan to sell unclaimed dogs and cats for medical research. Response was so great that an effective committee was organized and the plan defeated.

(2) Compose a clean, neat layout. Make the message of the ad easy to read and follow. Use a distinctive, readable headline and do not overload the ad with copy. Trying to "get your money's worth" by filling every available inch of space with copy can defeat your purpose. Remember, you ad will be competing for attention with everything else on the magazine or newspaper page. Don't make reading it a chore and don't complicate the message with too many superfluous details.

(3) Use direct, to-the-point copy. Be descriptive but concise. Use short, declarative sentences. Use familiar words; do not force the reader to refer to a dictionary, and do not use words that can have double meanings. Remember, too, that terms familiar to those of us in the humane movement may be totally foreign to someone unfamiliar with the issue. For example, *euthanize* sounds more genteel than *kill* but it is not a word used in everyday conversation. A copywriting tactic that can backfire for a shelter-operating society's ad is placing blame on pet owners in general. Emphasize the service you are giving animals, not the feelings you may have for the people bringing those animals to you.

(4) Include a clip-out, return coupon. This should state the purpose of the group, give the amount of annual membership dues, and allow sufficient space for the contributor to fully write out his or her name and address. Again: in putting together the layout, emphasize the coupon by surrounding it with solid clip marks. State that you are a tax-exempt, tax-deductible group.

The discard. Hunters often proceed wholesale: here fourteen raccoons were skinned and then tossed aside.

Press Releases

The press release, a valuable aid in making sure positions are correctly interpreted and publicized in the press, is often overlooked or underused by humane groups.

Fear of writing is probably the main reason press releases do not become a regular feature of a group's publicity efforts, but it is not necessary to be a journalism school graduate to produce a successful release. Keep in mind that generally they are rewritten by a newspaper reporter if used; and, if not printed in entirety, they can be a source of quotes or inspiration for a feature story.

A release can get a group mentioned in the local press and, at the same time, act as an aid to the local media. Editors cannot always assign reporters to every newsworthy event in a community and appreciate the handed-in information.

It is important that the release writer have a working knowledge of the press in the community or state. Releases should be distributed at the same time to the television and radio stations and the newspapers. Keep in mind that in a large

It became a celebrated ad. It became an ad which angered people. Angered trappers. It became a symbol of the animal protectionist movement. People who didn't know they could care about raccoons looked at this ad—and did. PHOTO COURTESY MONTEREY COUNTY (CA) SPCA.

149

community reporters compete for coverage of the day's news events. Everyone wants a "scoop" or exclusive. If your event is covered by one station, for example, it may be ignored by another. Or, as often happens, the second station will be interested in a follow-up report on later developments within a few days.

Should the subject of your release be of statewide or even national importance, deliver a copy to the wire services as well. These are the Associated Press and United Press International; they have bureaus or representatives in most cities.

News is a matter of deadlines, and reporters' jobs involve the daily pressure of filling the pages of a newspaper or the six-to-six-thirty television or radio time slot. You will be competing with world and community events that day for time or space. Depending upon the content of your story, it may go in the wastebasket on a heavy news day; on a light news day your issue may get ten column inches of space in the newspaper and three minutes on the evening television news. Don't be discouraged if every item you send out is not given coverage. Many, many factors beyond the quality of your writing influence the space and time you will receive.

Basically, anyone can write a press release by following a few simple guidelines:

(1) The standby checklist for the composition of a news story is: Who? What? Where? When? Why? and sometimes—How? Have the answers before beginning to write.

(2) Use short sentences and short paragraphs. Be concise, but strongly state your position. Remember that controversy and the unusual are often what are covered by the media.

(3) Use adjectives that are descriptive. For example, "Three dead cats were found in a schoolyard today by a student" could be better written as "The battered bodies of three cats were found behind a garbage dumpster in a south-area schoolyard today. The bloody carcasses were discovered by a third-grader on her way to class."

(4) Fully identify anyone named in the release. Do not assume that names and titles will be known by the press. For example, "Frank Miller said a reward is being offered for information on the case" should read, "Frank Miller, executive director of the Society for the Prevention of Cruelty to Animals, said a reward is being offered for information on the case."

(5) Use direct quotes to emphasize your position. This may not be necessary in a short release but can add variety of writing style to a longer one. Quotes will also give a reporter or rewrite-man more "meat" for the story. For example, " 'We strongly feel anyone torturing an animal in this way should be prosecuted to the full extent of the law,' said Miller," has more strength than simply writing "The S.P.C.A. wants the torturers prosecuted."

(6) Accompany your release to newspapers with a photograph whenever possible. If your budget will not allow the free handing out of pictures but you do have them, make a notation on the release that photos are available upon request.

(7) Concentrate on learning how to write a good lead. In the journalism trade the lead is the first sentence or paragraph of a story or release. It should command attention and give a clear indication of the content of the story. Standard rules for writing the lead are given in journalism texts as: (a) it should contain within the first ten or more words a key to the story; (b) it should be short enough to sustain reader interest; (c) it should present the most interesting aspect of the story.

The local reporters will not expect you, as publicity director for a humane group, to be able to give them copy completely ready to be set in type. Still, learning a few of the gimmicks of the journalism craft can be a decided asset in keeping your group before the public.

Releases can be written and distributed in advance of an event and marked for publication on a certain date by including a special notation. Before beginning the body copy of your story, type in all capital letters, "FOR RELEASE ON

SATURDAY, NOVEMBER 4, 1978." Always specifically give the day and date. Releases ready for printing on the day they are handed out should be headed, "FOR IMMEDIATE RELEASE."

It is important that reporters be given the name and telephone number of a person whom they can contact for more information. Generally, this is the writer of the release. In the upper, right-hand corner of your release write, "For further information contact: Jay Jones (916) 422-1921."

Finally, another trick of the trade is to begin the body copy of your release about a third of the page down. This gives the editor sufficient white space to write in a head or other comment. Always double-space all copy and indent paragraphs. Should your information require the use of two pages, do not break the copy between the two pages in the middle of a paragraph.

Letters to Editors

A simple way to use your local newspaper for publicity purposes on a regular basis is by writing letters to the editor. Practically all newspapers have letters columns and these are widely read.

A letter to the editor does not necessarily have to be your comment on something appearing in the paper itself. This forum can be used to call public attention to an animal problem, tell about a proposed piece of legislation, give basics on pet care, support a local ordinance, or simply state your position on an issue.

Most newspapers have length or word limitations on such letters. Stay within those limits and you have a good chance of getting your message printed as written. Longer letters are sometimes edited—usually by someone unfamiliar with your topic—and this can detract from the punch of your message.

One word of caution: Don't flood such columns with letters. Readers will begin to skip your comments if they appear on what seems to be a continual basis. Also, diversify your topics.

Television and Radio

Television and radio provide ready access to the public through the use of public service time. Under a Federal Communications Commission ruling, television and radio stations must donate a percentage of air time to messages promoting the public good. This time is commonly used for announcements from nonprofit or charitable groups or for information on community activities.

The amount of time given to public service is categorized into ten-second, twenty-second, thirty-second, and sixty-second units. These are fitted by station program directors into time slots at the beginning and the end of programs and during commercial breaks at the quarter hour.

The preparation of public service messages is not difficult, and many television and radio stations like to promote the work of community humane groups. After all, nearly everyone likes dogs and cats, and no one wants to see animals suffer.

Just as with a commercial, the public service message is geared to arouse emotion and persuade. The copy should be clear and grammatically correct. One of the basic guides is that the message be "in good taste." Interpretation of taste differs, however, with every individual. Some stations will show shots of dead dogs and cats euthanized at a shelter (API has used this technique in a spot to shock viewers into action); others will think this grim reminder of the reality of humane work too gory and too emotional.

In structuring a public service announcement, five steps should be followed: (1) get attention; (2) hold attention; (3) define the problem; (4) show means of solving the problem; (5) finish with a strong emotional or logical appeal for action.

The following is a thirty-second public service announcement produced and distributed by API.

Script for PET POPULATION TRAGEDY

Length: 0:30 secs

VIDEO	AUDIO
FADE IN ON SERIES OF SHOTS OF DOGS AND CATS	**SLOW DRUM BEAT UNDER AND THEN ANNR:** Dogs and cats are a part of our lives.
SHOT OF BOY PLAYING WITH DOG.	They provide companionship and affection.
SHOT OF GIRL PLAYING WITH CAT.	
SHOT OF MOTHER DOG WITH PUPPIES.	Yet this year nearly 17 million
CLOSE UP OF PUPPIES.	
CLOSE UP OF DOG BEHIND FENCE AT POUND.	unwanted dogs and cats will
SHOT OF PILE OF DEAD DOGS AND CATS AT POUND.	die in pounds and shelters.
SHOT OF STRAY CAT IN ALLEY.	Others will end up as strays.
SHOT OF DOG RUMMAGING FOR FOOD.	
CLOSE UP OF DOG AS IT TURNS TO CAMERA.	What kind of life is this?
SERIES OF PROGRESSIVELY CLOSER SHOTS OF A DEAD CAT. LAST ONE VERY TIGHT.	**LOUD CRASH. DRUM BEAT STOPS.** Stop this needless suffering.
DISSOLVE TO CLOSE UP OF DOG IN CAGE AT POUND. SLOW ZOOM BACK TO SHOW THE CAGE IS VERY CROWDED.	Have female pets spayed and male animals neutered. End America's Pet Population Tragedy.
DISSOLVE TO ART CARD OF BOOKLET AND ADDRESS OF API	For this free booklet, write Animal Protection Institute. . .Box 22505. . . Sacramento, California.
FADE TO BLACK	FADE

Generally, the copy written for a television announcement can be adapted for radio as well. Radio, because of its lack of visual aid, requires more descriptive words. If, on the other hand, radio announcements are taped rather than just read by the announcer, background sounds such as a dog's bark or a cat's meow can serve as excellent attention-getters.

Many television and radio stations incorporate public service messages into station identifications. These are ten- or twenty-second announcements like the following:

"KCTC reminds you that someone with a cold nose and a warm heart needs your help! Send a contribution to the Humane Society today."

Once they were the most populous of all California animals. The coming of the white man changed that with a vengeance: by the mid-twentieth century only a few specimens of the tule elk remained. The drive to save this midget elk was spearheaded by Beula Edmiston and the Committee for the Preservation of the Tule Elk and eventually resulted in federal protective legislation. PHOTO BY GERRARD BAKER, COMMITTEE FOR THE PRESERVATION OF THE TULE ELK.

"This is KABT reminding you that there are many homeless puppies and kittens waiting at the SPCA shelter on Fourth Street. Drop by today."

Television stations use somewhat the same technique, incorporating a message and the station logo on a flashcard. Nonprofit, community service groups can often have the cards prepared by a graphic artist for the station's use. The important point is to allow space for the station to insert its identifying symbol or logo.

Voice messages to be read while the flash card is shown can differ. For example, for a card reading "Be Kind to Animals," the speaker would announce, "WHLT and the Humane Society remind you it is illegal to abandon or dump animals in our state." The same card could be used to announce a pet show or an open house.

Public service films and tapes are best produced by a professional. Occasionally, advertising agencies or production companies will work for a humane group at reduced rates or at cost. Unless a society has no financial worries, this possibility should be explored.

Other sources of help are the public service directors at local radio and television stations, who are often willing to give freely of their time and expertise to help a community group.

Radio and Television Interviews

Another type of television and radio publicity is the interview, either live or taped. The news style here is brief and to the point and there's little time for detailed explanations. Generally, the scenario is a rapid discourse between the reporter and the interviewee, filmed or taped for later showing, and all but the most sensational statements get left on the editing room floor.

In talking to electronic media reporters, be explicit and forceful. Nearly always you are being interviewed because you think the way in which certain animals are being treated is cruel. Say so. Don't waffle or leave yourself open to an editing job that could misrepresent your issue.

For example, never open a statement by acknowledging the opposition's statement as factual or true. Make *your* point first. If you are picketing on behalf of the whales and a reporter asks why you are doing so, the answer is that the great whales are being hunted to extinction. They have decreased drastically in number, are cruelly killed by explosive harpoons, and everything made from the bodies of dead whales can be made from substitutes. The whales are going to disappear from the face of the earth in the immediate future if something is not done.

It would dilute your position to respond to the question by saying that the people of Japan eat whale meat, but you think they should stop and turn to some other food source. While that statement may be true, you have not elucidated your main point and the reporter might permanently divert you into a mere discussion of protein percentages instead of the fact that whales are endangered.

Demonstrators at city pounds — protesting either conditions or euthanasia methods — sometimes lose ground by being unable to speak with the press. The spokesperson for such a group should always be prepared beforehand. When a reporter asks why the group is there, the spokesperson should be able to quickly delineate all the problems. For example: "Conditions in the pound are brutal. Cages are overcrowded and the animals are lying in their own excrement. Sick and injured animals receive no veterinary care. Feeding is done only once a day and many of the cages do not have water. The manager of this pound should be charged with cruelty to animals!"

Once the charges have been laid on the line, the reporter may ask for specific examples and then for your recommendations. Here, go into detail, but initially take a good shot at your main points. Even if your interview gets edited down to a minute or two, chances are your first statement will be used.

Another factor to keep in mind in dealing with television and radio interviewers is that they are "stars" of sorts. They generally do not like long, detailed answers — no matter how necessary they may be to a full understanding of the problem. The reporter will want to question you and to have the opportunity to appear curious or well versed on the issue. Help him or her and you will probably get better press coverage. If possible, try to discuss the issue fully with the reporter before the actual on-camera interview or radio taping.

Right of Reply Re Broadcasting

The Federal Communications Commission's Code of Federal Regulations requires television and radio stations to give "right of reply" time to individuals or groups misrepresented or attacked on the air.

Since the treatment of animals is often a controversial subject, and, as API has learned, these attacks can often move from the subject and become personal in nature, animal activists should be aware of this regulation.

Section 73.123 Personal attacks; political editorials.
(a) When, during the presentation of views on a controversial issue of public

importance, an attack is made upon the honesty, character, integrity or like personal qualities of an identified person or group, the licensee shall, within a reasonable time and in no event later than one week after the attack, transmit to the person or group attacked (1) notification of the date, time and identification of the broadcast; (2) a script or tape (or an accurate summary if a script or tape is not available) of the attack; and (3) an offer of a reasonable opportunity to respond over the licensee's facilities.

(b) The provisions of paragraph (a) of this section shall not be applicable (1) to attacks on foreign groups or foreign public figures; (2) to personal attacks which are made by legally qualified candidates, their authorized spokesmen, or those associated with them in the campaign, on other such candidates, their authorized spokesmen, or persons associated with the candidates in the campaign; and (3) to bona fide newscasts, bona fide news interviews, and on-the-spot coverage of a bona fide news event (including commentary or analysis contained in the foregoing programs, but the provisions of paragraph (a) of this section shall be applicable to editorials of the licensee).

Should a television or radio station ineffectively handle a complaint or if further interpretation of the regulation is needed, write the Federal Communications Commission, Washington, D.C., 20554.

Public Speaking

In the career of every animal protectionist there comes a time when speaking before an audience is necessary. Whether the purpose is to explain a humane group's functions to the local Lions Club or to persuade a legislative committee to enact a new law for the protection of animals, the animal crusader has to swallow the lump in his or her throat and "squeak up."

While most of us are apprehensive about accepting speaking engagements, there is one point we must keep in mind: people are almost always sympathetic to the problems of animals. Animals touch everyone's life — as companions, like dogs and cats, as wild creatures affording us a glimpse of survival and freedom, or just as the steak on our dinner plates. One way or another, we all have an interest in animals.

A common practice with many speakers is to "wing it." Basically, this means standing up before an audience after you have been introduced and frantically searching the recesses of your mind for something to say.

No matter how well-versed you may be on the problems of animals in your area, state, or country, this can at best be a jumbled, hard-to-follow talk and will probably not impress your audience. Speakers who use this tactic waste everybody's time and accomplish little for their subject or cause. Keep in mind that a good proportion of your audience has also had to present a talk a time or two; if you are unprepared, they are uncomfortable. Our human tendency is to sympathize with a speaker and agonize with him or her rather than listen to what is being said. Spare your audience and yourself; think ahead.

The first step is to evaluate your audience. Open the talk with something with which they can identify. If you are addressing the Kiwanis, Lions, a women's club, or other service group, emphasize the *services* a humane society provides the community. If your audience is a church group, make a connection between treatment of animals and some of the Bible's teachings, or use St. Francis as an illustration. If you are talking to a high school honor club, stress the intelligence of many animal species. Find the common ground between your audience and your topic.

Next, make an outline and define your objectives. Time will probably be limited and it is extremely unlikely you'll be able to cover the whole realm of animal welfare work. Choose the topics of interest to your group or community. Should you not cover issues of special concern to a member of the group, chances are it will be brought up in the question period following your presentation, or the concerned individual will seek you out afterward.

Once the outline is completed, you can either write out the entire speech or talk directly from the outline notes. This choice depends on your experience. If you are not an experienced speaker, definitely write the talk and practice it beforehand. In preparing, do the following.

(1) Involve the audience's feelings — perhaps by stressing human dependency on animals.
(2) Research your facts, using local figures and issues whenever possible.
(3) Use short sentences; watch modifiers; avoid tongue-twisters.
(4) Don't use the words if you are unsure of meanings. Check the dictionary. Archie Bunker malapropisms are funny on television, but they can totally undo a speaker unaware that the joke is on him or her. One anecdote I recall is an individual describing an octopus' tentacles as "testicles." Another fellow was trying to condense the gist of his explanation but, unfortunately, he was calling it the "jest."
(5) Interject some humor. A few laughs always help.
(6) Don't use stuffy, business-letter type sentence structures. Get to the point with simple, concise phrases — the type we all use. Instead of saying, "I would like to ask your permission now to show you this short film," condense it to, "I'd like to show you a film."
(7) Avoid using the jargon of the humane movement unless you fully explain it. Initial terms like PTS (put to sleep) are foreign to someone who has not worked in an animal shelter. In talking about state and national agencies and departments that control the fate of animals, explain the structure fully. For example, BLM is the Bureau of Land Management, an agency of the Department of the Interior; NMFS is National Marine Fisheries Service, a division of the Department of Commerce.

Once your talk is ready, learn it. Never plan to read to your audience. You can read to emphasize short excerpts or comments or quotes from another source, but *never* give an entire speech in this manner.

It is often wise to practice the presentation on a friend, spouse, or co-worker a time or two. Vary your tone of voice, emphasize emotional words, and change your pace. One point to keep in mind is that many of us have mannerisms we unconsciously use that can distract an audience. Pointing fingers, pulling at beards or mustaches, clicking ballpoint pens, or jamming both hands into pants pockets are all little manifestations of nervousness that can irritate listeners. A friendly critique could vastly improve your rapport with an audience.

If a talk is to be accompanied by audio-visual aids, it is best to check out the type of equipment beforehand. Make sure the available projector is the right one for the film you are bringing. Place the screen where it is easily visible to everyone. Put your slides in order and consider asking for a remote control so you can turn them yourself. If you want to use graphs or charts, keep them simple and large enough to be read by everyone in the room. If you are bringing an animal, ask a friend or co-worker to accompany you and assist in the handling. It is impossible to give a convincing lecture on proper cat care with a frightened cat digging its claws into your shoulder.

Finally, with your homework done, you'll find stage fright is not a problem. When you step to the podium, you'll be in command, and you will be convincing.

Petitions

Petitions are a means of expressing wants, feelings, or directives to an individual or to a governmental body. They can have tremendous impact in changing attitudes or laws, and they can work most effectively in helping animals.

Assistant Secretary of the Interior Nat Reed (left) and Belton Mouras examine a sampling of 188,264 signatures asking protection for ocean mammals. The collection effort by API members preceded and helped ensure passage of the federal Marine Mammal Protection Act of 1972.

There are basically two types of petitioning. The first is the legal or official petition drive, called either an initiative or a referendum. It asks that a measure be put on the ballot, that a new law be passed, repealed, or considered by the state legislature.

As defined by the *Encyclopedia of Social Sciences*, the initiative is a "device by which any person or group of persons may draft a proposed ordinance, law or constitutional amendment and by securing in its behalf a designated number of signatures may require that such proposal be submitted to the voters for their acceptance or rejection." The number of required signatures is usually based on a percentage of the number of voters voting for some officer-holder, like the governor, in the preceding election. In the states that allow initiatives, the measure must be filed, usually with the Secretary of State, and all signatures verified as being from registered voters before the issue is put on the ballot. Definite legal steps must be followed in the drafting of the proposal and in the format used to obtain signatures.

When the collection of signatures is done to repeal an existing law, the action is referred to as a referendum.

Humane and environmental groups have only recently begun using the legal initiative as a means of changing laws. In June 1976, Californians, as a result of such an effort, voted on whether or not the building of nuclear power plants could continue in the state until it was shown the plants are absolutely safe. In South Dakota, the mourning dove was removed from the list of game birds and listed as a protected species thanks to the results of an initiative campaign.

Initiatives can be used in nearly half the states: Alaska, Arizona, Arkansas, California, Colorado, Idaho, Maine, Maryland, Massachusetts, Michigan, Missouri, Montana, Nebraska, Nevada, New Mexico, North Dakota, Ohio, Oklahoma, Oregon, South Dakota, Utah, and Washington.

The procedure is one means of direct participation in our system of democracy and should be evaluated in terms of what it may accomplish for animals. In many instances, control over so-called game animals is so tightly entrenched in management-oriented fish and game departments that it is almost impossible for protectionists to change laws by means of the legislature. More often than not, public sentiment is on our side about any particular animal, and this sentiment could be effectively used in an initiative effort.

The major drawback to mounting an initiative is the possible loss of tax-exempt status because of excessive lobbying. In many cases, this could be circumvented by formation of a "citizens committee" or by having a federation of humane groups, rather than an individual society, spearhead the movement.

Carefully weigh all aspects, however, before initiating such an effort. It requires a great deal of time, legal assistance, and coordination. Primarily, you need the unending devotion of a force of volunteers willing to scour the countryside for signatures. But, your chances of success on many animal issues are excellent.

The second type of petition used by humane groups is of the informal variety, those circulated to put pressure on governments or individuals and to help spread the word about animal treatment. Such petitions enable an individual to "do something" immediate for animals. Additionally, they get action from persons who may feel strongly about an issue but would not take the time to express those feelings in a protest letter.

API has utilized the petition package a number of times in campaigns. Members have petitioned the governments of Canada and Norway to end the baby seal slaughter, the government of Japan to stop killing whales, individual legislators to support a bill that would end the use of the steel-jaw leghold trap as well as congressional committees having control over this bill.

Following are a few pointers for composing an informal petition.

(1) Choose an influential or identifiable target. Emphasize the name of the addressee at the top of the message. Signers will want to know to whom the petition will be sent or directed. Boldface or larger type helps make this more obvious.

(2) If possible, identify the people signing the petition. Examples are, "We, the undersigned citizens of the U.S., ask. . ." or, "We, the undersigned residents of the County of San Mateo. . . ."

(3) Forcibly and uncompromisingly state the issue, but keep the wording to a paragraph or two. Petition signers, especially on animal issues, do not want to plough through long explanations. More often than not, they already know where they stand on an animal abuse and are signing to express their opinion.

(4) Allow sufficient room for signatures, addresses, city names, and zip codes. Trying to save effort or paper by placing signature lines a quarter-inch apart will merely result in totally unreadable petitions. Many people have stylized methods of signing their names and need space.

The presentation of petitions is an opportunity to get media coverage, especially on the community and state government levels. Call the local press and tell them the petitions will be given to the mayor at such and such a time or your group will appear before the city council at its next meeting. If the presentation is made to an individual where the press may not be allowed in, send out a press release on the day of the presentation.

One sure method of getting publicity is to use a gimmick to transport the petitions to their destination. One Canadian group trucked over a million petition signatures for the seals from Montreal to Washington, D.C., and the Norwegian embassy. A bundle of petitions asking for an improvement in city pound conditions could be carried into the mayor's office by a St. Bernard. Photos of abandoned animals scrounging in garbage cans or killed on the city's streets could accompany petitions asking for a municipally funded spay clinic (these same photos should be released to the press).

Like any effort involving a number of people, conducting a petition drive requires careful coordination. Consider setting a time limit on the effort to give it more urgency and impetus.

Should the petition subject be one that may not be familiar to all group members, give full backup information that will enable circulators to answer all questions intelligently.

Demonstrations

Placard-carrying demonstrators, whether they be union workers protesting a contract disagreement or citizens trying to make a point with a governmental official, have become an accepted part of the American system of freedom of speech and expression. Demonstrations focus attention on an issue in a dramatic fashion and, because they are news, demonstrations, pickets, vigils, can all be effective tools in publicizing an animal issue.

Following are step-by-step guidelines for planning a demonstration.

(1) Choose an easily accessible site that gets public exposure. Your purposes are to be seen by passersby and to get the message to your target.
(2) Appoint a coordinating chairman and a publicity chairman.
(3) Check with local law enforcement officials as to whether or not a permit is required. You will probably have to inform the police or sheriff of the date, location, and approximate number of persons involved in the demonstration. Ask about any regulations regarding such displays; there will be some—such as not impeding traffic, not blocking the sidewalk or right-of-way, not crossing onto the private property of the establishment being picketed, and not blocking crosswalks.
(4) Select a time of day during which there is public activity, the lunch hour, for example. Saturday, too, is usually a busy day, and it gives people who work a chance to participate.
(5) Set a time limit on the gathering. Make it a two-hour vigil, a three-hour picket, or whatever will give you a sufficient amount of time to make your point. Do not expect demonstrators to spend an entire day on the effort, unless you stagger the times at which they are to show up. Demonstrations have a way of losing effectiveness when participants begin thinning out or trailing off. Keep your people within a specified area for maximum visibility.
(6) Send out postcards or a mailing to all your members or to all individuals you expect to participate. This is much safer for a large demonstration than relying on word of mouth. List the purpose, date, time, location, whether or not participants should make their own placards or posters, and the phone number of the coordination chairperson. Where to park can also be helpful

information if people are unfamiliar with the area. Having those who plan to come so notify the chairperson can save a lot of worry about whether anyone will show up.

(7) Picket signs can be individually made or preprinted by the sponsoring group. The best public presentation is done when the signs are a combination of both. Many times an individual's own expression of feeling about an issue is more poignant than that on a mass-produced poster. Diversity in the messages is also more effective when television news crews cover the demonstration. Often, the cameraman can shift from placard to placard. Mount your placards or posters with a sturdy backing on sticks so they can be easily seen and read and are comfortable for the participants to hold.

(8) Compose a hand-out sheet to be given to passersby and to the press. Provide full background on the issue and, if possible, state what an individual can do. If a number of groups are participating in the demonstration, list their names. These sheets can be cheaply printed or mimeographed, but make certain they explain the issue and are easy to read.

(8) Compose a hand-out sheet to be given to passersby and to the press. stations, and television stations in the area at least four days before the demonstration. If postal service in your city is bad, give yourself an extra day or two on the release. A couple of days before the demonstration, have the publicity chairperson call news directors and editors to mention the news release and again give details. The publicity chairperson should be capable of answering any questions they might have and should express the hope that someone will be assigned to cover the story. Include on the press release the name and phone number of an individual who can be contacted for further information.

(10) At the demonstration itself, the chairperson, publicity chairperson, or another individual should be assigned to deal with reporters. Keep in mind, too, that occasionally a reporter will disagree with your point of view and may be antagonistic. Make certain you have clear and unequivocal answers ready for all anticipated questions. When the issue is animal cruelty, you can't compromise. You must be forceful in your statements and position.

(11) During the demonstration, the coordinating chairperson should be continually alert to any city ordinances or regulations that must be followed. If your issue is a volatile one, there may also be disagreements with passersby or derogatory remarks made by them. Discussions are fine, but arguments can become extremely uncomfortable for all concerned. The coordinating chairperson should try to head off any potential incidents.

(12) If the press does not arrive when the demonstration is in full swing, the publicity chairperson should again make a round of phone calls to the editors and news directors. Again explain the issue, note how many people are participating, and politely try to persuade the person in charge that your event will make a good news story.

(13) When the demonstration is completed, pick up all litter. Leaving placards or hand-out sheets laying about not only reflects unfavorably on your cause but could also get your group a citation for littering.

(14) Thank everyone!

13

Government's Role in Protection and Persecution: The Key to Humane Reform Lies in a Labyrinth

By far the most frequently asked question at API is, "What can be done?" The answer often boils down to whether or not a law exists. If so, who enforces it? On the national level, stipulations regarding animals can issue from two sources — rulemaking by government agencies and lawmaking by Congress.

At the outset, however, it should be stressed that the federal government cannot "lay down the law" with respect to any and all animals. It has jurisdiction only in the absence of state controls — when there are questions of foreign import/ export, of interstate shipment, of marine or multistate populations, of animals handled by federal institutions or those which receive federal funds.

There is no single federal office that handles all animal problems, nor is there one that deals exclusively with humaneness — contrary to what many people envision.

Different agencies of the federal government have been assigned responsibilities for various animals. Such agencies function as a part of the executive branch, having as their heads members of the President's cabinet. The structure — notwithstanding bureaucracy's bad name — is not complicated. Each cabinet member is secretary of a department; each department is divided into services, bureaus, and offices — spreading out like a family tree in reverse.

Almost any department can, at one time or another, become involved in animal issues — as the Department of Defense discovered when it was bombarded with criticism of the Army's plans for exterminating blackbirds at two military sites in Kentucky and Tennessee. However, the departments of Agriculture, Commerce, and Interior are those with which protectionists are most concerned.

Under the umbrella of the Department of Agriculture, the Animal and Plant Health Inspection Service (APHIS) operates as a quality control for meat and poultry products intended for human use and regulates animal and plant health as these relate to the benefit of man.

Specifically, APHIS programs provide for: inspection of food animals at time of processing and of slaughter facilities (legally required only when resulting products are shipped in interstate or foreign commerce); supervision of pest control or eradication programs, including a constant check on imported plants and animals; detection and control of outbreaks of communicable diseases affecting food animals;

161

certification of imported and exported animals; administration of federal law pertaining to humane handling of food animals and to the transport, sale, and handling of animals used for laboratory research and for exhibitions (zoos, circuses); enforcement of the Horse Protection Act, which prohibits soring of show horses shipped in interstate commerce.

Within the Department of Commerce, the National Oceanic and Atmospheric Administration (NOAA) is charged with exploring, utilizing, and conserving marine resources and with monitoring and reporting atmospheric, oceanic, sun, and space conditions. Under NOAA, the programs of the National Marine Fisheries Service (NMFS) have to do with living marine resources, including those marine mammals having commercial value. This situation is largely the result of directives of the Marine Mammal Protection Act of 1972, which awarded the Department of Commerce custody of whales, dolphins, porpoises, and seals. It is NMFS that regulates United States participation in the annual clubbing of Pribilof Island seals, under terms of the North Pacific Fur Convention (other signatories are Russia, Japan, and Canada).

The responsibilities of the Department of the Interior include: administration of over five-hundred million acres of federal land; conservation and development of mineral and water resources; conservation, development, and utilization of fish and wildlife resources; preservation and administration of the nation's scenic and historic areas.

One of the Secretary of the Interior's helpers is the Assistant Secretary for Fish and Wildlife and Parks. Under his jurisdiction lie the National Park Service, the Bureau of Outdoor Recreation, and the U.S. Fish and Wildlife Service (FWS). The latter is undoubtedly the executive service most familiar to protectionists, for it presides over animal species not specifically assigned elsewhere.

FWS (up to July 1974, the Bureau of Sport Fisheries and Wildlife) is responsible for wild birds, mammals — except those overseen by Commerce — and inland sport fisheries. The Service develops and manages national wildlife refuges for migratory birds and endangered species and enforces the Endangered Species Act, the Lacey Act, the Marine Mammal Protection Act, and the Migratory Bird Treaty Act.

A division of FWS is the Office of Endangered Species, which monitors and classifies animal populations as rare, threatened, or endangered.

At the other side of Interior's organizational chart, under Assistant Secretary for Land and Water Resources, is the Bureau of Land Management (BLM). BLM administers the public land, located primarily in the West and amounting to sixty percent of all federally owned land. Land uses include outdoor recreation, fish and wildlife production, livestock grazing, timber, watershed protection, and mineral production. The Bureau, in conjunction with Agriculture's Forest Service, is charged with enforcement of the 1971 Wild, Free-Roaming Horse and Burro Act.

Other, independent agencies may be established by law or by treaty to oversee particular problems. Examples are the Marine Mammal Commission, the Migratory Bird Conservation Commission, the International Commission for the Northwest Atlantic Fisheries, and the International Whaling Commission.

When people think of federal regulations, they tend to focus on the legislative process. Yet, a majority, perhaps eighty percent, of federal decisions regarding animal welfare are nonlegislative, formulated by the very agencies just described. Considering the lengthy and complicated legislative process, this imbalance is fortunate indeed.

CONGRESSIONAL CONVOLUTIONS

During each Congress, which is composed of two one-year sessions, only a small percentage of the many bills introduced are eventually enacted. In the 91st

Careful driving—observing speed limits, watching for animals—can lower highway kills. Figures aren't readily available, but in 1975 Colorado reported road kills of 5,000 deer and 100,000 other animals; 29,914 deer were killed in Pennsylvania, and 39,000 animals died in Georgia. TEDWARD PHOTO.

Congress (1969-70), of 4,616 Senate bills introduced, only 464 were passed; in the House, 762 laws resulted from 20,015 various proposals.

When a bill is introduced in either chamber, the presiding officer routinely refers it to the appropriate committee, the chairman of which, in turn, assigns it to a subcommittee. It is at this juncture that many bills die from inattention. It takes no great expertise to have a bill introduced; many—termed "constituent bills"—are the result of outside pressures. However, once a bill is assigned to a subcommittee, only a subcommittee chairman can decide whether or not it will receive hearings—the first step in the passage process.

During hearings, witnesses with knowledge of the subject under consideration read prepared testimony, stating their support of or objections to the bill, or offering suggestions for improvement of its provisions. At the conclusion of the hearings, the subcommittee members meet in closed, executive session. If the legislators decide to take no action, the bill is effectively killed; if they favor the legislation, it is reported, with any changes, to the full committee. The latter considers the measure, also in closed session, and often approves the subcommittee's finding without further debate.

When a bill is reported out of committee in the Senate, it is placed on the Calendar of General Orders, which is an agenda of pending legislative business. When a bill is reported out of a House committee, it is assigned to one of several calendars. If the legislation requires an appropriation, it is placed on the Union Calendar, in which case it reaches the floor through a "special order" or rule from the House Committee on Rules. The House Rules Committee holds a hearing on the legislation to determine ground rules — the amount of debate allowed and the kinds of amendments that can be offered from the floor. If the special order is adopted in the House, the measure can be debated outside the time sequence of the calendars.

Once the bill reaches the floor of the House or the Senate, debate is held. The floor manager of the legislation, often the subcommittee chairman, tries to ensure its passage and stave off crippling amendments. Following debate, a vote is taken.

In order for a bill to be sent to the President for approval or rejection, it must pass both houses in identical form (the usual procedure is to have the same measure introduced in both houses, which is quicker than having a single bill acted on by first one chamber and then the other). If the legislation passes in different forms and neither body will accept the changes offered by the other, a Conference Committee, composed of members from both houses, is formed to iron out differences. The House committee members are appointed by the Speaker, Senate members by the Vice President or the President Pro Tempore. When a majority of the conferees agree on the language of the bill, a report is sent to each chamber, where it may not be amended when called up for consideration. This bill then becomes a high priority measure and is acted on almost immediately.

If the proposal passes both houses in its new form, it is put in enrolled form, which means it is certified and printed on parchment. It is signed by the presiding officers in the House and Senate and sent to the President. The Chief Executive may approve the bill with his signature, making it law, or he may veto it by returning it to Congress or refusing to sign in a specified time ("pocket" veto). In the latter case, the measure cannot become law unless it is passed again in identical form by two-thirds of the members present and voting in each chamber.

It's a complicated process and often, especially where animal issues are concerned, a sluggish one. Years can pass from introduction of a measure to its eventual passage; antileghold-trap bills languished for over four years before even being heard in subcommittee.

INFORMATION ON FEDERAL MATTERS

How does one find out what is happening on the national legislative scene? The simplest route is to subscribe to the publications of a national humane group that monitors bill introductions and progress. Such reports may not always include every bill affecting animals, but worthwhile listings will give the vital statistics — provisions, committee assignments — of proposals that have the best chances of being enacted. For individuals desiring greater detail or wishing more background on the entire federal process, there are several helpful publications, many of which are available at public libraries.

Both the *Congressional Record* and the *Federal Register* are compiled on a daily basis. The former covers happenings in both houses of Congress while the latter records proposed rules, approved rules and regulations, and notices of executive branch agencies. The *Digest of General Bills and Resolutions,* prepared by the Library of Congress, summarizes bills and lists legislative action taken on them; it is published during each session in five or more cumulative issues with supplements and a final edition. The *United States Government Manual* describes purposes and programs of government agencies (including structural charts) and lists top personnel for each Congress. All the preceding publications, as well as records of subcommittee hearings, are available from the Superintendent of Documents, U.S. Government Printing Office.

The *Congressional Quarterly Almanac* is an annual publication that gives detailed accounts of major congressional action and lists voting charts, newly passed laws, and lobby reports. The 1973 edition, for example, lists API as an opponent of the Alaska pipeline and reports the National Woolgrowers Association paid its lobbying firm one thousand five hundred dollars per month, not including expenses. Congressional Quarterly's *Guide to the Congress of the U.S.* carries a history of Congress and descriptions of the legislative process, committee structures and rules, powers of Congress, and election processes. A former member of Congress publishes an annual *Congressional Staff Directory* that contains "all you ever wanted to know" about who works for whom — biographical information on legislators, their committee assignments, the staffs of legislators and committees, key personnel of executive branch agencies, and staff biographies. This is a yearly directory.

If the information you're seeking is not generally distributed, take the direct approach — ask your legislator(s) for help. Congressmen have access to government research facilities and a substantial portion of their mail counts involve information requests. Incidentally, many legislators maintain mailing lists for news releases and periodic newsletters; if you're interested in a particular lawmaker's views, ask to be included.

Another tack is to contact a government agency for the desired material. Under the 1967 Freedom of Information Act (F01), certain records of executive branch agencies are available to the public. Items of interest might be: final orders or opinions resulting from any agency adjudicative proceeding; scientific or factual studies prepared for, by, or on behalf of, an agency; any statement, opinion, study, or record relied upon as precedent by an agency in making a policy determination. 1974 amendments to the Act require executive departments and agencies to publish an index of generally available documents, which may be had at your library.

To make a request, write the head of the agency that has the records you seek. Cite the FOI Act and be as specific as possible regarding the material requested. Under law, the agency should respond within ten working days. If your request is granted, you may be charged for photocopying where numerous documents are involved. However, you may have your request denied for one or more of nine reasons, the FOI Act exemptions. These are: (1) the material is classified for reasons of national defense or foreign policy; (2) the material pertains to internal personnel rules and practices that do not affect a member of the public; (3) the material is exempted from disclosure by some other statute; (4) the material involves trade secrets or commercial or financial information given by a person with a government guarantee of privilege or confidentiality; (5) the material is a nonfactual interagency or intraagency memorandum of opinion; (6) the material involves personnel, medical, or other information that cannot be disclosed without an unwarranted invasion of privacy; (7) the material involves investigatory records that, if disclosed, might damage pending court adjudication, cause injury to a law enforcement official or informer, or otherwise invade personal privacy; (8) the material involves information prepared by or for an agency responsible for the regulation or supervision of financial institutions such as the Securities and Exchange Commission; or (9) the material pertains to geological or geophysical information and data, including maps concerning gas and oil wells.

If refused at the initial level, you may appeal to the head of the agency for consideration. After twenty working days you should receive a response. If this, too, is negative, the only alternative is court litigation. If you have particular difficulty with an agency at the initial or appeal level, you might inform the House of Representatives Committee on Government Operations, Subcommittee on Government Information and Individual Rights. If you contemplate litigation, there are two organizations you can contact regarding the advisability of the action and possible assistance. These are the American Civil Liberties Union (headquarters or a state affiliate) and the Freedom of Information Clearinghouse, a Ralph Nader enterprise.

Animal protectionists and environmentalists make their point with the postal department as well as with other federal agencies.

THE STATE SCENE

State legislatures can vary considerably in structure, rules, and procedures. Know yours. A good starting point is your library, which can furnish reference books and state governmental publications. If you want to delve more deeply into the subject, check for classes and seminars that may be offered by colleges and organizations or associations involved with the public sector.

As a rule, state governments publish "histories"—brief descriptions of bills introduced, including number, author, and subject. This publication can be obtained from the documents section or bill room of the capitol building and is available to the general public, although there may be a small charge. A copy of any bill that mentions animals can be ordered from the bill room or from the bill's author. Additionally, your state legislature probably compiles publications concerning the legislature's schedule, background on its members, composition of committees, and other supplemental information. If you require particular material, contact the documents section, your library, or your state congressmen for help.

The equivalent of federal agencies can be found on the state level in conservation or fish and game departments. Generally, the policy-making body for such departments is a fish and game or conservation commission, the members of which are appointed by the governor. The slant of these agencies has traditionally been toward propagating and regulating hunting of game animals, although there is evidence this attitude is changing—as nonconsumptive users of wildlife make themselves heard—via efforts to initiate or revitalize nongame programs.

If you have questions about population and habitat of a state's wildlife, try this agency. Other sources of information on animal issues exist. Check with national organizations to see if they have chapters or branch offices near you. Your library should have directories of environmental/conservation/humane groups—both Audubon and National Wildlife Federation publish such—from which you can pick out applicable state organizations. (A caution: The tendency to lump all animal and environment groups together ignores the use-or-protection issue, so careful inquiry may be needed.)

A hunter of big game can spend a lifetime telling how he tracked the big cat. But, if your methods are efficient, you may have more than one to tell about. On this hunt a pack of hounds lowered the mountain lion count by half a dozen.

There may also be individuals or organizations engaged in lobbying for state laws; these are generally required to register with the Secretary of State. If information you require is connected with state departments, it may still be obtainable—many states have freedom of information acts similar to the federal law described earlier.

Knowing what humane issues are in the forefront and being aware of any changes being made in the status of animals gives you a leg up in being able to recognize and respond to illegal actions involving animals. This is where a little research and effort bear fruit.

ADDRESSES

Department of Agriculture
14th Street & Jefferson Drive
Washington, D.C. 20250

Information Service
Animal and Plant Health Inspection Service
Department of Agriculture
Washington, D.C. 20250

Department of Defense
The Pentagon
Washington, D.C. 20301

Department of Commerce
14th Street & Constitution Ave., N.W.
Washington, D.C. 20230

Office of Public Affairs
National Oceanic and Atmospheric Administration
Department of Commerce
Rockville, MD 20852

National Marine Fisheries Service
3300 Whitehaven Parkway
Washington, D.C. 20240

Department of the Interior
C Street bet. 18th & 19th, N.W.
Washington, D.C. 20240

Office of Public Affairs
Fish and Wildlife Service
Department of the Interior
Washington, D.C. 20240

For Senators:
  The Honorable_____
  Senate Office Building
  Washington, D.C. 20510

For Representatives:
  The Honorable_____
  House Office Building
  Washington, D.C. 20515

The President
The White House
Washington, D.C. 20500

Office of the Federal Register
National Archives and Records Service
Washington, D.C. 20408

Superintendent of Documents
U.S. Government Printing Office
Public Documents Department
Washington, D.C. 20402

Congressional Quarterly, Inc.
1414 — 22nd Street, N.W.
Washington, D.C. 20037

House of Representatives
  Committee on Government Operatio
Subcommittee on Government
  Information and Individual Rights
Rayburn House Office Building B-349
Washington, D.C. 20515

American Civil Liberties Union
22 East 40th Street
New York, N.Y. 10016

Freedom of Information Clearinghouse
2000 P Street, N.W., Suite 515
Washington, D.C. 20036

14

Some Inhumanities Are Illegal: Laws to be Enforced and Added To

A Pennsylvania doctor receives a brochure from a New York company offering whale steaks for sale. An Indiana woman has seen men jack-lighting deer and shooting from pickup trucks along the road to her home. A Colorado tourist enters a curios shop and finds eagle feathers for sale. A California woman watches helplessly as a neighbor's dog is left without food or shelter for a week.

These people have one thing in common—they are witnessing violations of laws to protect animals. Each should report what he or she has seen to a law enforcement agency. But to which agency? It's often not common knowledge, and, as pointed out in the previous chapter, the governmental structure is a complicated one.

Animal protection laws exist on the city and county level, the state level, and the federal level. Because of specialization and conflicting jurisdictions, it can sometimes take a few tries to reach the right enforcement officer. However, many times, when the report does reach the appropriate agency, officials are grateful for such outside assistance. Citizen awareness plays a major role in making sure the laws do protect animals.

The following is a breakdown of animal protection laws every animal lover should know about. Also offered are guidelines for reporting violations.

FEDERAL LAWS

Department of the Interior

Most federal regulations and laws for the protection of wildlife and migratory birds and waterfowl are under the jurisdiction of the Fish and Wildlife Service, a division of the Department of the Interior. To contact the Service, check your phone book under the heading "U.S. Government, Interior, Department of." If the incident you want to report took place in another area, your local agent-in-charge will give you the address and phone number or relay your message himself to the proper officer.

The Fish and Wildlife Service has enforcement responsibilities for several important laws.

(1) The Migratory Bird Treaty Act implements treaties with Great Britain (for Canada) and Mexico for the protection of all migratory birds. Practically all songbirds are protected by the treaty, the hunting of insectivorous birds is prohibited, and birds considered injurious to agriculture may only be killed under permit. Migratory waterfowl, like ducks, geese, and cranes, can only be killed during a specified hunt-

Don't be a litter-killer.

The Animal Protection Institute urges you to dispose of plastic six-pack holders properly.

The California-Hawaii Elk Photo.

When your party's over,

don't end an animal's life.

The Animal Protection Institute urges you to dispose of plastic six-pack holders properly.

Feline and Canine Friends, Inc. Photo.

Even seemingly innocent devices, like plastic six-pack holders, can be deadly to animals if carelessly discarded. These public service announcements were prepared and distributed to outdoors publications by API; members were also urged to run them in local newspapers.

ing seasons. In March 1972, thirty-two additional families of birds, including crows, eagles, hawks, and owls, were added to the Act's protected status. With the exceptions of the English sparrow and the starling, nearly every bird is now covered.

Anyone seeing waterfowl being shot out of season, hawks or owls being used for target practice, or even boys shooting songbirds with BB guns, is witnessing a violation of this Act and should make a report. Also, no items made from the feathers, claws, beaks, or other sections of these birds can be offered for sale, barter, or trade. Curios, including pictures and jewelry made from feathers, offered for sale in souvenir and craft shops should be especially noted. You can report what you've seen to the Fish and Wildlife Service quickly by telephone, and all reports are treated confidentially.

(2) The Bald Eagle Act of 1940 is an additional law protecting bald and gold eagles, and agents sometimes work under this law in confiscating curios made from parts of eagles. This law does not prohibit the use of eagle feathers by American Indians, provided the objects are not offered for sale; the Fish and Wildlife Service gives eagle parts and feathers free to the Indians to make headdresses and other traditional objects.

(3) P.L. 92-159, an amendment to the Fish and Wildlife Act of 1956, forbids shooting wildlife from aircraft, except as authorized by federal or state governments through a license or permit. The exemption is intended only for emergency predator control situations and has been invoked in a few states for the taking of coyotes. Any other shooting from aircraft, including helicopters, is illegal.

(4) The Endangered Species Conservation Act of 1969 establishes policy for a comprehensive program to conserve, restore, and propagate selected native fish and wildlife threatened with extinction, and gives authority to acquire habitat land for threatened animals. Under the Act, the importation of animals or by-products from animals the Secretary of the Interior determines to be threatened with extinction is prohibited. The Secretary maintains a list of endangered species throughout the world and new animals are constantly being added. Over four-hundred species are now officially listed.

The importation ban applies not only to commercial operations but to American tourists traveling abroad as well. Souvenirs or hunting trophies of endangered animals cannot be brought into the United States. Such items are confiscated by Customs officials. The rationale, "The animal's already dead," is not acceptable. The intent of the law is to cut off a market for products from endangered animals; allowing tourists to make such purchases would simply increase the demand, which would result in more killing.

The offering of the whale steak for sale is probably a violation of this act, as is the importing of skins from spotted cats such as margay, cheetah, leopard, tiger, and ocelot. The sale of crocodile shoes or belts or combs, eyeglass frames, and jewelry from the hawksbill turtle's shell is also forbidden. If you find a store dealing in any items you suspect may be from a threatened animal, make a report to the authorities. Nearly all raids and confiscations of this type of merchandise are the result of tips from the public.

(5) The Marine Mammal Protection Act of 1972 establishes a moratorium on the taking and importation of marine mammals and products made from them. The Department of the Interior is responsible for protecting sea otters, walrus, polar bears, dugongs, and manatees. Seals, sea lions, dolphins, porpoises, and whales come under the jurisdiction of the Department of Commerce's National Oceanic and Atmospheric Administration. The only exemptions are for native peoples, Eskimos and Aleuts, to continue killing these animals for their traditional food, clothing, and handicraft needs.

Anyone seeing porpoises and dolphins shot at, and sea lions indiscriminately killed, should report such incidents to authorities. When the shooting is done from a boat, try to get the registration numbers as well as a description. Any harassing of marine mammals is illegal.

Again, the importation restriction of this law applies to tourists traveling in foreign countries. Do not buy sealskin toys, purses, wallets, jackets, or other items made from seals or sea lions. Whale bone, ivory from walrus, polar bear rugs and trophies, and clothing or novelties made from sea otters are forbidden. Such items will be confiscated by Customs.

(6) The Lacey Act of 1900 prohibits importation of wild vertebrates and other animals declared by the Secretary of the Interior to be injurious to humane, agriculture, or wildlife resources of this country. Animals in this category can only come into the United States under special circumstances.

A 1969 amendment to the Act outlaws shipping, transport, sale, or purchase of wildlife or their products taken or possessed in violation of federal, state, or foreign law. For example, if a poacher shot a bighorn ram out of season in Montana and shipped the head to a client in another state, he would be charged with federal counts under the Lacey Act as well as with state violations. Transporting poached deer across state lines is a common violation of this law.

(7) P.L. 92-195, the Wild, Free-Roaming Horse and Burro Act of 1971, mandated protection of wild horses and burros. Responsibility for carrying out provisions of the Act is shared by the Bureau of Land Management, another agency of the Department of the Interior, and the Forest Service, part of the Department of Agriculture. Both agencies have jurisdiction over public lands.

An earlier law, P.L. 86-234, banned use of aircraft or motorized vehicles for hunting, capturing, or killing any wild burro or horse. This law was passed in 1959 and is known as the "Wild Horse Annie Law" in recognition of Mrs. Velma B. Johnston, whose fight to save the wild horses and burros resulted in its passage.

Shooting wild horses or burros, driving the animals from waterholes, and running them with airplanes or snowmobiles are violations of these laws. In the past, such treatment was common because the creatures were considered "worthless vermin" competing with domestic livestock. Values have changed, and anyone learning of harassment of wild horses or burros or planned illegal roundups should notify authorities.

Department of Agriculture

(1) P.L. 91-579, the Laboratory Animal Welfare Act of 1970, is enforced by the Department of Agriculture, another federal agency entrusted with ensuring humane treatment of animals.

The Department licenses and inspects the facilities of animal dealers and breeders who sell dogs and cats to any pet shop or research facility. Inspections are carried out through the Veterinary Services Division. This agency also has the responsibility of checking public animal displays, which include zoos — the roadside variety as well as those municipally funded — and wild animal parks. Regulations require that housing for the animals be properly constructed to allow adequate ventilation, space, and shade, and the animals must be properly fed.

Veterinary Services can be especially helpful in areas where there is no humane society to check out pet-store or captive-animal displays. The agency is listed in your phone book under "U.S. Government, Agriculture, Department of." It is a section of the Department's Animal and Plant Health Inspection Services, and you may have to call this number if there is no separate listing for Veterinary Services.

(2) The Horse Protection Act of 1970, prohibiting the shipment of sored walking horses in interstate commerce and the showing of horses treated in such a manner, is also the responsibility of the Department of Agriculture.

Soring is done to alter the gait of Tennessee walking horses. By applying blistering compounds to the front feet or legs of the horse, placing chemical agents, tacks, nails or wedges on the hooves, or putting boots or chains on the horses, the animals can be made to perform because of pain. They will throw their weight toward their back legs and quickly lift their front feet—the desired gait for walkers.

The Act forbids transporting sored horses across state lines, showing sored horses, or permitting such horses to be shown. Department of Agriculture agents may inspect a show if just one horse in the entire show was shipped across state lines. The agent, however, must personally view and check the sored horses. Charges cannot be pressed on the word of a witness. Because of very limited funding appropriated by Congress for enforcement of this Act, the Department cannot inspect every show and, in fact, is actually only able to cover a very small percentage of them. An individual learning of a show where sored horses are expected to be shown should notify the Department, even though there is no guarantee an inspector can be sent.

STATE LAWS

Livestock and Pets

Every state has some laws requiring decent treatment of animals. The two most basic are protection from malicious, intentionally cruel treatment such as beatings, and a requirement that animals be provided food and water. Although it would seem shelter from the weather would be a basic consideration as well, a substantial number of states have no law to this effect.

The other major areas covered by state laws are poisoning, dog-stealing, dog-fighting or baiting, and humane slaughter. Abandonment of a healthy animal, typically the dumping of a dog or cat, is only illegal in about twenty-eight states.

Familiarize yourself with your state's anticruelty laws. If you see an animal being abused, contact the law enforcement agency for your area—either the city police or the county sheriff—and file a complaint. If there is a local humane society, you might ask it to investigate; however, some local humane groups do not have the manpower or authority to take on cruelty investigations.

If the police or sheriff cannot get relief for the animal or will not see the case through, you can file a citizen's complaint with the district attorney. Whichever course of action you take, it is necessary to have a first-hand witness to the act of cruelty or neglect.

Wildlife

All states have laws protecting game animals like deer and rabbits, and furbearers such as raccoons and mink. Such laws allow for the killing of these animals only during specified hunting seasons.

Poaching—the illegal, out-of-season shooting or trapping of fur and game animals—is becoming a major problem. In some states it is estimated the illegal take of deer by poachers equals the number legally shot by hunters during the hunting season. There have been reports of poaching rings in a number of states—in one instance they were thought to be supplying venison to restaurants. Wildlife refuges are frequent targets, with poachers going to such extremes as using citizen-band radios to keep in contact with each other.

If you encounter any activity you suspect may be connected with poaching, report it to your area's game warden or the sheriff or police. Whenever possible, try to give descriptions of any vehicles involved.

CITY AND COUNTY LAWS

Cities and counties are responsible for animal control. Through the passage of or-

173

dinances, they require the licensing of dogs (in some areas, cats too). City and county laws can also require that a dog owner have his or her pet vaccinated for rabies, keep the animal under voice control or on a leash when outside the owner's property, and limit the number of animals a single household may keep. Municipalities often establish regulations for kennels as well, and these must generally meet certain sanitary specifications.

Local laws and ordinances can often be used to quickly clean up situations where a number of animals are being kept in filthy conditions. Often, one of the best places to report such an incident and bring some immediate relief for the animals is your city or county health department.

Aside from dogs and cats, local ordinances can also limit the keeping of livestock in certain zones and the sale of chicks or other infant animals at Easter time.

LOBBYING FOR LAW CHANGES

Frequently, activities are legal that shouldn't be, or laws on the books are inadequate. A person working for such legislative changes is called a *lobbyist*—an emotion-evoking word that causes people to bristle or smile, depending on where they stand on issues of the day. The term has often been a maligned one, spoken amid mutterings of "pressure politics" and a "breakdown of democracy," but in modern, complex society lobbyists do make a contribution to the operation of the legislative branch of government.

It is impossible for individual lawmakers to be totally unfamiliar with all aspects of society's needs; the problems are just too numerous. If no one tells a legislator about the difficulties of reporting child abuse, or the need for adequate housing for the elderly, or underground dogfighting, chances are he or she will never learn about them. Pressure groups—whether they be working for humane laws or against the outlawing of handguns—must maintain communications channels with lawmakers. Yet, because of vague and often unclear Internal Revenue Service standards regulating tax-exempt organizations, most humane societies tremble at the prospect of dealing with legislators.

What is lobbying? It is any activity that influences the passage or consideration of bills in the legislative branch of government. The emphasis is on legislation.

Recalling from civics books, our federal government has three branches— executive, legislative, and judicial. The executive arm consists of the President, his administrative offices, and his cabinet. Within the cabinet are the departments of State, Justice, Interior, Agriculture, Health-Education-Welfare, Defense, Commerce, and Labor. These agencies are responsible for carrying out policies, providing services, *and* enforcing laws already on the books. They also issue regulations under laws and treaties in effect.

Activity within the executive branch by special-interest groups is not defined by IRS as lobbying. The laws have already been passed and the executive branch is dealing with their administration. Thus, humane organizations can testify at Department of the Interior hearings on the importation of exotic wildlife, the limitations of the waterfowl hunting season, or even the use of steel rather than lead shot. Getting a law passed is only a minor part of the total battle. There are numerous laws—the Wild, Free-Roaming Horse and Burro Act, the Marine Mammal Protection Act, the Endangered Species Conservation Act—that require constant monitoring by humane organizations for effective enforcement.

Within the judicial branch, humane societies can seek injunctions, restraining orders, and other court actions to prevent an act considered detrimental to animals. Additionally, groups can file suit against executive departments thought to be remiss in administering animal protective laws. One such suit to which API was a party was

174

filed against the Department of Commerce for its lax regulations, under the Marine Mammal Protection Act, restricting the incidental kill of porpoises by tuna fishermen. Again, such actions are not considered lobbying.

On the state level, the executive and judicial branches are, respectively, the governor and the state departments (fish and game, agriculture, health, etc.), and the courts. The same guidelines apply regarding lobbying state governments.

What activities, then, constitute lobbying? Basically, those involving working with lawmakers to effect the passage of a bill. Such efforts include:

(1) Direct contact with legislators;
(2) Appearances as witnesses at hearings;
(3) Dissemination of information to legislators;
(4) Dissemination of information to the public to elicit expressions of support such as mass letter-writing or packing a hearing room (common methods of such dissemination are radio and television announcements, letters to newspaper editors, paid advertisements, billboards).

In determining to what extent a group has engaged in lobbying, IRS considers the amount of staff time spent working for the legislation as well as the amount of money used. The specific limits are hazy, but a safe guideline is thought to be less than five percent of a group's total time and expenditures. Roughly, this means that if an organization employs twenty people, one could be a full-time lobbyist. Or, if a society's total expenditures for the year were one-hundred thousand dollars, approximately five-thousand dollars could be spent influencing legislation without endangering the group's tax-exempt status. *

Realistically, however, there are a good many parameters influencing the attention IRS pays to an organization's activities, the major one being how influential the opponents of the legislation you are seeking happen to be. A common practice of opposition groups is to seek the removal of a society's tax-exempt status. If there is enough power behind the request—usually substantial economic interests—they seem to get results. Just before the antileghold-trap bill came to hearings in Congress in 1975, most humane organizations were audited by IRS. The threat is implicit: If tax-exempt status is removed, contributions will dry up and the organization will cease to function.

The tactic does not always work. One battle-scarred veteran is the Sierra Club, which took on the loggers and the timber industry in trying to save the redwood trees. The Club lost its tax-exempt status in the process but has remained a potent force on the conservation scene, and, in the long run, is probably more respected for having fought the battle.

IRS does not audit every tax-exempt group yearly, and most efforts local humane groups take would hardly bring the type of opposition API encounters in its campaigns. However, it would be foolhardy for any group to become involved in legislative projects without fully understanding the possibilities.

---

*The Tax Reform Act of 1976, passed late in the year, is intended to set clear standards for lobbying activity. Tax-exempt organizations may elect to either come under the Act's provisions or continue under the "insubstantial" test (which will still exist in the law).

The core of the Act is a sliding percentage scale for permissible lobbying. Briefly, an organization with annual expenditures of $500,000 can spend up to $100,000 on lobbying; with $5 million, up to $400,000; with $15 million, up to $900,000. No organization, regardless of size, can spend more than $1 million on lobbying.

There are other important provisions in the Act. Officials of nonprofit organizations should contact a lawyer or a tax analyst to ascertain this law's conditions and ramifications.

The reasoning behind the establishment of tax-exempt organizations is that they are incorporated to serve the public good and society's welfare. To encourage support of such programs, our government—on both the national and the state levels—allows individuals to contribute to these groups without paying a tax on the money donated. The understanding is that government cannot undertake all the services the public needs and through the tax-deductible system is subsidizing independent groups performing such activities.

American colonists once made "No taxation without representation" a rallying cry eventually leading to our system of government; the slogan becomes somewhat convoluted when applied to tax-exempt groups. "Severely-limited representation without taxation" is the result. Organizations whose purpose is to work for the public good—nearly always necessitating passing or changing laws—are greatly hampered. The only avenue left is to take an issue to the public and let the public agitate for change. This is the basic premise on which the Animal Protection Institute was founded and on which most humane groups must work.

There is an alternative to the hassle imposed by IRS limitations on animal groups involved in lobbying: the establishment of a separate branch or committee to deal with legislation. These can be incorporated as nontax-exempt, with lobbying as their express purpose.

Several national humane groups have such committees. Depending on the bylaws of the sponsoring society, financial support can sometimes be directly channeled to its legislative committee. Others must depend on the services of volunteers. Any local society interested in doing legislative work should consider the possibility of incorporating a separate branch to avoid IRS limitations.

With a down-to-earth grasp on what lobbying is, the next step is to master the mechanics. Although your heart may be pure and your cause just, do not expect legislators to await you with open arms.

A cynic (or a realist, depending on your point of view) once remarked that a legislator's first job is to get reelected. His or her primary interests will be those of the voters in his or her district. People's incomes—even whole industries like furriers, tanners, pet-food companies, meat packers, and farm suppliers—can depend on animals, and nobody likes regulation. Thus, a good many legislators shy away from animal protective bills because of their inherent controversy.

If your organization decides to actively lobby, the best way to go after animal laws is with a full understanding of the legislative process and with the willingness to spend long hours researching and working for your bill. At first glance, this may seem an oppressive and impossible assignment, but it can, in fact, be a stimulating and rewarding experience.

There are basic points to be considered and steps to be followed.

(1) Know how the legislature functions—when it convenes, length of sessions, deadline for introducing bills, if special sessions are held.

(2) Query legislators for possible sponsors of your bill. Keep in mind the economic interests that may be a power in the lawmaker's district. Study the past performance of a legislator who may be a likely sponsor. Sometimes bills are undertaken for political or "show" reasons and nothing further is done with them; also, legislators will occasionally take on a bill as a constituent request and only half-heartedly support it. Some legislators, too, have a habit of sponsoring a great many bills, issuing press releases on them, and accomplishing nothing—such individuals are well known to their colleagues and their measures are never taken seriously. Don't be misled by fanfare; look for performance.

(3) Research the attitude of the committee to which the bill will be assigned. If it is strongly unfavorable, consider rewriting the measure or renaming it to obtain a different committee assignment. Most state-level, antitrap bills, for example, have fail-

ed because they have gone to committees long imbued with the "harvest" theory of the usefulness of wildlife. It is not always possible to reroute a bill, but do check. Lobby the committee members; make sure they all receive copies of your arguments.

(4) Be prepared to testify in support of the bill when it comes to hearings and, if possible, have other expert witnesses lined up. On the federal level, many bills die because the chairman of the assigned committee does not want to consider them. It is sometimes necessary to pressure him or her with press stories or letter-writing. On the state level, bills are usually granted a hearing. Be aware of the fact that your opposition will show up. Have facts and figures to back your premises. If the bill will require an expenditure by the state, be ready to justify it. If it will save the taxpayers money, make this one of your major points.

(5) If a bill is unacceptable to a majority of committee members, weigh the possibility of compromise. With humane issues, some immediate alleviation of pain and suffering can be more beneficial than insisting on a full bill that may take years to enact. It's possible that when your compromised bill is considered by the other house of government it will remain intact, with no further changes, and the compromise need not be devastating.

(6) Be alert to maneuvers by the committee that can delay the bill. One California committee voted to send a trap bill back to another committee because the legislators said they could not understand it as amended; they themselves had insisted on the amendments. When such shenanigans cause the loss of a bill, let the press know. The public should have the opportunity to evaluate lawmakers' behavior—after all, the public pays them. Should a maneuver to kill the bill seem likely, sometimes the sponsor can request that action be delayed and the bill reconsidered at a later date; this can also allow for amendments that would save the measure.

(7) When a bill goes out of its initial committee with a yes vote, don't relax. In most cases, proposals are heard first by a part of a committee, a subcommittee, and then by the full committee. Yours may also have to be considered by a fiscal committee. Follow the same steps on this second round; make sure every member is informed, and, again, be prepared to testify.

(8) The next step will be a vote by the full legislative body on the floor. If possible, try to get a reading on the number of votes in your favor. In nearly all cases, a simple majority is required for passage. Letters sent to individual legislators are the best means of gauging support. Those who seem undecided in their responses should receive a personal visit by you or, even better, by someone from their districts supporting the bill.

(9) Be prepared to follow this same procedure in the second house of government—either state or federal.

(10) Make sure the governor or the President knows of the grassroots support your bill has. When it appears the bill will pass, get as many letters and other expressions of support to the President or governor as possible. With the exception of North Carolina's, all governors can veto bills, as can the President. Governors are less bound by regional sentiment than legislators, and people from all over the state should communicate their feelings. One authority feels press coverage of a controversial piece of legislation is especially important as the bill approaches the governor's desk. Editorials can be particularly persuasive.

The President, on the other hand, will veto bills on the advice of agencies within his cabinet. Agency support, such as from the departments of Interior or Commerce, becomes essential to the passage of many animal bills, and such support needs to be cultivated, usually through public opinion. With animal issues the question is often one of decent treatment, and agencies are cooperative.

Throughout the process of getting legislation passed, the backup of community-, state-, or national-level citizens groups is essential. Use the press and use civic clubs.

Get letter-writing campaigns going, to individual legislators and especially to the members of all committees. Always communicate positively with your supporters. Consider composing an emergency-alert mailing or telephone list of persons willing to respond immediately to a call for help; you may, for example, need to bombard one legislator or committee member with communications of support. Also consider using rallies, pickets, and other demonstrations to attract public attention to your issue, but make sure any such gathering is well attended and presents a solid public image.

Finally, thank any legislator who has been outstandingly helpful. Cultivate goodwill for the next time 'round!

15

Forming Your Own Chapter, Making Your Own Crusade: Toward that Garden of Earthly Delights

The poet Robert Frost said that a poem begins in delight and ends in wisdom. Some of the crusades for animal rights have had the same pattern. Some haven't. Some have begun in rage, and the wisdom that came out of them was partly the wisdom of knowing you really get nowhere until you're organized.

Let's get organized! It's a favorite catch-phrase of the twentieth century. Good advice, too, for an animal rightist of almost any stripe—but what do you do and where do you start? An even more pertinent question is: *What would it take to start you?*

In Shell Knob, Missouri, Stanley G. Patterson, chairman of the Committee to Outlaw Steel Traps, explains why he decided that some sort of an organization was needed. He reached that conviction, he says, in December 1971, "when several of my dogs were caught in leghold traps.

"The search for the missing dogs, which went on daily for about two weeks, gave me a close look at some of the horrors of fur trapping. The pitiful look in the eyes of one particular raccoon will haunt me always.

"Subsequent events—the almost total lack of enforcement of trapping regulations, the hypocrisy of the professional 'wildlifers' who staff the Missouri Department of Conservation, the realization that 'game management' is a special interest ripoff—this and much more has been ample incentive to carry on the fight against fur-trapping and to expose to public view the fraudulent aspects of our present system of wildlife conservation."

As rapidly as he decided to form an organization, Stanley Patterson discovered that the road ahead was strewn with difficulties. It was also strewn with people who would try to block the road.

He found "complex problems. . .massive apathy of the public." The farmers' attitude toward wildlife was, in a great many cases, careless or callous or cruel or all three. He found that "many otherwise good individuals will kill any wild furbearer on sight, without the semblance of a reason for doing so." He found that, when the Department of Conservation becomes aware of this attitude, "rather than cope with it, they simply go along with it." He found that the high price of fur causes state officials to turn their eyes away from even the most rampant cruelty. He found it was a prevailing belief of "the game managers" that "to give in on the trapping issue would only open the flood gates to anti-hunting forces." (This is a persistent apprehension

Friendly persuasion. Most youngsters will expend hours of loving care if someone sets an example—and gives them the facts.

wherever animal welfare people operate—the sportsman-hunter sometimes feels challenged when the kind of large-scale slaughter that organized animal-rights groups come down on is actually far afield from his own activities.)

When Patterson noticed "the dependence of the Department of Conservation on the sale of game permits and the excise tax on sporting goods as its major source of revenue," he concluded: "In short, the whole system of conservation and wildlife management needed a major shakeout." He founded the Committee to Outlaw Steel Traps with three members—himself, his wife, and his son, Joe.

This is a rather typical development, and there are at least two lessons to be drawn. One: No one should underestimate the power of a single individual to seek significant change—most organizations have, at their center, at least one driving individual who is not discouraged by lack of initial support. Two: The fundamental problem for the organizer in the animal rights crusade is to be able to set clear goals, name his or her group accordingly, and *get going*.

In this chapter, we will examine the ways in which the one-person organization becomes more than that in the hands of a skillful organizer. We will look at the techniques of founding such a group—and we will look at the pitfalls.

CHOOSING THE ACHIEVABLE GOAL

Robbins Barstow, a Ph.D. whose beard would do credit to an old-time whaler, has been notably successful in helping reconcile New England to losing a whaling trade but gaining something better—an appreciation of the whale as an endlessly fascinating creature. In 1974, says Barstow, the Connecticut Cetacean Society was "formally initiated by a handful of committed persons" and he believes "the key to our activity was having a single, simple, achievable goal—to get the state legislature to pass a one-sentence bill, designating the sperm whale as the state animal."

It went along swimmingly.

Just sixteen months after this gambit was adopted, and in spite of a setback during the 1975 session when the state Senate ducked and the proposal ricocheted back to committee, the Cetacean Society—and the school children of Connecticut—had their way. "Miraculously," declares the whale society, "the bill was resurrected and returned." There was an eruption by public and press when it appeared that the whale proposal had been harpooned by sharpshooters in the legislature. Substitution of the white-tailed deer or the grey squirrel, or *homo sapiens* himself, as the state animal was side-stepped. The sperm whale—whose silhouette had influenced the history of New England and the eastern seaboard from the outset of the Colonies—was now the official state animal of Connecticut.

An important aspect of this is to recognize that the crusade was "a gambit"—a gambit being that tiny but significant ploy which can lead to a great victory elsewhere. *State animal* is only a phrase in a reference book; but the public airing that this pursuit of an "achievable goal" brought to the whole question of whales and their preservation—this lifted the campaign out of the trivial.

Says Barstow: "The broader objectives behind this goal were to publicize both the wonder of whales and the desperateness of their present plight—to raise citizen consciousness about cetaceans. The goal required action by a majority of the one-hundred eighty-seven Connecticut state representatives and senators. We utilized every proper means we could think of to influence them, both directly and indirectly." Flyers, letters, petitions, questionnaires were broadsided in all directions. Capitol reporters were wooed, says Barstow, and they came to believe in the cause themselves, creating openings for public discussion that an unaided whale society could not have.

181

"It was a natural topic for controversy and coverage. We did everything we could to assist the media. . .we solicited resolutions of support and communications from all appropriate groups and organizations we could think of. The backing of concerned, conservation-minded school children from many parts of the state was a crucial factor. We queried every candidate for the state legislature in advance of the November 1974, election."

As Barstow notes, however, in pursuit of this "achievable goal," there are some

In honor of the sperm whale's 1975 designation as Connecticut state animal, the Connecticut Cetacean Society presented Governor Ella Grasso (sixth from left) with a Richard Ellis print of the mammal. CCS members include president Donald Sineti (fifth from right) and program coordinator Dr. Robbins Barstow ((fifth from left).

ditches the unwary can fall into. Lobbying efforts — direct intervention with legislators constituted lobbying — could not be anonymous. The Cetacean Society registered with the Connecticut Secretary of State as a lobbyist on behalf of the sperm whale as state animal.

In the long run, even though the goal adopted by the organization might have seemed limited, it brought an unlimited amount of attention to the underlying questions about treatment of the whale — and those questions are as broad as the planet itself. Instead of a parochial discussion in one little corner of New England, the issue

Events like California Whale Day in Sacramento tell the public what's happening to whales—and let individuals know how they can get involved in the movement.

transformed itself into debate with ramifications for more than one state and more than one nation.

Barstow himself concludes: "A flexible, viable, fast-acting organizational base is essential—together with the active involvement of as many other individuals and groups as possible. A leader who is on the spot and free to move rapidly—but with an accessible corps of backers—is vital. Continual written communication and updating to an ever-expanding network of supporters, can transform a small trickle into a strong stream. It does take time, patience, and painstaking creative effort. . . .Having succeeded in our initial goal of having the sperm whale designated as Connecticut's official state animal, our emphasis is now changed to using this as a springboard for education. . . .This has involved preparing materials for teachers in schools, films, meetings, governor proclamations, literature, lectures, news releases and building a life-size 60-foot whale model at the West Hartford Children's Museum."

So an original "achievable goal" led in very natural order to a second one. Well before Christmas 1976, the Children's Museum had this massive present ready for the youngsters of the nation: an impressive, man-built whale that serves as a symbol of a dramatic worldwide struggle. One of these days it will be possible to walk inside that whale at the Children's Museum and know a whale inside out. "Furnishing its insides" is the next step. The goals of the Cetacean Society leap on ahead of them.

A description of how Conny the Whale was built gives some notion of how the whale society organized to acquire support in many directions. The tail of this sixty-foot whale towers eighteen feet in the air and, declare its builders, it is a scientifically faithful reproduction. At one point, over one-hundred volunteers worked for nineteen hours straight to raise Conny on high.

The scaffolding was lent by Patent Scaffolding of Hartford. A first layer of chicken wire came from Porch and Patio of Wethersfield, Connecticut. The "endless rows" of steel reinforcement rods were from Shepard Steel. Concrete blocks on which the body rests were built from sand donated by Silica Sand and Gravel of South Windsor. This is not a polite bow to the helping firms—there were many others—but just an indication of *how many friends need to be made* by the animal rights group that is organizing to serve its goals.

Volunteers can secure mighty accomplishments, but let's also listen to Larry Foster of General Whale, an organization that has mounted some remarkable displays, again with the aim of making the nature of the whale in the ocean depths luminous to mankind.

Says Larry: "Show me a group that isn't seeking funds and I'll show you a group that is either already wealthy or isn't doing anything."

FUND-RAISING TIPS

Spirit alone won't win the animal wars. Even a letter needs a postage stamp. And rare is the campaign that doesn't need thousands upon thousands of letters.

(If it should happen that you inherit the chore of raising money for a given project, you might find it useful to become acquainted with several publications available for that purpose. Aside from books written by professionals, the American Humane Association publishes an excellent guide entitled, *The Animal Welfare Agency and the Public: Publicity and Fund-Raising.*)

Most organizations have an angel or two, at least in the beginning, but to be altogether dependent on them invites a crash. If some effort isn't made to help the angels shoulder the load, their wings may become droopy—may even fall off. My experience indicates that eighty percent of the operational cost of an animal welfare organization comes from twenty percent of the membership. This in no way diminishes the importance of that twenty percent of cost coming from eighty percent of the members.

There was a time when membership dues were looked upon as part of the fund-raising effort. Quite frankly, with inflation running wild, the usual five dollar or ten dollar annual dues serves only to administratively sustain a member. Normally, if revenue from dues is not expanded on acquisition of the member, his or her payment "just to belong" can easily be eaten up simply in the printing of absolutely necessary informational material such as periodicals, magazines, or news bulletins. When the member asks for information that requires research by a staff member—and he or she should be encouraged to do so to increase awareness—the time involved in acquiring specialized information, dictation, and typing, outruns the dues.

Except for the fact that in a large organization most members do not request these special services, membership dues would never begin to cover the mere cost of *having* members. This is a paradox that lies at the core of all efforts to achieve large-scale goals through a large-scale membership. Your financial plan must avoid an overload that causes you to strangle your own efforts accidentally. Members *help*; members *cost*—two horns of a dilemma. Add to all this a horrendous rate of attrition, annually, if your organization is attempting to be national in scope, and you have the ingredients of bankruptcy in short order.

API has a unique approach to solving the high cost of coping with the membership-dues problem. The first time a member pays dues—say, in April—the anniversary for renewal would normally be the following April. If, in the meanwhile, the member contributes again—for example, in August—to a special project, then the anniversary date is automatically advanced to a year from *that* month. This elim-inates costly renewal reminders and it holds down badgering of members. And, it works.

One more point to consider relative to membership dues: It may be better, for cer-tain types of crusades, to solicit a small contribution rather than try to enroll a member. As all who indulge in fund-raising soon discover, a percentage of those who contribute really have in mind a quid pro quo—very likely, they will be hitting you later for a return gift for their own charity. Well—touché!

In my early career, I was prone to be excited by such projects as bake sales, raffles, and rummage sales. They were, in addition to being hard work and hard to organize, a never-ending challenge. With few exceptions, the result was hardly much more than a covering of costs—and you wound up with a bunch of weary and frustrated workers. There were other flies in the ointment: the chumps who ended up with the residue in their garage, the publicity grabbers who saw the whole event as a chance to get their names mentioned, the bargain-hunters who neither worked nor contributed but gobbled up the "good stuff" before the sale started. Et cetera, ad nauseam.

The late Howard Pattee, retired professional fund-raiser for Pomona Colleges, thought it best, instead of a rummage sale, to get pledges of twenty hours from the participants and then collect ten cents per hour—roughly the value of rummage sale labor. That raised just as much money and, in addition, the donors of rummage could save it one more year and sell it as antique. The more I reflect on the Pattee policy, the smarter it seems. Too many ten-dollar-an-hour people have let themselves in for the hustle and bustle of a poorly conceived "fund-raiser"—and discovered, in the long run, that all their hours didn't bring back ten dollars of honest aid. How much better to have just made a contribution from the top!

But this doesn't mean that conventional methods are necessarily bad methods. An extremely effective and efficient way to develop funds, long-term, is to set up a part- or full-time small business, operating on behalf of an organization. The most popular (and sometimes the most workable) version of this is the thrift shop. The ingredients are: merchant, space, and merchandise, in that order. The key, of course, is the merchant: a person knowledgeable in the trade. The space needs to be in a location having good traffic—otherwise, the whole operation can be time-wasting and costly. The merchandise should consist of items actually saleable—not piles of old shoes that no one will ever put on again. Mix these ingredients with the humane spirit and membership support, and the result can be a small but steady income. Such a commercial outlet has utility, also, as a beehive for dispensing information—spreading the word a bit further on what can be done in the animal cause you're promoting. A casual customer may become an ardent supporter of your cause.

Never forget the elements of publicity in seeking funds. What people don't hear about, they can't contribute to. Announcements to press, radio, and television; letters to the editor; notices posted in supermarkets and many other spots—all of these serve due notice and also help establish the legitimacy of an event, for a jaundiced eye is often turned on those seeking to rouse financial support.

You *must* be aware of the rules that apply to fund-raising in your community and acquire any permits required by local ordinance. Before you start, visit city hall. It can save you a grand embarrassment later.

WHO AND HOW—SOME THOUGHTS ABOUT LEADERSHIP

Wild Horse Annie Johnston, cited earlier in this book as an example of the great self-starter who was able to infect a nation with a sense of justice, knows better than anyone that the leadership in the animal rights movement must adopt the same methods as leaders in other fields.

Yes, passion spins the plot. Yes, without a great emotional thrust, most of the animal rights leaders wouldn't have started their crusades to begin with. But the passion must be channeled; it must be guided along that channel by reason; it must be flexible—knowing when the time is ripe, knowing how to create an opening, knowing how to take adequate account of all the antiarguments and of all the currents that are running against your campaign and can defeat it.

"My first recommendation," says Annie, "would be to know your subject. Then eliminate, to the greatest extent possible, overemotionalism. And never resort to exaggeration. Be completely sure of the facts and be prepared to submit documented evidence. . . .One must be inexhaustible, both physically and mentally, with an ability to withstand harassment, ridicule, and rudeness. There must also be a willingness to listen to all sides of an issue without losing sight of the eventual goal, and the courage to stand firm in a decision once it is made.

"Diplomacy works better than aggressiveness. Integrity must be maintained, for it is the firm foundation upon which an entire campaign is built."

Diplomacy works better than aggressiveness. This should be engraved somewhere for the battlers in this work to reflect upon. Many have imagined that shouts and venom will carry the day—and they rarely do.

The animal rightist frequently lands the role of special pleader. The cause so familiar to him or her may be exotic indeed to the listener—a hard-pressed city councilman, an obtuse bureaucrat, a determined rancher. On the average, the person with leadership qualities will know how to use the very exoticness of the subject to stir the imaginations of those who have set out to be the foe.

All around the United States, individual leaders rise up who fight with skill and eloquence and a nice sense of reality on behalf of many creatures. Stan Minasian is a hard-hitting young man who produced the film *The Last Days of the Dolphin?* When he addresses an audience, he takes the stance of a shortstop, ready to block quickly and gracefully any remark hurled in his direction. Beula Edmiston, who finally stopped that outrageous chapter in American history which reduced the Tule Elk from

California's dominant species to an almost-vanished species, is both funny and wise as she depicts the struggle to tell a large and varied population about an animal grown so rare that *many of the people working to save it have never seen it.*

The leaders in the animal protection movement are often self-appointed leaders—all the more reason why they need to make a careful study of the techniques of persuasion and effective administration.

Those who take the pivotal position in steering their own societies come in many forms. Not a few of the profound spokesmen for animal causes in this country fit within a psychologist's definition of charismatic individuals—the persons who wrap themselves in strength and whose inner dynamism creates a glow around all their activities. On the other hand, the noncharismatic, highly motivated, straightforward organizers can often accomplish as much through skills in mediating and administration as can the fiery leaders with their eyes on distant horizons.

For the moment as a whole to go forward, it needs a liberal sprinkling of both: visionaries not above forming a personal cult and the less dramatic step-by-step people who look forward to immediate gains.

There is a style of leader who basks in headlines or even notoriety, who feels entirely at home amid swirling controversy, who may begin to mope if he or she thinks "someone else is getting the credit." But I can think of a young man who moves all around the world, pursuing his goal to save a particularly rare form of wild bird, and he is selflessly determined that his picture shall never be shown in a newspaper. He wants no *personal* publicity whatever. These traits of character make for interesting discussion at times, but they are not right or wrong in themselves. Whether the leader wishes credit and acclaim or hopes to remain anonymous through all eternity, is he or she getting action? Do his or her methods bring the goals in closer range?

Because so many of the animal campaigns began with a single person whose eyes were suddenly opened to overwhelming injustice, the crossroads for the fledgling organization is apt to be that moment when it passes from personal crusade to a group commitment. The weakness in the animal rights movement is often an organizational weakness—the top management doesn't represent a sufficient variety of skills to get things done over a wide spectrum. After all, an animal rights group will immediately come up against questions involving mass-persuasion psychology, legality, fund-raising techniques, the logistics of animal handling—a vast complex of questions, nearly all of which require knowledge in highly specialized subjects. As the group expands, therefore, it should try to acquire special skills. It should contain within it those who will understand business operations, the law, photography, and other topics, and no one person can spread himself or herself successfully across all these fields. One person *can* gather a forceful group whose combined expertise, and a free play of discussion, will aid in coming to wise decisions.

The "kitchen cabinet" method of arriving at policies for your organization may start as a very loose alliance, but sooner or later you will probably want a formal board of directors.

I know of no legal requirements stipulating the qualifications for someone to sit on the board of an animal welfare organization. However, since the fifty states are not required to have uniform statutes for incorporating a nonprofit organization, it would be wise to check out with an attorney the ramifications of any appointments being considered. The directors—or the trustees, as they are sometimes called—do have legal responsibilities and can, in certain respects, be held accountable for the activities of the organization and its financial operations. Each member of the board should understand clearly what his or her responsibilities are and aren't.

You don't have to move in the dark on this subject. There is a more than adequate rundown available on the selection of leadership and the duties and responsibilities of a board of directors. This information, based on years of experience, can be obtained from the American Humane Association.

Keeping in mind that the setting of policy is the board's main task, any present leaders of the organization will do well to seek experience when they are reaching out for board members to amplify their own skills. They may also find special benefits in acquiring board members with a wide acquaintance in the community — persons experienced in dealing with those in many walks of life. Animal protectionists are seeking change or restoration. Out there somewhere may be foes as varied as ten thousand rabbit-boppers, a single recalcitrant dog warden, or an environment-be-damned governor. The change or restoration that you desire may well strike them as galloping idiocy on your part: Don't you understand how *business* operates? Don't you see that rabbit-bopping is a social necessity and a heck of a lot of *fun*? Are you trying to bankrupt the whole community to mollycoddle a bunch of mongrels? Primitive emotion — and the most primitive arguments you'll ever hear — invade every question involving animal rights, and dealing with these from a standpoint of ab-solute logic is only the beginning of your solution. Board members who are sophisticated enough to know what people are like can give you a flexibility of approach that can overcome many different types of obstructionist foes.

Should the recruit to the board of directors be experienced directly in animal welfare? That will help — but it's not imperative. The sympathy should be there. The person accepting a post should not do so just for the sake of adding another position. The board member you're looking for will probably have at least a mild acquaintance with Robert's Rules of Order, either in letter or in spirit. Chances are, he or she will own a dog or cat — if his or her life is entirely animaless you might have reason to question how deep the commitment is.

You've probably heard the expression, "The more I know about animals, the less I like people." Watch out for it, especially if it seems to be more than just a chance phrase. People, too, are within what the biologist ordains as the animal kingdom, and it's doubtful that someone who thoroughly deplores people can actually have a great reservoir of love for animalkind. We do know that the misanthrope is easily at-tracted to any strong crusade, but the consternation that a people-hater can cause may totally outweigh any advantage. Even if he or she is packing fat checks for the movement, don't end up being the prisoner of such spites. When the organization begins to reflect spite instead of love, it will cease to be effective and cherished goals will be pushed far out of reach.

WHY TAX-EXEMPT?

Definite financial advantages come with the tax-exempt status available to the nonprofit organization. The serious donor to an organization is usually looking for a way to make a considerable difference in a cause he or she believes in — but how much of a difference, will be eroded greatly if the gift is eaten away by taxes. Recognition of this by the government has led to an encouragement of philanthropy firmly embedded in the tax laws.

As pointed out in chapter 14, there are other things embedded there, too: restric-tions. Every group, therefore, that organizes as a nonprofit group must necessarily begin (and continue through its lifetime) a study of tax laws. If it doesn't, it will shortly be in conflict with the authorities. Even if it does — since there are areas in which the rules are not as clear-cut as they might be — it will probably have occasion to debate the fine points with its attorneys or with the Internal Revenue Service.

Obtaining tax-exempt status from city, county, and federal government is quite straightforward. The required forms can be obtained from the government office involved. Obtaining tax-exempt status from the federal government usually has the highest financial implications. Contributions coming in from members and donors are hugely encouraged because they are subject to deduction as charitable contributions. At the same time, the government assuredly watches for ruses in such procedures.

It is not just smart tactics to "take advantage" of the tax-exemption provisions. It is the obligation of the organization, supported by philanthropic moneys, to make the tax laws accomplish what they were intended to accomplish in this respect. What can be achieved through private charity as a matter of individual goodwill will not *have* to be done by government under a system of coercion. What is a greater demonstration of the value of money than to be able to do good works with it? Giving *does* make people feel good. Giving *is* a way of returning to a society a tangible personal thanks for what that society has conferred. The same thrill certainly *does not* arise from the mere paying of taxes, so there is justice and sensibility in this general human urge to use philanthropy as a way of earmarking what will be done with a sum of money that might otherwise wind up as income or inheritance tax.

Don't, therefore, ever feel sheepish about putting forward the tax advantages of donating to a worthwhile nonprofit organization. It is not only a part of our system, but many of the finest accomplishments of that system are an outgrowth of inspired philanthropy. To endow a great project as you leave this life is truly to achieve a degree of immortality. And to endow an important project while still alive is at least as admirable. Projects like API's Museum of the Lost can only exist through visionary gifts. Such special-interest institutions are not likely to be underwritten by hard-pressed legislatures. At this stage in our national history, they occur mainly through private action by the individual.

Once an organization has been granted a tax-exempt letter from the Internal Revenue Service, caution should be exercised with respect to its activities, as mentioned in the previous chapter. A modicum of interaction with the legislative process may be permissible but should only be approached with clear legal advice. This is necessarily an important consideration because a campaign of many years standing by an animal rights group can eventually climax in action by legislators to pass a law. At this stage, a fine-point interpretation may be put on what activity is or is not permissible in effecting the "coup de grace" that puts that legislation over the top. Public persuasion and political tactics have an unclear middle ground where persuasion *could* become lobbying. You must keep your priorities clear, and get sound legal advice so as to strictly observe the tax-exemption provisions.

I should point out here that while a group like the Animal Protection Institute is permitted a minimum of activity that has a bearing on legislation, it would certainly not act on any issue except that with a direct bearing on the welfare of animals. A tax-exempt organization cannot, under any circumstances, participate in the political process by campaigning for the election of an individual. (This does not apply to individuals—it does apply to the organization.)

UNBALANCED BUDGETS AND BALANCED PROGRAMS

A nonprofit organization can't print its own money, so it doesn't have the option of long-term deficit financing. You make yourself organizationally strong not only by building up a cash reserve but by developing a varied program to maintain this reserve while spending as widely and wisely as possible on the crusades you have adopted as your own.

The unbalanced budget will lead almost immediately to an extinct organization. But so will an unbalanced program.

You organized in order to go somewhere—to get something done. Whether the goal is a cat shelter in Minneapolis or a worldwide system to protect the stork, your program should take off from a realistic appraisal of your budget and intermediate goals based on present and projected moneys.

Don't leave this program in the air as something that is "generally understood" and never committed to paper. The board of directors should periodically make a statement of program and appraise the organization's ability to carry it out. Are you doing all you can to exert leadership? Are you approaching your goal from more than a single angle? Are you supportive of other organizations who may be as close or closer than you are to the same goal — and need the little extra push your support could give them? Are you using the full talents of your membership to achieve your program (sometimes the leaders are so intent on acting they forget to involve other people).

Your program should be based on a "projection of the possible," but this needn't be regarded as a sink-or-swim proposition. Your time-table for achieving a particular goal may be often upset, but in the animal wars it's those who endure who win. It takes grittiness to stick to a program of action in the face of repeated failure, but almost every important advance in the field of animal rights has come at the cost of many defeats along the way.

Propose and estimate ambitiously (but not bankruptingly) with the recognition that the board of directors can modify the goals and extend the time-table as need be. A tangible program, well spelled out, will guard against those impromptu involvements in activities that are *not* well thought out — and that often drain a treasury without a tangible result. The animal actionists who have had a pervasive influence aren't helter-skelter in their approach. They recognize that they're in a struggle not for a day but for the decades. They program with that in mind.

AVOIDING THE TRAPS

The day you decide to be more than an individual — in clambering to the defense of the golden eagle, the mountain goat, or the puppies in a grimy pet store — can be quite a glad day. It will be followed with disillusionment unless you are prepared. Brain-picking those who have involved themselves in such a campaign will forewarn you of much that can be expected.

For Ted Sorich II, who organized Citizens for Low-Cost Spay and Neuter Clinics, the discoveries came swiftly.

"In 1970 while in graduate school," Sorich reported, "I found two abandoned female dogs and each subsequently presented me with seven puppies." He then had sixteen reasons to concern himself with the high cost of that minor operation that prevents the unwanted litter. He had no trouble building a case for the low-cost spay and neuter clinic based on (1) sympathy for the animals born only to be wiped out and (2) the sensibleness of spending community money to control pet population through birth control methods rather than euthanasia. Cost-benefit studies clearly indicated his community would be ahead by establishing the kind of clinic he wanted. But sensibleness and sympathy do not, by themselves, carry the battle.

"A great many people, in a relatively few occupations and fewer professions and industries, reap tremendous financial profits," concluded Sorich, "from the dog and cat overpopulation problem. Yet all profess that they want to see the problem solved. Statewide symposiums and national conferences in which such factions participate cause the general public and government officials to *think* that meaningful solutions are being developed and that governmental intervention is unnecessary.

"There will be no significant progress until there is widespread governmental financing of public spay clinics and, especially, until the federal government develops and controls distribution of low-cost chemical contraceptives."

Those who will lose money should the problem itself recede do not just sit on the sidelines while such issues are debated. Sorich found that wherever he turned these people with "vested interests in animals" had used their "extreme willingness" to secure posts on municipal humane commissions. "With such conflicts of interest," he argues, "humane concerns become subordinate to financial interest. Spay and neuter clinics are studiously avoided."

Beyond these entrenched, overinterested parties, he found the entrenched and highly uninterested politicians. "Public officials are so accustomed to labeling animal issues unimportant," he said, "that they are unapproachable on the pet overpopulation problem—a problem costing local governments an estimated $250 million a year and other organizations an additional $100 million in animal control efforts."

Sorich was hard at work on possibly the most common problem of all—but its commonness, like the commonness of the cold, has not led to its eradication. Nor is the less common problem any easier to solve. In Pacific Palisades, California, one of the most beautiful residential areas in the United States, J. Richard Hilton described what it's like to form an organization called the Society for the Preservation of Birds of Prey.

"We are probably one of the most specialized organizations in the world," said its founder. "Our only vocal concern—hawks and owls. We *are* interested in all wildlife but this is the thrust. . . .By publishing a regular newsletter and sending it to target individuals at no cost, we thought it would attract and unite those interested. It has been ten years, at a cost of more than ten-thousand dollars, and we are only beginning to attract support."

His organization numbers only two-hundred members, but it has the scope of a jet aircraft, for its members are flung all about the globe and it considers itself a worldwide society. Hilton's words echo the difficulties encountered by many who have organized groups of two or twenty thousand.

"The problem with any new organization," he says, "is to attract capable leadership and sympathetic supporters. Few people will invest faith and trust in a new venture. They want organizational prestige and fame before they will join to help. . . .Bird-watchers, and we've dealt with many of them, seem fanatical about traveling great distances to observe and record a bird in their life lists. Yet these same people have no interest in the conservation of the very birds they admire. In the past few years, we have deliberately tried to breed militancy among bird enthusiasts, but we have overwhelmingly failed to muster the birders' support. They are not at all concerned with that which is beyond sight of their scopes and binoculars.

"They love birds in the wild but they do not understand that it often takes action and debate to keep them there."

To form an organization on behalf of birds of prey is, even on the face of it, a lonely struggle. Hilton does not recommend that others go and do likewise; he sees the path as a hard one. Yet his Society casts a trail in the world more powerful than its two-hundred members would suggest. Without spectacular agendas, it nevertheless leaves afloat some observations that the world would do well to listen to. It finds messages in the long-ago extinction of the La Brea stork, a flightless auk, and the Merriam teratorn (a large vulture). It chances the view that there are "senile species" that sometimes cannot be saved by Man even if he would. This rare organization has become an assembler of rare facts. And so it has found a purposeful role.

Those who organize campaigns out of a fretful desire to make this world conscious of what it is losing are a diverse bunch and they have their normal complement of human faults. But I am often happily surprised to note how many believe that they haven't yet done enough—that they can do more. Smugness is not the most common of our sins.

Stan Minasian of Save the Dolphins, Inc., says: "Our organization is definitely not satisfied with its progress. We feel that we have a long way to go before conquering

Blue whales are the largest animals ever to inhabit the earth. They can reach lengths of 100 feet and weights of 120 tons—three times the size of the largest dinosaur. In the twentieth century, populations of blue whales have been drastically reduced; although almost complete worldwide protection measures were initiated in 1966, there is some doubt whether the species can survive. DRAWING BY LARRY FOSTER, GENERAL WHALE.

and resolving the problem against which we organized. Things operate slowly and we must be patient. But at the same time we must be demanding and adamant."

In the early 1970s, Stan was extremely adamant in demanding that the United States government give up the filmed evidence that was the one and only effective depiction of the porpoise massacres actually occurring. For two years, he and supporting organizations hung tough through a tense legal struggle with the Department of Commerce.

"Had all sides just sat down and talked about it," Stan thinks, "the problem (getting the film out where the public would see it and know what happens) could have been solved in two days. The court system does not allow parties to do this. It is frustrating, expensive and stupid."

Frustration, expense, and stupidity do come the way—and will continue to come the way—of those who organize on behalf of animal rights. It often takes two years to get the two-day discussion. Sometimes it takes twenty years to get the two-day discussion. This is what organizers of animal welfare groups let themselves in for.

Why?

Because, in the end, it's worth it.

Appendix
A Handbook Of Animal Care
And First Aid*

Anyone receptive to animal problems and having a knowledge of preventive measures will probably be called on, at some point, to administer treatment to an injured animal—perhaps because a neighbor or friend knows of one's interest, perhaps because humanitarians are simply more alert to signs of distress.

Emergency medical care or first aid is a skill that provides immediate treatment for injured or severely ill animals. The objectives of this type of treatment are to preserve life, ease suffering, and prevent aggravation of the abnormal condition until professional assistance can be obtained. *First-aid measures should not be used as a substitute for professional veterinary medical care.* The following is an attempt to familiarize the average person with proper basic procedures to follow in emergency situations.

It is vitally important for the person administering first aid to be sure of techniques. Many well-intentioned but misinformed people have attempted to aid animals in distress with disastrous results because they were not educated as to what should and should not have been done. On the other hand, many animals' lives have been saved by a conscientious first-aider knowledgeable in his or her skills. If you are unsure of the proper procedure to follow in a certain case, DO LITTLE OR NOTHING—seek professional assistance immediately.

Note: Each section in this chapter is designed to discuss a particular animal. Even though one species may in some respects resemble another and treatments may be similar, do not suppose treatments will be the same. Unless specifically directed to refer to another section, do not attempt to improvise medical treatments from those suggested for other animals.

THE DOG

Anatomy of the Dog

To be able to recognize an abnormal condition, knowledge of the normal state is necessary. The following diagrams are simplified schemes of the dog's anatomy; refer to them when necessary. An overall familiarity with the structure and location of key points will be essential in practical applications. Practice learning important areas on the animal; be gentle.

*Illustrations in the Appendix are the artist's reproductions and not anatomical drawings.

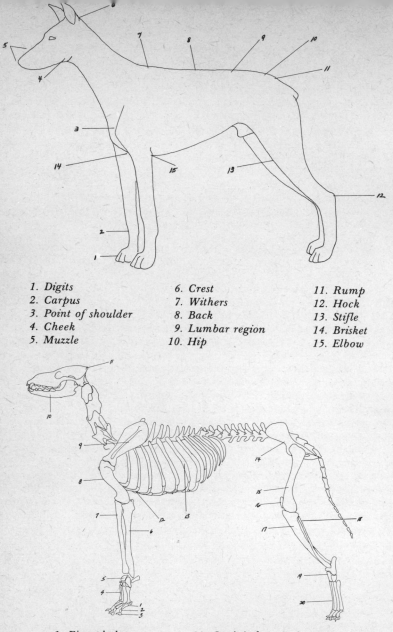

1. Digits	6. Crest	11. Rump
2. Carpus	7. Withers	12. Hock
3. Point of shoulder	8. Back	13. Stifle
4. Cheek	9. Lumbar region	14. Brisket
5. Muzzle	10. Hip	15. Elbow

1. First phalanx	11. Occipital protruberance
2. Second phalanx	12. Sternum
3. Third phalanx	13. Ribs
4. Metacarpals	14. Pelvis
5. Carpals	15. Femur
6. Ulna	16. Patella
7. Radius	17. Tibia
9. Scapula	19. Tarsals
10. Mandible	20. Metatarsals

194

Approaching an Injured Dog

If an animal has been injured, his or her temperament will usually change due to the trauma and pain involved, so even if you know the animal you are approaching, BE CAREFUL. Make your initial approach very slowly and calmly; if feasible, do not attempt to catch the animal initially. Let the dog know you want to help; talk to him or her and call him or her by name if you know it. Offer the back of your hand with your fingers curled under for the animal to sniff. Keep your face away in case the dog snaps. If approaching a strange dog or a particularly aggressive one, cover your arms and hands with gloves, a blanket, a pillow, or newspaper.

Catching and Restraining the Injured Dog

After your initial approach, the next step is to catch and restrain the dog. He or she will probably be unnerved and resist your attempts to help. Be as gentle as possible to avoid aggravating injuries but firm enough to restrain the animal.

The first method to try, especially if the dog is your own or one familiar to you, is luring him or her toward you or to an open car. If this procedure fails, you will probably require a lasso, a come-along, or a restraining stick. Construction of one of these devices is simple (see diagrams), and they allow you to catch an animal from a distance. Position yourself so you can slip the open end of the loop over the dog's head and neck; tighten the loop by pulling on the loose end of the cord. Work quickly and use as little force as possible to avoid choking the animal or upsetting him or her further. As soon as the dog is in a confined space, loosen the come-along.

Use of a lasso or come-along throws some dogs into a frenzy. If this reaction occurs, it may be necessary to seek skilled assistance in restraining the animal.

If the injured animal is in extreme pain or seems overly excited, it is wise to place a temporary muzzle on him or her. The following diagrams show how to do this, using any soft flexible piece of material such as a scarf, handkerchief, or roll of gauze. If you have a choice, use material about one inch wide. Be sure the muzzle is on tightly and positioned correctly — do not put it too far back toward the angle of the mouth or too far forward on the soft spot of the nose. If the muzzle is positioned properly there is no danger of suffocating the animal because nasal bones protect the respiratory passages. Note that snub-nosed dogs require a slight modification of the muzzle (see cat muzzle, page 219) to prevent its slipping off.

Transporting the Injured Dog

After an animal has been injured, he or she will usually sit or lie in the most comfortable position, so it's best not to alter that position too much when moving the animal. There are several ways an animal can be carried, depending on size and extent of injuries. Means of transportation include carrying in the arms, using a container such as a box or basket, using a stretcher or wheeled transport. When a dog is carried in the arms, the injured side should be toward the person.

When lifting a small dog, place the right hand around the body and under the breastbone. Place the left hand on the collar or the scruff of the neck. After lifting in this manner, a small dog can be carried under the right arm. *Do not* use this method if spinal injury is present.

With larger dogs the person kneels and places one arm across the back of the dog's buttocks around the tail; the other arm goes across the front of the animal. The carrier then presses the dog against his or her body and, after rising, carries the animal's front quarters slightly higher, so that the weight is thrown on the animal's buttocks. *Do not* use this method if the dog is suffering from injuries to the pelvis or hindquarters — in such cases, pressure on the injured area will cause severe pain. A restraint method may have to be applied before the animal is lifted.

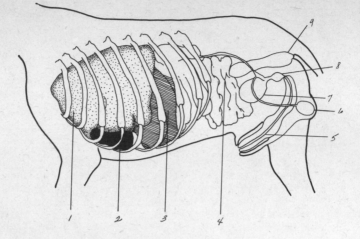

Viscera of the Dog
Male dog, left lateral view

1. Lung
2. Heart
3. Liver
4. Intestine
5. Urethra

6. Left testis
7. Urinary bladder
7. Prostate
9. Rectum

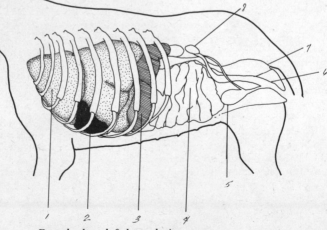

Female dog, left lateral view

1. Lung
2. Heart
3. Liver
4. Intestine

5. Bladder
6. Vagina
7. Rectum
8. Left ovary

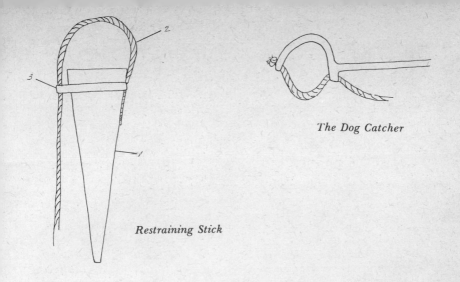

The Dog Catcher

Restraining Stick

Wood is 1" thick, 3' long, with the top end 3" wide and the bottom 1/2" wide.

Strap is 3/4" wide, 6' long. Attach to right side of wood with four 1 1/2" No. 10 wood screws and thread through metal loop on left side of wood.

Use a 9" piece of flat metal, with both sides flush with right side of wood. Attach with two 1/4" bolts 2" long.

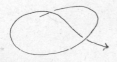

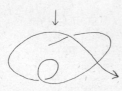

Making a Lasso
(Use 9' of rope.)

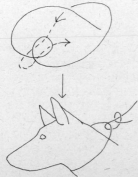

Boxes and baskets may be used for small dogs. If these are unavailable, a sack or a pillowcase may be used, provided proper care is taken to ensure plenty of fresh air for the victim. Stretchers made of canvas, and wooden poles with a boxlike structure on top to enclose the animal, are ideal for larger dogs. Variations are possible. A plain board is usable if care is exercised so the animal doesn't fall off. A blanket or a coat is also suitable. Be careful when moving the animal from the ground to the stretcher. Inch the stretcher under the animal. Disturb him or her as little as possible.

Emergency Situations and Procedures

A. Hemorrhage (Bleeding) and Lacerations

Hemorrhage or bleeding is usually caused by injury but may be the result of diseases affecting the clotting process. Most small scratches and cuts will stop bleeding on their own in a few minutes and require little, if any, care. If the bleeding is severe and obviously isn't stopping, your help will be needed. When severe bleeding occurs, the possibility of shock being present is high. Dogs in shock require immediate veterinary care (see section on shock treatment).

There are three types of hemorrhage, but serious wounds will usually involve all three, so don't spend a lot of time trying to trace the blood source.

1. *Arterial bleeding* — The blood will be bright red in color since it is freshly oxygenated blood. It will emerge from the wound in spurts, corresponding to the beats of the heart. Careful examination will usually reveal a definite point of bleeding.

2. *Venous bleeding* — The blood issuing forth from a vein will be dark red — deoxygenated blood returning from the tissues to the heart. It will flow from the wound in a continuous manner. As with arterial bleeding, a definite point of bleeding can usually be found.

3. *Capillary bleeding* — Capillaries are the tiny blood vessels in the blood tissues, so this bleeding will be seen to some extent in all wounds. The blood will ooze from the wound with relatively little force, and examination will usually reveal no definite point of origin.

4. *Mixed bleeding* — As noted above, most severe wounds will involve all three types of hemorrhage due to the closeness of the various blood vessels. In such cases, the volume of blood coming from the wound will not permit you to see the characteristics of each type of hemorrhage.

If you are able to identify the source of the bleeding, it will be helpful to the attending veterinarian later. The force of the blood flow will depend on the size and depth of the wound.

Treatment for hemorrhage can follow one of several courses. The first method you should try is direct pressure. Place a clean piece of gauze or other material directly over the wound and apply pressure with the palm of your hand. (If a foreign body is present or a fracture is suspected, be careful, since applying pressure may aggravate the situation.) If the injury is to the tail or other extremity, a pressure bandage may be applied: Place a clean piece of cloth or a gauze pad over the wound and wrap the entire extremity with another strip of material. If extra layers of material are needed, *do not* remove old bandages; just place the new layers directly over the old ones. Removing old bandages interrupts clot formation.

If direct pressure does not seem to be working, the next step is to apply pressure to one of several pressure points. These are areas where it is possible to press an artery against a bone, thereby decreasing blood flow to areas below. Three pressure points in the dog are (see diagrams):

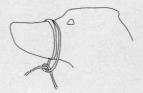

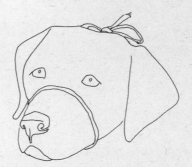

Making an Emergency Muzzle

1. *Tie a loose knot in the middle of the material, making a large loop.*
2. *Slip the loop over the dog's nose, bringing it past the soft part of the nose.*
3. *Quickly pull the ends to tighten the loop.*
4. *Bring the ends down and under the chin and knot them there.*
5. *Take the ends back under the ears and tie them together behind the head.*

Small dog

Medium dog

Large dog

1. The *brachial artery* as it slants over the inside of the lower third of the humerus, one to one and one-half inches above the elbow joint; pressure at this point will arrest hemorrhage from below the elbow.

2. The *femoral artery* as it slants over the femur on the inside of the thigh; pressure at this point arrests hemorrhage from below the stifle joint.

3. The *coccygeal artery* as it passes backward along the underside of the tail; pressure at the root will arrest hemorrhage from the rest of the tail.

Pressure should be applied to the pressure point located nearest the wound on the side between the wound and the heart.

The final and most dangerous manner in which bleeding may be stopped is by application of a tourniquet. This technique should only be used as a last resort, and extreme care must be taken to ensure proper application. Tourniquets may only be used on extremities. A flat strip of cloth, rubber, or other suitable material about one and one-half inches wide should be fixed around the limb and tightened just enough to slow the flow of blood appreciably. The tourniquet should be applied between the body and the wound and, if possible, just above a joint, since this helps prevent slippage. When the blood flow has been sufficiently reduced, try to replace the tourniquet with a pressure bandage. Most veterinarians recommend loosening the tourniquet every ten to fifteen minutes to allow reoxygenation of tissues below the tourniquet. Remember, THIS IS AN EXTREME MEASURE and should only be used when all else fails.

All wounds, whether incised (clean-cut wound with well-defined edges), lacerated (jagged-edged), punctured, or contused (with bruises), run the risk of infection and should be cleaned. It may be necessary to clip away hair from the wound and apply an appropriate antiseptic. Hydrogen peroxide is a good cleaning agent. Clean wounds by flushing or swabbing with hydrogen peroxide until they appear clean and free of debris. Leave the wound uncovered unless it is constantly irritated by the animal. Severe lacerations that do not appear to be responding to normal care should be examined by a veterinarian.

If the animal continually aggravates the injury it may be necessary to apply an Elizabethan or "Peter Pan" collar to prevent the dog from reaching the wound. These devices are fairly simple to make from a piece of cardboard or an old bucket. Do not be too hasty in applying these collars, since a certain amount of licking and cleaning by the dog is good for the wound and promotes healing.

B. Shock

Shock is a condition whereby the circulatory system disfunctions, resulting in a lack of oxygen being circulated to the brain and other body tissues. This is a very serious condition and should be readily recognized. The animal may or may not be completely prostrate. A certain degree of shock will almost always be present following accidents. Before treating for shock, make sure severe bleeding has been stopped and artificial respiration and external heart massage have been administered, if necessary. The following signs are indications of shock.

1. Glassy-eyed appearance with a vacant stare.

2. Respiration and heart rate increased with respiration being shallow.

3. Rapid and weak pulse that may disappear altogether in advanced cases of shock.

4. Subnormal temperature; rectal temperature may fall below 100 degrees F., and extremities will be cool to the touch.

5. Slow capillary-refill time. To test for this, press your finger firmly against the gums, causing them to turn white beneath your touch. Quickly lift away your finger and note how long it takes for the color to return. Normally this should take only a couple of seconds. If capillary refill time is poor, chances are some degree of shock is present.

Arteries of the Pelvic Limb

Medial View

1 *Femoral artery*
2. *Pelvis*
3. *Femur*
4. *Tibia*

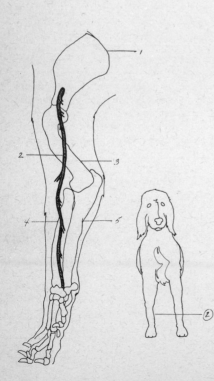

Arteries of the Forelimb
Medial View

1. *Scapula*
2. *Brachial artery*
3. *Humerus*
4. *Radius*
5. *Ulna*

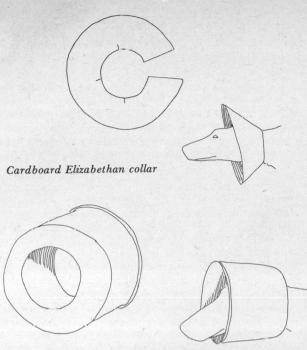

Cardboard Elizabethan collar

Plastic bucket

If you believe the animal is in shock, it is extremely important for him or her to receive professional care immediately since the condition necessitates intravenous fluids and drugs. Due to poor circulation, body heat is lost quickly, so keep the animal warm by wrapping him or her in blankets, coats, newspapers, or anything else that is handy. Lack of oxygen to the brain will result in irreparable damage after only a few minutes, so lower the animal's head in respect to the rest of his or her body to facilitate blood flow. Keep the dog quiet and transport him or her to a veterinarian as soon as possible.

C. Artificial Respiration

When breathing has stopped, artificial respiration must be started at once. Usually, it will be necessary for you to combine artificial respiration (AR) with external heart message (EHM), so become proficient at doing both at once. A veterinarian should be contacted immediately if the animal has a chance of being saved, for it's unlikely you will be able to revive the dog on the spot.

Method I:

First, open the dog's mouth and pull out the tongue so you can see as far back as possible into the pharynx. Check carefully to see if any obstructions are present. Clear away all mucus and blood. Close the dog's mouth. Inhale and cover the front part of the animal's nose and mouth with your own. (With large dogs you will probably only be able to cover the nose; if you wish, you may cover the nose with a handkerchief before beginning.) Make sure your mouth completely seals the nose area. Exhale, forcing air into the animal's lungs. Watch for expansion of the chest.

After the chest has expanded, allow it to return to its original position. The process should be repeated five or six times per minute as long as required.

Method II:

There is a second, less satisfactory method. Place the dog on his or her right side. Using a handkerchief or your bare hand, pull the tongue forward to keep it from obstructing the air passage. Extend the head and neck. Kneel by the animal and place your palms on the chest over the ribs, directly behind the shoulder blade. Press down, compressing the lungs and forcing air out. Quickly release the pressure, allowing the lungs to expand and take in air. Continue the pressure and release at the rate of about twenty times per minute for large dogs and thirty times per minute for small dogs. This process may be long and tedious, but do not give up too soon.

D. External Heart Massage (EHM)

As previously noted, this technique will probably be used in conjunction with AR. External heart massage attempts to maintain circulation after the heart has stopped. It is used when no pulse or heartbeat is discernible, but EHM must be initiated within three to five minutes after the heart has stopped to prevent irreparable brain damage. Place the dog on his or her right side on a firm surface. Depending on the size of the animal, use one or two hands. Place your palms on the chest wall directly behind the elbow. Press firmly and release, at the rate of about seventy times per minute. If your technique is correct, you will be able to feel a pulse with every compression.

It is possible to break an unconscious dog's ribs by external cardiac massage; be sensitive to the size of the dog and visualize what you are physically trying to do. Use only that degree of chest wall pressure necessary to get a good pulse.

Seek immediate veterinary care. (Notice that positioning of the hands for EHM is lower on the chest wall than for AR; see anatomy diagram for positions of the lungs and heart.)

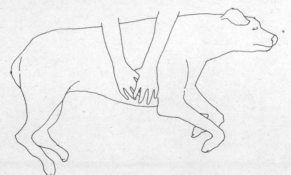

External Heart Massage

E. Checking Vital Signs

Vital signs are indicators of the bodily functions necessary to sustain life. They can be important clues to the health of an animal but, at the same time, an abnormal vital sign should not be taken as an absolute signal of illness. Be familiar with your pet's vital signs. Write them down for reference and comparison when you think he or she might be ill.

An animal's pulse and heartbeat will have the same number of pulsations per minute, but they will be felt in different places. To feel the heartbeat, place your hand on the chest wall as if you were going to give EHM. To feel the pulse, place your fingers on the inside of the thigh, over the femoral artery (see diagram page 202). The pulse of a resting dog will vary, depending on size, breed, disposition, sex, age, and other factors. The normal range is eighty to 120 beats per minute.

The respiration rate of a resting dog is about ten to thirty times per minute. Again, this rate depends on a number of variables; watch the movements of the chest to determine it.

Taking a dog's temperature is a fairly simple procedure. Use a rectal thermometer (oral thermometers break more easily). Make sure the instrument is clean, and shake it down to below 99 degrees F. before using it. Lubricate the tip of the thermometer with petroleum jelly or soap. Lift the dog's tail and insert the thermometer with a firm but gentle push. Leave it in place for two to three minutes if possible; however, readings taken after one minute are usually correct. Remove the thermometer and wipe it off. Roll it between your fingers until you can see a thin mercury column, the end of which will correspond to the temperature. Normal temperature readings will be between 101.0 and 102.5 degrees F.

F. Foreign Bodies

Some injuries are associated with a foreign body being lodged in a cut or body aperture. Whenever feasible, these should be removed; but in some cases removal attempts may cause more damage. Following are examples of foreign-body injuries and treatments.

1. *Fishhooks*. Due to their construction, fishhooks will not fall out on their own once they become lodged in the skin. It will be necessary to push the hook through a second puncture site if it isn't already completely through the skin. Cut off the barbed point, then remove the shaft of the hook through the original point of entry. This process can be very painful, and you may need the assistance of a veterinarian who can administer an anesthetic. Fishhooks are usually dirty and are thus a source of infection. Clean fishhook wounds carefully. Antibiotics may be needed, so consult a veterinarian.

2. *Porcupine quills*. These are very painful and can also cause infection, so be sure to remove the whole quill and clean each resulting hole. To remove the quills, grasp them near the point of entry with a pair of pliers and give a quick pull. Again, be sure the entire quill is removed.

3. *Bones*. Many well-intentioned but misinformed people give dogs bones, which tend to fragment and become lodged in the throat, stomach, or other portions of the digestive tract. Bones that are stuck in the mouth can usually be easily removed unless the animal panics or they are wedged too tightly. Bone fragments lodged further down the digestive tract will require removal by a veterinarian. Do not feed or water an animal suspected of having a foreign object lodged in his or her throat until a veterinarian has made an examination.

4. *Foreign bodies in the eye.* Eye injuries are extremely serious and should be treated as such. If only a small piece of dirt or matter is causing the irritation, the eye may be irrigated with olive oil, boric acid solution, or some other suitable eyewash to remove it. If, however, the eyeball has been scratched or punctured or a large foreign body is embedded in it, keep the animal from rubbing or scratching the eye and take him or her to a veterinarian.

5. *Foreign bodies in the ear.* Dogs tend to get irritants such as foxtails or other grass parts in their ears if they are not checked regularly. Foxtails, if they enter via the feet or trunk, can migrate throughout the entire body, disrupting correct organ function and causing infection. API's Program Coordinator once helped with extensive surgery on a dog that had two foxtails migrating through muscle, liver, and other parts of his body; each operation revealed the foxtail had already moved to a new location, and the animal finally died after four operations.

If a foreign body is lodged in a dog's ear, he or she will shake the head, scratch at the ears, and possibly cry out if you touch the injured ear. Use a flashlight to look into the ear canal. If you can see the object causing the problem, remove it with a pair of tweezers. A dog's ear canal makes a turn part way down and is not straight like the human ear. If the object has worked in too far, a veterinarian's special training and tools will be required to remove it. A dog's ears are very sensitive, so be extra careful when examining them. If a veterinarian is not immediately available, a few drops of mineral oil or vegetable oil in the ear will usually soften a foxtail and ease the pain until help can be obtained.

G. Poisoning

Poisons come in all forms, including certain plants, household items, and chemicals. First aid for poisoning cases will require immediate attention; get veterinary attention as soon as possible. Due to the variety of potential poisons, it will be necessary to be fairly certain of the poison involved, inasmuch as treatments differ accordingly. If at all possible, take the veterinarian a sample of the material involved in its original container.

Poisons may be taken into the body in several ways—through the mouth, the lungs, the skin. Types include corrosives, irritants, narcotics, and convulsants, and, while each has definite symptoms, an irritant may, for example, also be a corrosive. The number and variety of poisons and antidotes prohibit detailed discussion here, but some general comments will be helpful to the first-aider.

If you know what type of poison was ingested, follow the container's directions for treatment. In some cases a general anesthesia will be necessary to subdue and relax the animal before treating, so the lay person will be unable to help. DO NOT try to give solutions or other substances to partially conscious or unconscious animals.

Certain words are used in connection with poisoning cases. A *demulcent* is a substance allaying the irritation of inflamed tissues; milk and raw egg white or olive oil are effective demulcents. An *emetic* is a substance that causes vomiting. A reliable method of inducing emesis is administering by mouth about a teaspoon of three-percent (household) hydrogen peroxide per five pounds body weight. If vomiting does not occur within ten minutes, repeat the dose up to two more times. Another, less effective, way to cause vomiting is to place a teaspoon of salt on the back of the dog's tongue.

1. *Corrosive poisons.* These are poisons that cause burning at points of contact with body tissues; they may be either acid or alkali. Tell-tale signs of ingestion of corrosives include blisters and burns around the mouth. Shock often follows. For alkali poisoning, give large quantities of diluted acid such as five-percent acetic acid or

citric acid or vinegar. Acid poisoning should be treated with a dilute alkali such as baking soda in water, limewater, or chalk. Any burns should be flooded with water, then treated with dilute acid or alkali solution. Subsequently, administer liberal amounts of demulcents. EMETICS SHOULD NOT BE GIVEN.

Examples of corrosive acids are sulphuric acid, hydrochloric acid, and nitric acid. These substances can be found in etching fluids and car batteries. Examples of corrosive alkalis are ammonia and sodium hydroxide, which can be found in cleaning substances such as ammonia and drain cleaners.

2. *Irritant poisons.* These inflame or otherwise irritate the tissues they contact. They may be in the form of decaying plant and animal matter, poisonous plants, or chemicals. If a dog has ingested an irritant poison he or she will probably vomit, since these poisons act as emetics. Again, if the type of poison is known, follow the antidote directions on the container. In other cases, administer a suitable emetic and demulcent, treat for shock if necessary, and get the dog to a veterinarian.

3. *Narcotic and hypnotic (sedative) poisons.* With barbiturates, emetics may be of little value due to the effect of the drugs on the stomach. The animal may also be in respiratory distress, in which case artificial respiration must be started. If the dog is fully conscious, try to administer an emetic. If the emetic works, keep the dog warm and try to get him or her to drink a stimulant such as strong coffee. Do not try to exercise the dog. If the animal is unconscious, a veterinarian will be needed to insert a tube to empty the stomach.

4. *Convulsant poisons.* This type of poisoning is fairly common and is quite serious. Convulsants include strychnine, metaldehyde, and prussic acid. Strychnine is used in poisons for small animal pest control and is the type of poison most often used in malicious poisoning cases. The animal will be restless and twitch at first. Later, the muscles will contract, causing the limbs to stiffen and the neck to arch up and back. The interval between spasms will gradually decrease, and without prompt treatment the animal will die. As soon as poisoning symptoms occur, a general anesthetic is needed prior to treatment, so rush the dog to a veterinarian. The pet of an API staffer, maliciously poisoned, was experiencing respiratory paralysis when found. The owner was able to massage the dog's throat, aiding breathing, while driving to the veterinarian. The latter said this emergency measure was the only thing that saved the dog. Prevention is the best way to ensure against poisoning. Do not let animals run loose.

5. *Rat poisoning.* These compounds can contain various poisons. Animals may be poisoned by eating rat bait, poisoned rat droppings, or a poisoned rat. Most rat poisons are extremely toxic and there is at least one, zinc phosphide, that has no known antidote. Immediate professional help is mandatory if the animal is to be saved.

Other poisons dogs may come in contact with are cyanide, DDT, lead, mercury, nicotine, petroleum products (antifreeze, gasoline, kerosene), detergents, arsenic, aspirin, bleaches. Keep toxic substances out of reach, in animal-proof containers.

In all poisoning cases it is vitally important to obtain immediate veterinary care. Don't forget to take with you what is left of the poison in its original container.

H. Burns

Burns may occur in a number of ways, including fire, electric shock, and chemical burning. Burns of animals, like those of humans, may be of varying degree and cover small or large areas. Treatment and recovery time will vary with the type of burn. In general, it is a good idea to have all burns examined by a veterinarian, since you may not be able to ascertain their severity. Blisters may not occur on animals but a burn may, nevertheless, be very serious.

Burns will remain sterile for some time after they occur if treated properly. All materials used for treating burns must be clean if not sterile; try not to touch the burned area with your hands until they've been thoroughly scrubbed. Use commercial preparations, if available, for burns that are not severe or extensive. If these items are not handy, soak a clean piece of linen in a strong infusion of tea and apply it to the wounded area. The tannic acid in tea helps reduce pain and minimize fluid loss. Note, however, that tannic acid can be toxic to cells and, therefore, should not be used on large areas or in cases of severe burning. Another first-aid treatment is egg albumen—apply a thin covering of albumen to the burn, then cover the area with a sheet of cellophane followed by a light bandage.

Fluid loss is a serious problem related to burns, so the injured animal should be offered fluids. DO NOT try to attend very serious burns yourself. Cover the area with a piece of clean material that will not stick to the wounds, and take the animal to a vet as soon as possible. Slight burns should be cleaned if debris or matted fur is clinging to them. When the burn is caused by a chemical, flush the area with copious amounts of water. If you happen to know that an acid or an alkali was involved, flush the burned area with the appropriate weak acid or alkali solution (see section on corrosive poisons).

As in all traumatic situations, shock will probably be present to some extent, so look for the symptoms and treat accordingly. With electric shock, insulate yourself well before attempting to remove the animal from the shock source. Turn off the current if possible. Use a wooden stick such as a broom handle to pry the animal from the source. Electric shock may cause respiratory arrest, so administer artificial respiration if necessary.

I. Fractures

All breaks or cracks in bones, however large or small, are technically known as fractures. Pain around the area of the fracture, loss of function of the part, unnatural movement, deformity of the limb or other area involved, a shortened limb or swelling are all clues to a fracture. If you suspect one, handle the area as little as possible. Do not try to reduce (place into proper position) broken bones. If necessary, a splint or bandage may be applied to prevent further injury, but be very careful. Any stiff piece of material such as cardboard or wood will do, but materials shaped for the area needing the splint are best. If a wound is present along with the fracture, cover it lightly with a clean piece of material to reduce the chance of infection. Keep the animal quiet and take him or her to a veterinarian, who will be able to determine the extent of the fracture via X rays. Injuries to the spinal column are very serious, for paralysis is always a possibility and is usually present to some degree. BE EXTREMELY CAREFUL when moving a dog with a spinal injury; transport him or her to a veterinarian IMMEDIATELY.

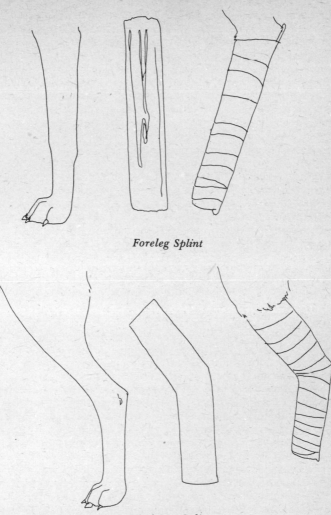

Foreleg Splint

Hind Leg Splint

J. Sprains, Strains, and Dislocations

Sprains are a result of damage to the ligaments and other soft structures surrounding a joint. Strains are caused by tearing or stretching a muscle. In both cases, movement of the joint or muscle involved will be painful. The treatment approach to sprains and strains is: *cold* at the time of injury to reduce inflammation, and *heat*, especially moist heat, during the convalescent period to help mobilize the body's defenses at the affected area. Apply cold compresses at the time of injury; a properly applied pressure bandage will also help by restricting movement and providing support. Heat applications via a heating pad or hot water bottle will speed healing when used twenty-four hours or more after the initial injury and applied two or three times daily for ten to twenty minutes.

Luxations (sprains) result when a bone is displaced from its normal position in a joint. Try to have the animal seen by a veterinarian within twenty-four hours, or permanent contraction of the muscles and other structures involved may occur. When in doubt as to whether a sprain, strain, dislocation, or fracture has occurred, treat the injury as if it were a fracture.

It is generally safe to give aspirin as a pain-killer. However, use it only when signs are not treatable in other ways, for aspirin irritates dogs' stomachs and can cause vomiting and stomach ulcers. The proper dosage is five grains per thirty-five pounds of body weight no more often than every six hours. Give aspirin with a little milk, cottage cheese, or egg to help reduce stomach irritation. (Do not give aspirin to cats.)

K. Insect Bites and Stings

An area of sudden localized or diffuse swelling with pain may mean a bee or wasp sting. If the stinger is still present, remove it with tweezers, being careful not to squeeze the poison bulb on the end. Application of a baking soda paste or undiluted hydrogen peroxide, and cold applications may help reduce pain and swelling of bee stings. For wasp stings, treat with vinegar. Another handy first-aid remedy is to rub wasp stings with moistened tobacco. If the dog has trouble breathing, if the swelling and pain persist for more than a couple of days, or if other complications arise, the animal may be having an allergic reaction and will need veterinary care.

Black widow and brown recluse spider bites should also be treated. Keep the animal quiet, apply cold packs to the area, and transport him or her to a veterinarian.

L. Snakebites

The four poisonous snakes of concern in the United States are the rattlesnake, the copperhead, the water moccasin, and the coral snake. The severity of the bite will depend on its location and the amount of venom injected. Bites on or around the head are most serious. Swelling, puncture marks, pain, weakness, paralysis, and vomiting are all signs of snakebites. Try to identify the type of snake or, at least, be able to describe it. Keep the animal quiet, for movement only speeds circulation of venom. Place an emergency muzzle on the animal before you proceed.

Treatment of a snakebite consists of constriction, incision, and suction. If the bite is on a leg, apply a constricting band—NOT A TOURNIQUET—that is loose enough to slip one finger under. Make linear incisions between the fang marks (for coral snake bites, a wide area of tissue around the marks should be cut away). Apply suction to draw out the venom. If no snakebite kit is available, you can improvise a suction device. Into a small glass, bottle, or canteen, put a twisted piece of paper you've lighted. Quickly place the open end of the container (the flame will go out) over the incisions, leaving it there until it falls off. The suction should be repeated a dozen times, minimum. Work quickly; slap the vessel down on the incisions before any fresh air can enter, or no suction will result. The bitten animal should be taken to a veterinarian as soon as possible. Antibiotics and pain relievers will be needed; antivenom and treatment for shock may be needed.

M. Choking

When an object is caught in the throat, hold the dog and pry open his or her jaws. To keep the animal from biting down, place a piece of cork, toothbrush handle, or other appropriate object between the molars. Look down the throat. If an object is visible try to pull it out, but be very careful. Do not pull too hard or push the object farther down the throat. Work quickly and carefully. If you are able to remove the obstruction, but breathing has stopped, administer AR. If unable to remove the object, RUSH the animal to a veterinarian.

N. Heatstroke

Prevent this situation by not keeping your animal in a hot car or other potentially hot place. Temperatures in closed cars may reach over 100 degrees F. on only mildly hot days. If an animal is overcome by heatstroke, remove him or her from the heat. Immediately immerse the animal in cold water or in some other way cool him or her off; don't worry about chilling. Massage the body. Take the rectal temperature several times to be sure it is normal before stopping emergency proceedings; an initial drop in temperature may be a false indicator.

O. Whelping Problems

Pregnancy in the bitch lasts fifty-eight to sixty-eight days. As with any pregnant mammal, the dog will need extra protein, vitamins, and minerals during part of her pregnancy if she is to produce healthy offspring. Ask your veterinarian to advise you on proper diet, exercise and other special care needed.

Make sure there is a specific area ready for the bitch to use for whelping. Disturb her as little as possible, and don't be alarmed if she acts rather strangely. Loss of appetite, vomiting, shredding of bedding material in the whelping box, and pulling hair from the body are all normal actions for a dog about to give birth. These signs may last up to a day. However, do not hesitate to contact a veterinarian if you feel something is wrong.

The next sign will be straining movements caused by contraction of the abdominal muscles. It may be as long as an hour before the first puppy is born. Once the head and front paws of the puppy appear (usual position), it should only take another ten to fifteen minutes before the rest of it is delivered. If it takes much longer than this you should call a veterinarian. After each puppy is born, the mother should see that the membranes surrounding its nose and mouth are removed; if she does not you must, or the pup will suffocate. The period between puppies will vary from fifteen minutes to two hours but shouldn't be much longer. Make sure all the placentas (afterbirths) are expelled, one for each pup. A retained placenta can cause many problems.

Most delivery problems should be attended by a veterinarian. If a veterinarian is not available and the bitch is having difficulty with a pup, lubricate one of your fingers with petroleum jelly and gently insert it into the dog's vagina. If you can feel the problem try to rectify it (the pup may be incorrectly positioned). Grasp the puppy by the shoulders and GENTLY PULL WITH EACH CONTRACTION. DO NOT pull when the mother is not pushing. Be EXTREMELY careful since rough treatment can damage both the mother and the puppy. If the problem is a retained placenta blocking the birth canal, grasp it with a piece of rough cloth or gauze and free it.

If the puppies are delivered normally but one of them is not breathing, take the pup in your hands or wrap it in a towel, supporting the head so it doesn't swing freely; then move the animal vigorously in a wide arch from about chest to knee level (at this point the pup's nose should be toward the ground). Other methods for removing excess fluids are putting your mouth over the pup's nose and mouth and sucking, or using an infant syringe to remove the fluid. After clearing the airways, rub the pup's chest and body with a rough towel. If the animal still does not start to breathe, place your mouth over its nose and mouth and blow gently until you see the chest expand; remove your mouth to let the pup exhale, then repeat. Have both the mother and pups examined by a veterinarian within a few days after birth to make sure all is well.

Orphan pups require special attention. A *very* warm environment and a proper diet and feeding schedule are imperative if they are to survive. Commercial bitch's milk substitutes are on the market and should be used whenever they are available. Plain cow's milk will not provide all the required nutrients, so do not use it by itself;

in addition, cow's milk (whole, nonfat, evaporated, etc.) causes diarrhea in most dogs and cats. Ralston-Purina suggests the following homemade formulas if a commercial substitute is not available:

A. Put twenty grams Purina Puppy Chow and eighty grams water in a blender and macerate into a gruel that can be fed by bottle, spoon or gastric intubation.

B. Blend: 1 cup milk
          3 egg yolks (no albumen)
          1 tablespoon corn oil
          1 drop high-quality multiple vitamins (liquid)
          Pinch of salt

Mix uniformly and warm to 95-100 degrees F. for puppies less than two weeks of age. Feed with a spoon, dropper, bottle, or gastric intubation. Keep unused formula refrigerated between feedings.

When hand-raising pups it will be necessary for you to stimulate excretion. Gently massage the excretory areas after each feeding; afterward, carefully clean each puppy. Don't feed formula too fast, and DO NOT turn a puppy on its back to feed. Three equally spaced feedings a day, minimum, are recommended for most puppies. Tube and hand-feeding can generally be terminated by the third or fourth week.

NOTE: With the pet population explosion as serious as it is, I suggest you have your pet neutered or spayed *before its first heat period*. These operations do not cause personality changes, or obesity if a proper diet and exercise routine are followed. There are often local organizations that will assist with the cost of the operation if you cannot afford it. Unwanted puppies and kittens usually die terrible deaths, so exercise your better judgment before breeding your pets or letting them run loose.

General Signs of Illness

Many times the key to whether or not an animal will recover from an illness or injury depends on how soon it is diagnosed; thus, it is very important to know your pet's behavior patterns. Each animal, of course, is an individual, but there are general signs that indicate something's amiss, among them:

Abnormal vital signs
Lack of appetite
Obvious anatomical abnormalities
Unusual discharges from body orifices
Abnormal mucous membrane coloring
   (e.g., pale gums)
Shivering (by itself, may only indicate
   nervousness or fear)
Difficult swallowing
Weakness
Abortion
Lameness
Sneezing
Abnormal lumps on the body
Slow capillary refill time
Listlessness
Paralysis
Abnormal eye appearance
Distended stomach
Foul smell exuding from body orifices
Vomiting
Constipation
Diarrhea
Raw areas
Weight loss
Coughing

Pilling a large dog

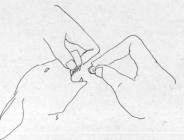

Pilling a small dog

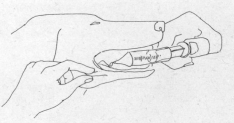

Liquid medication in cheek pouch

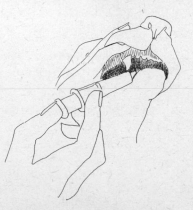

Liquid medication into mouth

Any of the above signs does not necessarily indicate illness when taken by itself but may in conjunction with other symptoms. When in doubt, call a veterinarian. The latter will also be interested in when signs of illness appeared and their progression — continuous, more frequent, more severe.

Miscellaneous Problems and Useful Information

Dogs may occasionally pick up ticks. To remove a tick, grasp it as closely as possible to its point of attachment and pull — do not twist. Do not be alarmed if the mouth parts of the tick are left in the wound, but be sure to watch for signs of infection. Do not try to burn ticks off or soak them with irritants such as gasoline. If you feel it necessary to apply anything, use a concentrated tick solution or put fingernail polish remover on the tick (not on the skin surrounding it).

Have a good dog brush and use it. Your dog can't be blamed for shedding if he or she is not groomed frequently. Familiarize your animal with grooming early so he or she will not fight you. Don't be afraid to cut off matted fur — it will grow back.

Dogs occasionally tangle with skunks. If your dog has been on the receiving end in such an encounter, bathe him or her well with soap and water. Follow this with a tomato juice rinse. Pour the juice on and let it sit for ten minutes before rinsing. If tomato juice is not available, a dog (not a cat) may be rinsed with a *dilute* solution of ammonia; keep it out of the animal's eyes and rinse it off well.

Removing tar, paint, and oil can be a problem. UNDER NO CIRCUMSTANCES should gasoline, kerosene, paint remover, or other strong substances be used on your pet. Small patches of tar or paint can be clipped off. An alternative is to soak the area in vegetable, mineral, or baby oil for about twenty-four hours, then wash it off with soap and water. For small patches of oil, sprinkle with cornstarch, allow it to soak up the oil, then brush it out.

Animals as well as humans are susceptible to numerous diseases and afflictions. Proper vaccination programs will aid in protecting animals against some communicable diseases. In the case of the dog, vaccinations for rabies, distemper, hepatitis, and leptospirosis should be administered on a regular schedule. Additionally, most cities require dogs to be licensed (many areas allow a discount of up to fifty percent of the license fee for animals that have been neutered).

Dogs should also be checked regularly for parasites. Take a fresh fecal sample to your veterinarian, who can analyze it and provide you with the correct kinds and quantities of antiparasite medication. The use of a flea collar or powder will help control external parasites such as fleas and ticks, but the animal's sleeping area must also be flea-free for these medications to work. Some dogs are sensitive to the compounds found in flea collars and tags and should not wear them; follow directions on the package and watch for irritation.

Do not allow your animals to run free unattended. Dogs running loose sometimes band together and destroy livestock, wildlife, or plant life. Even very docile dogs can become bold and destructive in the company of others. In some places it is legal for a person to shoot animals found molesting livestock or other personal property. Additionally, there is the chance that free-running animals will be poisoned, stolen, or hit by cars. Owners may even find themselves involved in a lawsuit as a result of negligence.

Sick animals will often need to be given pills or liquid medication. There are several useful techniques for administering treatments (see illustrations). Depending on the type of medication, it may be possible to give it to the animal in his or her food. Ask the veterinarian about this and for any special instructions.

When you bring an animal to a veterinarian, you should tell him or her anything that will help in diagnosis and treatment. Don't be afraid to ask questions or to relay

214

information, even that which may be embarrassing—your animal's life can depend on it.

Most important, be a responsible pet owner. Respect other people's feelings and do not be a nuisance. If you walk your dog in the park or some other public place, take along a scoop and a small plastic bag and pick up any feces your dog leaves.

If you find you are unable to keep your pet any longer, it is advisable to have him or her put to sleep by a veterinarian. Homes for mature dogs are few and far between, even for purebred dogs. If you place an advertisement in a local paper, especially for free animals, BEWARE. Such notices are drawing cards for dog dealers who claim they'll give the animal a good home but, in reality, will sell him or her to a research laboratory. If you have a choice, don't take your pet to an animal shelter either. These are already overcrowded, and an animal may simply undergo fright and stress before being put to sleep in a decompression chamber or sold to a research laboratory—neither a pleasant alternative.

Above all, do not abandon your animal. Domestic animals left on their own are usually unable to feed themselves, and chances are they will be hit by a car, shot, or starve to death.

THE CAT

Anatomy of the Cat

The anatomy of the cat differs from that of the dog in many ways, yet similarities between the two make it easy to identify analogous structures. Study the following diagrams and review the anatomy of the dog if necessary. Note differences and similarities between the two animals.

Approaching an Injured Cat

Catching an injured cat will probably be one of the most difficult aspects of the animal's first-aid treatment. If the cat is still able to move around fairly well, he or she will probably run away. Try to follow until you have an opportunity to catch the cat; if you are near home, attempt to lure him or her inside.

Restraining an Injured Cat

Knowing how to properly control a panicky cat will save you and the animal a lot of pain and frustration. The cat's defenses include retractable claws and a set of sharp, needlelike teeth. Wear a pair of heavy canvas gloves if possible when handling an injured cat. A blanket that has been folded several times and wrapped around a cat with only his or her head showing allows maximum protection for both of you. Be gentle and use the minimum amount of force necessary to restrain the animal. Sometimes, just grasping a cat by the scruff of the neck will cause him or her to succumb to your control; however, if you are not aware of the extent of the cat's injuries, handling in this manner may only worsen them. Two people can easily restrain a cat, but this will usually cause undue stress; try restraining him or her by yourself first.

It may be necessary to use a muzzle to keep the cat from biting you while you proceed with treatment. A muzzle for a cat (see illustration) is similar to that used on snub-nosed dogs. A roll of gauze, handkerchief, or other strip of cloth can be fashioned into a muzzle. Be sure it is tight enough and properly positioned before proceeding.

Transporting the Injured Cat

After catching and suitably restraining the cat, it will be necessary to transport him or her to the veterinarian. Most cats do not particularly like riding in cars. If you

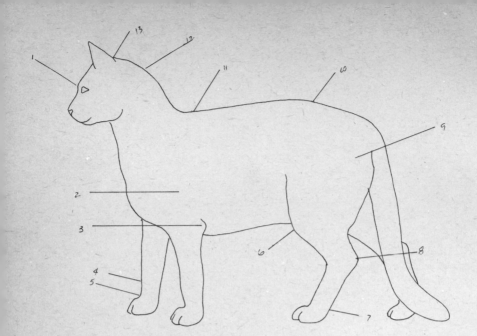

1. Forehead
2. Shoulder
3. Elbow
4. Carpus
5. Metacarpus
6. Stifle
7. Metatarsus

8. Hock
9. Rump
10. Back
11. Withers
12. Nape of neck
13. Occiput

Organs

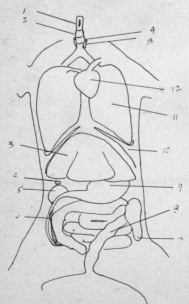

1. Larynx
2. Trachea
3. Liver
4. Adrenal gland
5. Kidney
6. Pancreas
7. Spleen
8. Rectum
9. Stomach
10. Diaphragm
11. Lungs
12. Heart
13. Thyroid gland
14. Parathyroid gland

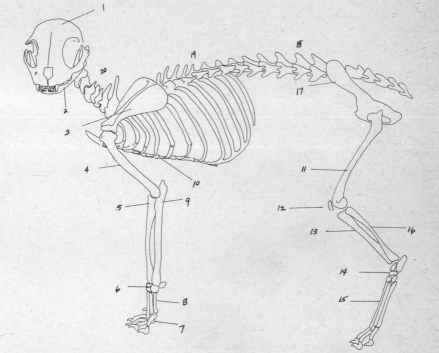

Skeleton

1. Skull	11. Femur
2. Mandible	12. Patella
3. Scapula	13. Tibia
4. Humerus	14. Tarsals
5. Radius	15. Metatarsals
6. Carpals	16. Fibula
7. Phalanges	17. Pelvis
8. Metacarpals	18. Lumbar vertebrae
9. Ulna	19. Thoracic vertebrae
10. Sternum	20. Cervical vertebrae

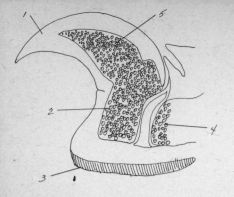

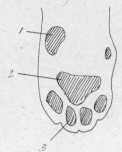

Cross Section of Claw

1. Claw
2. Third phalanx (bone)
3. Pad
4. Second phalanx (bone)
5. Ungual process dermis (quick)

Forepaw

1. Carpal pad
2. Metacarpal pad
3. Digital pad

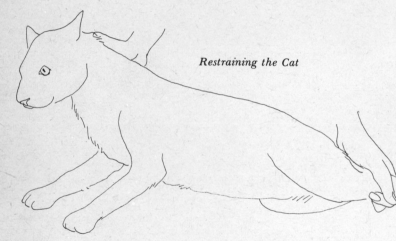

Restraining the Cat

1. Grasping scruff (nape) and hind legs
2. Holding front and hind legs

3. Grasping scruff

Muzzling the Cat

need to go only a short distance, carry the animal. For longer distances you will need a carrier. There are many commercially made cat carriers on the market, usually constructed of fiberglass or wicker with ventilation holes. You can also use a plain cardboard box, picnic basket, or other closed container, provided plenty of fresh air is available to the victim. Other suitable carriers include pillowcases, laundry bags, or duffle bags with just the animal's head exposed. How you decide to transport the cat will depend on the animal's temperament. A calm, docile cat can be transported by just about any of the methods mentioned, while an excited cat should be carried in a manner that will not panic him or her further, usually in a box or cat carrier.

Emergency Situations and Procedures

A. Hemorrhage Control and Care of Wounds

The types of bleeding—arterial, venous, capillary, and mixed—have been discussed in the section on hemorrhage control for the dog. They are the same for the cat. Treatment for profuse bleeding also follows the same courses as for the dog. First try direct pressure, then use one of the three pressure points (brachial, femoral, or coccygeal arteries). As a LAST RESORT, use a tourniquet. Follow the directions given on pages 198 through 201 for specifics concerning these methods.

If the cut is a small one, allow the cat to lick and cleanse it. If the cat is a long-haired animal, trim away the fur around the cut to prevent its becoming matted into the wound. Small cuts may be cleaned with soap and water or hydrogen peroxide and left for the cat to care for. Do check to make sure healing is taking place and infection isn't setting in.

If the cut is bleeding profusely or is inaccessible to the cat (face, back of the neck), treat it yourself, then take the animal to a veterinarian. Most gaping wounds will require suturing and should be attended by a veterinarian as soon as possible.

Wounds that are constantly aggravated by the cat should be protected. An Elizabethan (see drawings following) collar may be used in such cases. Some cats cannot eat or drink while wearing a collar of this sort, so be sure to take it off to allow for these activities.

B. Shock

Signs of shock are the same as those noted on page 201 for the dog. Be sure to check pulse, respiration, capillary refill time and temperature. Keep the animal warm and get him or her to a veterinarian immediately. Always suspect shock after trauma of any kind, but attend to profuse bleeding first.

C. Artificial Respiration

If respiration has ceased by the time you reach the cat, begin artificial respiration (AR) immediately. AR will follow the same basic course as it did for the dog. Check the mouth and throat for obstructions. Close the cat's mouth. Cover the muzzle with your mouth, making a tight seal. Exhale into the cat's nose and watch for chest expansion. Allow the chest to deflate. Repeat this process at the rate of ten to twelve times per minute. For details, reread the section on artificial respiration for the dog.

The mechanical method of chest compression may also be used. Using the flat of the hand, compress the chest, then release, at the rate of ten to twelve times per minute. Do not give up too soon. The mouth-to-muzzle method is, however, more efficient.

D. External Heart Massage

It will probably be necessary for you to perform this procedure along with artificial respiration, so practice doing both. Start external heart massage immediately after automatic heartbeat ceases, or irreparable brain damage will occur.

Place the cat on his or her right side on a firm surface. Place one hand (use your fingers) under the cat's body and the other hand above the cat's body, so that the heart area is enclosed (see illustration). Using both hands, compress this region, then release your grip. Repeat this procedure at the rate of about seventy times per minute. If you are applying EHM properly, you should be able to feel a pulse with each compression. Immediate veterinary care will be needed if the animal is to live. If possible, have someone drive you to the veterinarian while you attempt EHM. With small cats, using one hand may be sufficient.

E. Taking Vital Signs

Be familiar with procedures for taking vital signs. Following the same basic directions as given for the dog, you should have no trouble. Early training and handling of your cat will make it easy to monitor these important body functions.

Placing your hand over the heart (on the chest wall behind the point of the elbow—see illustration) will allow you to detect the heartbeat; another method is to wrap one hand around the lower chest as if you were going to perform one-handed

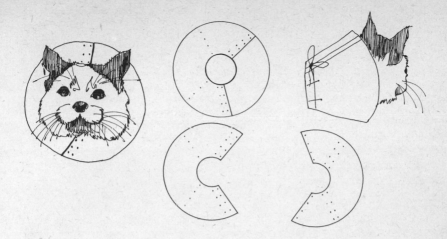

Devices to Prevent Self-Injury

An Elizabethan collar (left) may be improvised from thin plywood or sturdy card-board; or, a head funnel (right) can be fashioned from heavy cardboard or plastic. Some padding, such as sheet cotton, should be secured to that portion of the collar touching the neck, to prevent irritation.

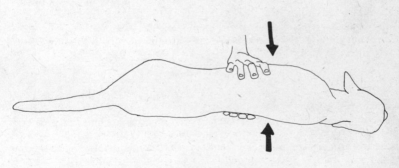

External Heart Massage

EHM. Do not use your thumb as a guide to the number of beats, since you might be counting your own pulse. The femoral artery is the best place to check the pulse. The normal pulse range is 110 to 130 per minute. This, of course, can vary according to sex, age, and activity.

Check respiration by watching movement of the chest. Normal respiration rates range from twenty to thirty breaths per minute.

Use a rectal thermometer to take your cat's temperature. Restrain the cat by using your forearm to press his or her body against yours. Hold up the tail and gently roll the thermometer to insert it. Depending on the size of the cat, the thermometer should be inserted about one or one and one-half inches into the rectum. Leave it in place for two minutes if possible, but a minimum of one minute. Normal temperatures range from 101.0 to 102.5 degrees F.

F. Foreign Bodies

Refer to the previous section on dogs; much of the first aid required is similar.

1. *Fishhooks, porcupine quills, bones.* See page 205.
2. *Foreign bodies in the eye.* Under a good light thoroughly examine the eye for ir-regularities or debris (see illustration). Compare the affected eye with the unaffected eye. If you can see the problem and the injury is fairly minor, remove the source of the irritation and irrigate the eye. For scratches or cuts on the eyeball (or when you suspect their existence), consult a veterinarian immediately. If problems persist after first aid has been rendered, consult a veterinarian.
3. *Foreign bodies in the ear.* Cats tend not to have the same problem with foreign objects in their ears as dogs do. They do, however, have more of a problem with irritation from ear mites. If an animal seems to have an ear problem, check for foreign objects and ear mites. If the problem is the latter, obtain proper medication and use it according to directions. If you cannot tell what the problem is, consult a veterinarian. Check the following "miscellaneous information" section for proper methods of cleaning and medicating the ear.

G. Poisoning

If you are fairly sure the poison involved was *not* a corrosive (see dog section), administer an emetic. Suitable emetics for cats are: one teaspoon of hydrogen peroxide given orally, to be repeated in ten to fifteen minutes if there is no result; or, one-fourth teaspoon of salt placed on the back of the tongue. Again, do *not* give emetics or any other substances to partially conscious or unconscious animals. Animals show-

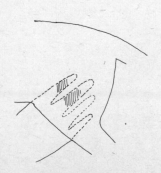

Feeling the Pulse

Feeling the Heart Beat

Restraint While Taking Temperature

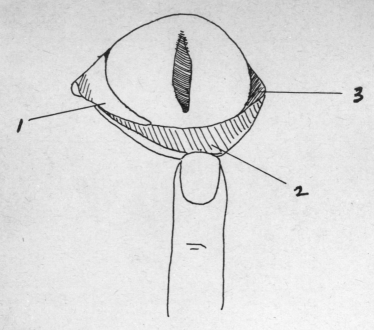

Examining the Eye

1. *Swollen third eyelid*
2. *Conjunctiva (forms sac when released)*
3. *Inflamed sclera*

ing signs of poisoning should be rushed to a veterinarian for treatment. Avoid using rat poisons around cats; they may eat the poison or the poisoned rodents. If you know what poison was ingested, take a sample of it in its original container to the veterinarian. Cats may also chew on houseplants, so be sure you have only nontoxic varieties. Check the section on dogs for treatment of specific poisoning cases, but be aware the emetic dosages for cats are lower than those for dogs.

H. Burns

See the section on dogs, pages 207 and 208, for information on burn treatment. Do not underestimate the severity of a burn. Blisters will not always appear and fur may remain attached even if a burn is rather severe. Have all burns checked by a veterinarian when possible. Remember to treat for shock if necessary.

I. Fractures

Usually, splinting a broken leg will cause you more trouble and the cat more pain than is necessary. However, if there is obvious danger in leaving a fractured limb unattended, apply a splint. Use any piece of stiff material to hold the limb in place, and secure it above and below the fracture site with tape, a handkerchief, or other suitable material. Transport the animal to a veterinarian as soon as possible. If splinting is unnecessary, just keep the animal still until he or she can be seen by a veterinarian. Refer to the section on dogs, page 208 for specific splinting and treatment directions.

J. Sprains, Strains, Dislocations

See the section on treatment for the dog. One big difference: DO NOT GIVE ASPIRIN TO CATS — it may poison them. Two aspirin tablets can be enough to kill an adult cat.

K. Insect Bites and Stings

See section on dogs, page 209. Be sure to watch for allergic reactions.

L. Snakebites

See pages 209 and 210.

M. Choking

See page 210.

N. Heatstroke

If you believe an animal is suffering from heatstroke, immediately cool him or her by immersing in, or spraying with, cold water. Monitor the animal's temperature to be sure recovery is complete; an initial drop in temperature may be a false alarm, so check several times before stopping emergency procedures. If the temperature has not been significantly reduced after twenty minutes administer a cold-water enema, but disregard rectal temperature readings after you give the enema. Have the animal checked by a veterinarian.

O. Queening (Delivery) Problems

The normal length of pregnancy in cats is fifty-six to sixty-five days. Have your cat examined by a veterinarian several times during her pregnancy to be sure everything is normal; have the veterinarian brief you on extra nutrient requirements and normal delivery procedures. Keep in contact with him or her in the event of a difficult delivery. BE FAMILIAR WITH NORMAL QUEENING PROCESSES, so you can spot trouble early.

When the cat begins to give birth, disturb her as little as possible. Render assistance only if it is required; otherwise, let the mother take care of things. It is a good idea to prepare a special area for the animal to give birth in and have her accustomed to it well before her due date. Reread the section on the care of the bitch during whelping so you will have a general idea of problems that may occur in the cat. A similar corrective procedure will work on the cat and kitten. For any kittens that are not breathing, follow the treatment prescribed for puppies. All animals require extra nourishment when lactating (giving milk), so provide an adequate diet, supplemented if necessary. Be sure to have the mother cat and kittens checked by a veterinarian soon after birth.

If you are left with orphaned kittens, remember that plain cow's milk alone is a dangerous milk replacer because it often causes severe diarrhea. Ideally, a commercial feline milk substitute, available in most pet stores, should be obtained and prepared according to directions (one trade name is Esbilac). If a commercial substitute is not available, *The Well Cat Book* recommends use of one of the following homemade formulas:

A. 26.5 ounces whole cow's milk
6.5 ounces cream (12% fat)
1 egg yolk
6 grams bone meal
4 grams citric acid
2,000 IU Vitamin A
500 IU Vitamin D

B. 16 ounces whole cow's milk
1 teaspoon corn syrup
1 egg yolk
Pinch of salt
Vitamin-mineral supplement
(according to vitamin package
or veterinarian's directions)

Formulas should be warmed to body temperature before being fed to the kittens; feed at least every six to eight hours. A baby bottle with a proportionately sized nipple or an eyedropper is a good formula dispenser. Stimulate excretion after each feeding by gently massaging the area around the excretory orifices. Do not feed formula too fast, and do not feed the kittens while they're on their backs. Make sure they are kept warm at all times, especially during feeding; baby animals require warmer environments than adults.

NOTE: Again, I urge you to carefully consider the fate of any kittens you bring into the world. There are many, many more kittens than there are good homes for them. Do not be swayed by old wives' tales stating it's best if your cat has one litter before being spayed. If you cannot afford the entire cost of the operation, consult your local humane society for the name of a low-cost spay program near you.

General Signs Of Illness
Although it is difficult to watch a cat as closely as a dog, try to identify normal behavior in your cat. Early detection of diseases and other problems may sometimes mean the difference between life and death for your pet. Know your animal's daily routine. The symptoms of illness listed on pages 211-213 of the dog-care section apply to the cat also. Once again, the list is by no means complete — you are the only one who can spot trouble early, so KNOW YOUR ANIMAL.

Miscellaneous Information
Part of a cat's natural grooming behavior includes scratching on rough materials. This behavior helps remove old and worn-out claws. If a cat is not trained early, you may later find your furniture and drapes in shreds. Scratching posts are available commercially, or can be easily built from a piece of fence-post lumber and a section of old carpeting. Cover the lumber with the carpeting and make a base so the post will stand by itself. Place the scratching post by the cat's sleeping area and praise him or her for using it; scold your pet when he or she uses anything but the scratching post. If training is started early, there should be no problem.

Cats occasionally get tar or paint in their fur or get sprayed by a skunk. See page 212 for specifics on tackling these problems.

All animals are more susceptible to some diseases than others. In many cases preventive disease control measures exist in the form of vaccination programs. Cats should be vaccinated against rabies and feline distemper (panleukopenia). A new vaccination for feline rhinotracheitis, a common upper respiratory tract infection in cats, was introduced a couple of years ago; consult your veterinarian about the benefits and disadvantages of this vaccine. Remember to follow a regular vaccination program, since most shots are effective for only a certain amount of time.

Although most areas do not require licensing of cats, it is advisable to have an identification tag on your cat; many flexible, stretch collars are available. If you do not want your cat to wear a collar and tag, have him or her tattooed for identification. This process is virtually painless when performed correctly and will allow for permanent identification of your pet.

Although cats are more independent and wander farther than dogs, it is best to train your cat from an early age to either stay inside unless attended by you or to stay

Pilling a Cat

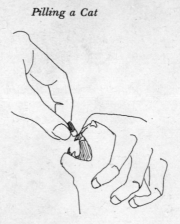

Tip the cat's head back and up.

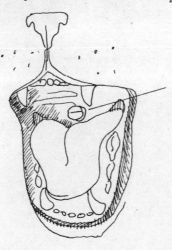

Drop the pill back in the mouth and close the mouth quickly.

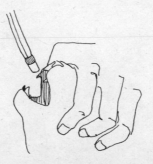

If the pill isn't swallowed, quickly but gently push it down with the eraser end of a pencil, hold the cat's mouth closed for a moment, and gently stroke the throat.

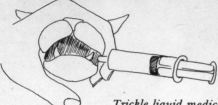

Trickle liquid medication into the back of the mouth.

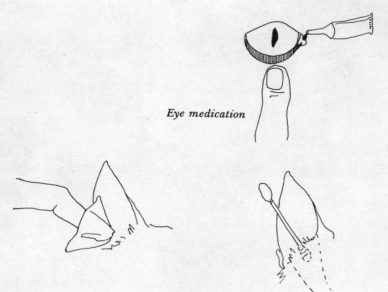

Eye medication

Clean the ear with a cloth (left) or a cotton swab (right).

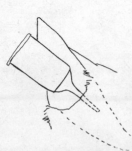

Ear medication

Massage

in your yard. At the very least, confine your cat during breeding season. Chances of your pet being hit by a car, poisoned, or shot are greatly increased if he or she is allowed to roam at will. Lawsuits may also be traced to you if damages are caused by your animal in direct or indirect ways.

In addition to following a regular vaccination program, your cat may need to be treated for internal parasites. Several commercial worming preparations are on the market, but read the directions to determine what kind of parasites they will control; many products cannot get rid of tough internal parasites. The best idea is to consult your veterinarian. From analyzing a fresh fecal sample, your vet can prescribe the correct kind and amount of medicine for your pet. In addition, check for external parasites such as fleas, ticks, and mites; obtain necessary medication for their control. The most common tapeworm is transmitted by eating a flea that contains a tapeworm egg.

The accompanying illustrations indicate the proper way to administer pills, liquids, ear medication, and eye preparations. Follow the directions on the bottle or package and ask your veterinarian if any special care is necessary while your pet is on medication.

If it is impossible for you to continue to keep your pet, take him or her to a veterinarian to be disposed of. Avoid giving animals away to just anyone, placing them in shelters, or abandoning them. Have a heart and have the animal put to sleep painlessly.

THE HORSE

Anatomy of the Horse
The following anatomical diagrams will help familiarize you with the horse anatomy. Study these diagrams as you have those for the dog and cat.

Approaching, Catching, and Restraining the Injured Horse
An injured and frightened horse is, due to his or her size, a very difficult animal to work with. Time permitting, professional help should be obtained before handling a frenzied horse. If the injuries are slight or immediate care is needed, attend to the animal yourself. Your job will be considerably easier if you and the horse are familiar with each other and he or she is in a small, confined area. If the horse is in a large pasture, attempt to lure him or her into a smaller enclosure before trying to catch the animal. If the horse is not too severely injured or scared and he or she will come to you for a bucket of grain or other treat, it will be a relatively simple matter to place a rope around the neck. Then lead the animal to a stall or other suitable place for treatment.

Frightened animals are only alarmed further by crowds, so have only one or two people approach the horse if he or she will not come to you. Do not try tricks or surprises; approach in full view. Talk to the horse in a quiet, relaxed manner. Do not make any sudden movements or loud noises. Offer a treat and cautiously touch his or her neck. Keep the rope or halter you plan to use out of sight until the horse is distracted or cannot see it; then inch it up and over his or her neck while you stand to one side. DO NOT use a slip-knot on the rope—the horse may panic, pull back, and choke. After a rope is around the animal's neck, try to replace it with a halter, putting the halter on before removing the rope.

If injuries are severe and the horse resists handling, you will probably need a tranquilizer or anesthetics to subdue him or her. Ideally, a veterinarian should administer any drugs necessary (at least initially); indeed, only a few drugs of this nature are available to the layman. Some pellet tranquilizing drugs are available and may be given in feed, but follow directions carefully.

229

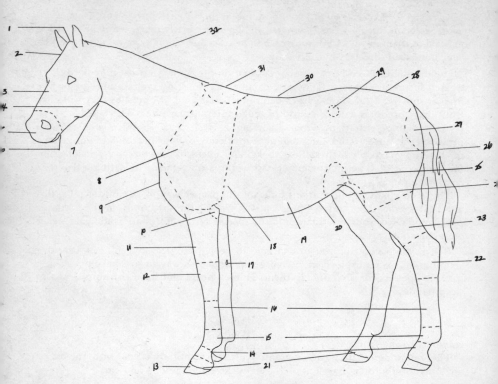

1. Poll
2. Forehead
3. Face
4. Cheek
5. Muzzle
6. Chin groove
7. Throat latch
8. Shoulder
9. Point of shoulder
10. Elbow
11. Forearm
12. Knee
13. Hoof
14. Pastern
15. Fetlock joint
16. Cannon
17. Chestnut
18. Heart girth
19. Barrel
20. Abdomen
21. Coronet
22. Hock
23. Gaskin or second thigh
24. Stifle
25. Flank
26. Thigh
27. Buttock
28. Rump or croup
29. Point of hip
30. Back
31. Withers
32. Crest

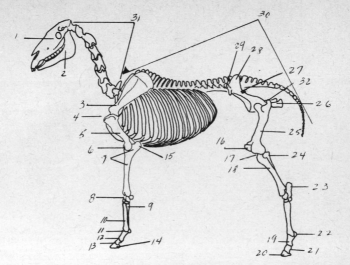

Skeleton

1. Skull
2. Mandible
3. Scapula (shoulder blade)
4. Shoulder joint
5. Humerus (arm)
6. Elbow joint
7. Radius and ulna (forearm)
8. Carpal joint (knee)
9. Fourth metacarpal (outside splint bone)
10. Third metacarpal (cannon bone)
11. Fetlock joint
12. Pastern joint
13. Coffin joint
14. Coffin bone
15. Point of elbow
16. Patella (knee cap)
17. Stifle joint
18. Tibia
19. Long pastern bone
20. Coffin bone
21. Short pastern bone
22. Proximal sesamoid bones
23. Tarsal joint (hock)
24. Fibula
25. Femur (thigh)
26. Point of buttock
27. Pelvis
28. Point of croup
29. Point of hip
30. Spinous process
31. Cervical vertebrae
32. Hip joint

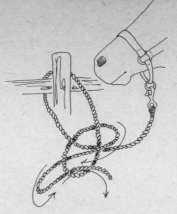

Slipknots may be used to tie a horse to a fence or hitching post. Be sure the post is sturdy.

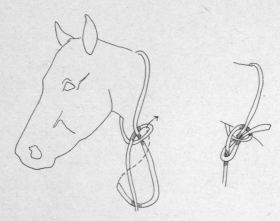

NEVER use a slipknot around a horse's neck. A bowline is easy to tie and safe.

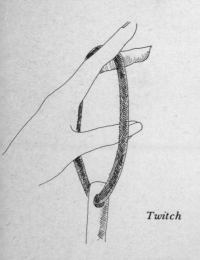

Twitch

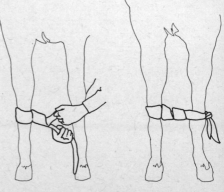

Hobble

Banding is placed around first leg and twisted twice, then second leg is enclosed and material is tied.

In the absence of any drugs, two other methods of restraining an uncooperative horse are available. It's possible these may cause fear or pain, but in some cases their use is imperative. The first method is to use a twitch, a device made of a length of wood or metal to which is attached a loop of rope or light chain. The twitch must be placed quickly and efficiently on the horse's nose before the animal learns evasive actions. Put your left hand through the loop of the twitch and firmly grasp the horse's nose, while holding the halter with the right hand. When your left hand has the horse under control, slide the twitch loop up over the left hand onto his or her nose. Then rotate the twitch handle toward the horse's nose, tightening it at the same time. Do not stand directly in front of the horse, and do not let go of the handle should the horse toss his or her head. To prevent the nose from becoming numb, loosen and retighten the twitch regularly. After removing the twitch, gently massage the nose to ensure normal circulation and to calm the horse.

The second restraining method is manipulation of the ears. By firmly but gently grasping the ear, a horse may be subdued for a short time. After releasing them, gently caress the ears and head to reassure the horse and prevent his or her becoming head-shy. Contact a veterinarian if long-term restraint is necessary. (Another form of restraint is throwing the horse, but I do not recommend that a novice try this—it may cause more damage to the horse and possible injury to the human.)

If you wish a horse to stand still, another simple procedure may do. If his or her legs are not injured, simply hold up one front leg. It may be possible to tie one leg up, but do not do this unless it's absolutely necessary. While the animal is being attended, speak gently and distract him or her by vigorously rubbing the animal's neck.

Hobbles are another device useful when treating a horse if he or she is apt to kick or strike out. See illustrations for proper application procedures. Use soft, flexible materials that will not cut into the horse's legs.

Transporting the Injured Horse

If the horse is not too severely injured, he or she may be either walked—not ridden—to the veterinarian if it is not far, or taken in a trailer. Trailers specially constructed for horses are best, but other livestock trailers may be used. Be sure the horse is securely tied in the trailer and all objects on which he or she may be injured are removed. NEVER transport a horse in a completely enclosed, multipurpose trailer—in which the animal may suffocate—or in the bed of a pickup.

Frightened, injured horses can be hard to load, even if they normally create no problems. Try regular loading procedures first. Place a favorite treat in the trailer and try to coax the horse in. Do not get in the trailer directly in front of the horse unless there is an escape route; stand to one side, passing the lead rope through to the outside of the trailer. If all efforts fail, pass a long length of rope behind the horse, slowly and gently tightening it around the horse's buttocks. While one person coaxes and pulls on the lead, the other person should tighten the rope. Eventually, you should be able to load the horse; keep trying, and BE PATIENT.

Emergency Situations and Procedures

A. Hemorrhage Control and Wounds

Hemorrhage control in horses consists of applying either a pressure bandage or direct pressure to the site of bleeding. Under no circumstances should a tourniquet be applied. A dog or cat can manage with three legs, but a horse cannot.

The severity of the wound depends, in part, on its location. Wounds of the face, neck, and body are generally less dangerous than wounds of the legs. Cuts on or near joints are particularly severe; if improperly cared for, they can result in impaired flexibility of the joint.

Wounds of the face, neck, and body, if deep and bleeding profusely, should be attended by a veterinarian; these will probably need suturing to prevent scarring. First, stop the bleeding as previously directed, using a clean gauze pad, a towel, or other suitable material. If the wound is gaping and flaps of skin have been pushed away from the cut, try to replace them. To minimize scar tissue formation, professional help *must* be obtained early. A veterinarian will usually treat severe wounds with antibiotics and a tetanus booster.

Wounds on the legs almost always require veterinary services. Even minor ones require greater care than more severe wounds on the rest of the body. Leg wounds have a tendency to produce more scar tissue, sometimes called "proud flesh" or granulation tissue; too much of this tissue can restrict movement. As mentioned earlier, injuries to the joints are especially worrisome, for joints can become easily infected. Disruption of their normal functioning may result in permanent lameness. CONSULT A VETERINARIAN EARLY. Stop bleeding by applying a secure wrap on the leg. Keep the horse quiet until the veterinarian arrives.

Since horses are kept in surroundings conducive to germ proliferation, extra care must be taken to ensure the cleanliness of a wound during healing. Most wounds will require AT LEAST daily care. Follow the directions the attending veterinarian gives you to ensure complete recovery; arrange for a follow-up visit if he or she feels it's necessary.

Minor wounds and abrasions should be treated with care. Wash them with a mild disinfectant and apply an appropriate medication to help keep flies away. Daily care and cleanliness are essential.

It may be necessary to fit your horse with a device that will prevent him or her from irritating the wound(s). A "cradle" consists of a frame of sticks of wood or other material placed around the neck to prevent abuse to a wounded limb. A "side-stick" is a stick attached to the horse's halter and the belly strap (surcingle) that prevents the horse from turning his or her head.

B. Shock

Shock in horses is very serious. Check for shock by taking rectal temperature (lower than normal if shock is present), looking at mucous membranes, and checking the appearance of the eyes (glossy in appearance with a blank stare if shock is present). CALL A VETERINARIAN IMMEDIATELY; stress the urgency of the situation and request that someone come immediately. Meanwhile, keep the horse warm.

C. Artificial Respiration

This is best handled by a veterinarian with an endotracheal tube, but artificial respiration can be given mechanically. Stand at the back of the horse. Reach across his or her body and grab the rib cage (see anatomy section). Pull up on the rib cage, thereby expanding the lungs. Release your hold quickly and press forward, causing expulsion of the air. Since the stomach of the horse is located farther back, there is no need to worry about causing regurgitation. Repeat this process rhythmically.

D. External Heart Massage

Unlike the dog and the cat, horses in the field can't be given EHM. The heart is located under the leg, and it's not possible to put pressure on the sternum (breastbone) in order to stimulate the heart.

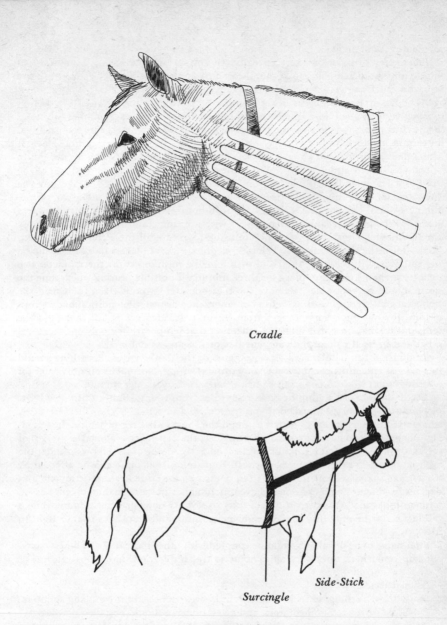

Cradle

Surcingle

Side-Stick

Side-Stick

E. Taking Vital Signs

Emergency situations make you realize the importance of having a well-trained horse, for first-aid care is greatly complicated by an unruly animal. Teach your horse to stand quietly so you can check his or her vital signs.

Although it is possible to use a regular rectal thermometer to take a horse's temperature, it's not wise. Such thermometers break and crack more easily than heavy-duty ones made for livestock. Livestock rectal thermometers can be purchased in certain livestock and veterinary supply stores, or ask your veterinarian. Have at least one in your first-aid kit. A livestock thermometer will have a ring on the end to which you should attach a cord. When using the instrument, tie the free end of the cord to a few strands of the horse's tail so it can be easily retrieved. Make sure the thermometer is thoroughly cleaned after each use, and follow any other care directions provided. Do not wash a thermometer in hot water; use a mild soap and warm water for the initial cleaning, then wipe it with a disinfectant such as alcohol. Rinse the thermometer with cool water before using to ensure all the alcohol is removed. Shake down the thermometer to below 95 degrees F., and place a dab of vaseline on the end of it. Lift the horse's tail and with a gentle push insert the thermometer two or three inches. Leave it in place for three minutes if possible, during which time the horse should be kept quiet. Remove the thermometer, wipe it clean, and read the temperature (practice reading before an emergency arises). The normal body temperature for an adult horse ranges from 99 to 101.5 degrees F.; on hot days the temperature may be a little higher. Remember that temperature is only one measurement and in itself cannot indicate whether or not an animal is sick.

Respiration can be observed as movements of the flank or ribs. Breathing should be noiseless and effortless; if it's not, something is wrong. Normal respiratory rates for a resting adult horse range from eight to fourteen breaths per minute.

The heart rate of an adult horse at rest varies from twenty-eight to fifty-two beats per minute. Do not be alarmed if you hear or feel irregular beats—they are fairly common. The heartbeat can be felt through the chest wall directly behind the left elbow. The pulse can be felt in one of three places; the best place is along the margin of the inside of the jaw, but it can also be checked at the inside of the elbow or under the tail (practice before an emergency arises). Remember that pulse can be affected by stress, fear, exercise, environmental temperature, the animal's temperament and size, sex, and age. Younger animals have much higher pulse rates than older ones—a six-month-old foal will have a pulse of sixty to seventy-one beats per minute while a yearling's may be only fifty to sixty-eight per minute and an adult's twenty-eight to fifty-two.

Vital signs, to be of value, should be coupled with other indications of illness, so do not stop your check after obtaining temperature, respiration, and heart rates.

F. Foreign Bodies

These are such things as rocks and nails in hooves, debris in the eyes, and splinters. They should be tended immediately, and a veterinarian should be called if necessary.
1. *Splinters.* These may go unnoticed until a small lump develops. If an opening can be seen and the tip of the splinter is near, pull it out with a pair of tweezers. Any pus that may have collected around the splinter should also be removed. Apply an appropriate antiseptic and check to make sure complications do not arise.
2. *Rocks and nails.* Areas that are going to be used to house horses should be checked thoroughly and regularly for any potentially dangerous objects. Examine fences for protruding nails and make sure boards and pipes are securely fastened to their posts. When making repairs in the area, keep track of all materials so none are left behind.

If a rock becomes lodged in a horse's hoof, it can usually be removed with a hoof pick. Check the other hooves at the same time.

If a nail or other sharp object happens to puncture the sole of the hoof or the area surrounding it, call a veterinarian. In the meantime, remove the nail if you can do so without causing more damage; treat the wound with a good disinfectant such as iodine or alcohol while you're removing the nail and again immediately after it's out. If the nail was deeply imbedded and hit a bone in the hoof, inflammation may be present. It's a good idea to place a cotton plug soaked in disinfectant in the resulting nail hole, and put a light bandage over the hoof to keep debris out. Contact a veterinarian as soon as possible when puncture wounds are noticed. Tetanus shots, antibiotics, and other medications may be needed.

3. *Foreign bodies in the eyes.* Be familiar with the appearance of the normal eye so you can quickly tell if something is wrong. Excess tearing is often a sign of eye irritation. If debris is present, use an appropriate eyewash to clean the eye. In the absence of a specific commercial preparation, dilute ninety grains (approximately one-fifth ounce) of boric acid with six ounces of freshly boiled and cooled water; administer with an eyedropper. Do not use eye ointments prescribed for a previous irritation or for another horse. Such ointments are very specific in nature and can cause more harm than good. If you cannot find the source of an irritation, check promptly with a veterinarian; he or she should also attend to all cuts located around or on the eyeball.

4. *Foreign bodies in the ears.* Even if the animal is cooperative, it will be difficult to examine the ear. Call a veterinarian.

G. Poisoning

Poisoning in horses is serious. Try to hinder or prevent further absorption of the poison either through the skin or through the lining of the stomach; wash off external poisons with plenty of water and soap.

If the type of poison is unknown, a general antidote can be prepared using four parts powdered charcoal, one part magnesium carbonate levis, and one part tannic acid. The horse should be given one-half pound of this combination mixed with water or gruel; the treatment should be followed later by milk, whipped eggs, or other bland fluid. This antidote uses uncommon ingredients, so have a supply of them in your first-aid chest for emergencies. Above all, contact a veterinarian at the first hint of poisoning.

The treatment for specific poisons such as strong acids or alkalis follows the basic treatment as for the dog; however, the medication dosage will be increased. Lead, arsenic, strychnine, and certain plants are all possible sources of poison. Detailed treatment instruction is not possible here. Again, CALL A VETERINARIAN at once. Prevent poisoning by keeping dangerous substances out of reach of horses and other animals. Pastures should be checked for poisonous plants before being used.

H. Burns

Minor burns on horses can be treated much the same way as burns on other animals. Cleanse the affected area and apply a suitable first-aid burn dressing. Commercial preparations are best, but a gauze pad soaked in a strong tea solution will also work. In cases where the hair has been singed off but the burn contains debris, it may be cleaned with a gauze pad soaked in normal saline solution (one teaspoon salt to one pint boiled cooled water). Burns are extremely painful, so be gentle.

Extensive burns—covering more than five percent of the body surface—should only be treated by a veterinarian. Cover the wounds with a clean (preferably sterile), dry, light bandage until the veterinarian arrives. Do not apply salves, creams or other substances. To ward off shock, keep the animal warm and coax him or her to drink water.

All burns should be seen by a veterinarian to ensure proper healing.

I. Fractures

Fractures are jobs for professionals. Unless veterinary care will be unavailable for a long time and the fracture is *very* bad, wait for the veterinarian before thinking of destroying the animal. New treatment techniques have allowed more and more animals with fractures to recover with little or no impairment of their normal movements; treatment is, nevertheless, a long, tedious, and expensive process. If necessary, splint the fracture so no more damage can be done. Keep the animal quiet until the veterinarian arrives. Wounds associated with the fracture should be covered with a clean, dry, light bandage to keep out debris.

J. Sprains and Strains

Leg sprains and strains, no matter how slight, should be looked after promptly. A veterinarian may be needed, but some cases can be handled by you. Sprained areas will be swollen, may feel hot, and will be painful when pressure is applied. A "sweat" (liniment) may be applied to the area to draw out the swelling, but this isn't always necessary — correct bandaging is the most important aspect of sprain treatment. If a liniment is used, follow the directions carefully to avoid blistering of the skin. For the bandage, obtain two sheets of cotton about fourteen inches wide and thirty inches long and either a roll of two-inch gauze or a two-inch wide elastic bandage (Vet Wrap). Carefully wrap the cotton sheeting around the leg, distributing pressure evenly over the affected area. Next, start winding the roll of gauze or elastic bandage over the cotton padding. This is the important part: A secure wrap with evenly applied pressure will provide maximum support and aid in recovery; a too-tight bandage will interfere with circulation. Be extra careful with elastic bandages for they tend to constrict after being on awhile (beginners should use gauze). Gauze and elastic bandages used together provide double support. After you have practiced bandaging legs a few times you will be able to tell when the tension is correct. Leave the leg wrapped for at least twenty-four hours before removing the bandage. Massage the leg and sprained area gently but vigorously. Check to see if the swelling has gone down and if the sprain still feels hot. Even if all appears well, it is wise to repeat the wrap several more times since sprains take a while to heal completely. During this time keep the animal quiet, in a fairly small area, and away from other sources of injury and animals that may harass him or her.

Strains usually occur where they cannot be treated with a wrap, such as shoulder injuries. Rub a liniment on the strained area and rest the horse.

Animals recovering from strains and sprains need time to readjust to normal routines. Do not work these horses heavily until they have been reconditioned.

K. Insect Bites and Stings

For bee, wasp, and hornet stings, remove the stinger if it is still present. Apply a paste of baking soda, a slice of raw onion, or a vinegar pack to the affected area. Stings on the nose may cause respiratory difficulty, and stimulants or antihistamines may be required; call a veterinarian.

L. Snakebites

Identify the snake or get a description of it, if possible, and contact a veterinarian at once. Apply a constricting band if the bite is on an extremity. Make incisions between the fang marks and draw out the venom and blood with suction (see section on dogs, page 209). Asphyxiation often occurs in horses after they've been bitten by a snake, so be prepared to administer AR; ideally, a tracheotomy should be performed by the veterinarian. To prevent rapid spreading of the venom, keep the horse quiet until the veterinarian arrives. The latter will also prescribe antiserum and other necessary drugs.

M. Heatstroke

This occurs most often during hot weather when horses are being shipped or confined in poorly ventilated stalls; overwork is also a cause. It is imperative for animals left in hot places to be removed at intervals, especially if traveling, and to have access to plenty of fresh water at all times. As with other animals, the important thing in heatstroke is to reduce the body temperature. The horse's body can either be sprayed with cold water or covered with towels soaked in water. Pay particular attention to the head and neck and place ice packs on these areas if the animal shows signs of noncoordination. Check body temperature regularly to tell when it's normal again. Dry the horse thoroughly after his or her temperature has been lowered to prevent chilling. If the animal appears to be in shock, call a veterinarian immediately.

N. Foaling

Place the expectant mare in a large box stall supplied with ample bedding. Leave the mare to herself and disturb her as little as possible when checking on her. Familiarize yourself with normal foaling procedures and notify the attending veterinarian of the expected birth so he or she can be summoned in case of emergency—this is especially important if the mare is expected to foal on a holiday or weekend. The mare's external genitalia should be thoroughly washed with warm water and a mild disinfectant and her tail should be almost completely wrapped with gauze. Keep an eye on the mare while she is foaling but do not interfere unless a problem arises.

If the foal is born normally but is ignored by the mother, you will have to clean it. Clear the nose and mouth of mucous, blood, and other debris and make sure the foal is breathing. Rub it down with a rough towel. Before leaving the mare and foal alone, be sure the mare will accept and nurse it. If the veterinarian was not on hand for the foaling, have him or her come by within a day or two to check both animals and administer any medication.

O. Hoof Injuries

The legs and hooves of the horse are extremely important parts of the anatomy and any problems with them can seriously impair or completely prohibit use of the animal. Thus, proper attention to any problem is essential. Nail punctures and rocks in the hoof have been discussed. Other problems are hoof diseases, most of which result from unsanitary conditions and consequent bacterial infestation. Obviously, the best medicine is preventive treatment—making sure stabling areas are clean and dry.

Horses that have to stand in constantly damp places are susceptible to many hoof problems, one of which is "thrush," a degenerative hoof disease. Symptoms include the presence of a thick, blackish-colored, foul-smelling discharge from the crevices of the hoof. The sensitive frog is the usual place of attack, but thrush can spread to other parts of the hoof. If left untreated it can cause permanent lameness. Treatment consists of placing the horse in a dry, clean environment, cleaning the hoof with a disinfectant, and applying a dressing such as Kopertox (trade name) to the hoof. Treatment must be continued for some time on a regular basis.

If proper hoof care is not observed, many other foot diseases and disorders, including grease heel, sand cracks, and split hooves, can occur. Hot, dry weather can cause special problems, for dry hoofs crack easily and do not allow for proper expansion and contraction of the frog. Application of a softening agent (pure lanolin is good) will help prevent this.

Regular hoof trimming will help ensure proper foot-to-ground contact and focus attention early on potential problems.

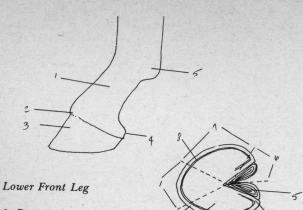

Lower Front Leg

1. Pastern
2. Coronet
3. Hoof
4. Bulb
5. Fetlock

1. Toe
2. Wall
3. Sole
4. Bar
5. Frog
6. Heel
7. Quarter
8. White line

Structure of Lower Front Leg

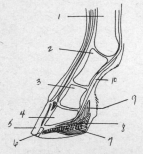

1. Cannon bone
2. Long pastern
3. Short pastern
4. Coffin bone
5. Sensitive laminae
6. White line
7. Insensitive frog
8. Sensitive frog
9. Plantar cushion
10. Deep flexor tendon

1. Coffin bone
2. Lateral cartilages

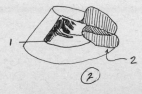

P. Leg Problems

The legs of the horse are amazing collections of muscles, tendons, nerves, bones, and blood vessels, all of which must work together in four very small, thin spaces to support and propel the animal. It is impossible to list and describe treatment for all potential leg problems, but they are a constant concern to the horse owner.

One very serious abnormality, resulting from a misstep or from overexertion, is a "bowed tendon." This can affect either one or both of two very important tendons, which normally act to flex the hoof and run along the back of the leg by the cannon bone. If something happens to rupture these tendons or their protective sheaths, a bowed tendon results. The disorder is very serious and should not be treated by an amateur. Call a veteriarian and apply cold compresses to the affected area until he or she arrives. Keep the animal quiet. DO NOT ATTEMPT TO TREAT A BOWED TENDON YOURSELF.

Q. Colic

Colic is a general term used to indicate a problem associated with pain in the abdominal cavity; it is one of the major causes of death in horses. The illness has varied causes, among them acute parasitic infestations, feeding moldy or dusty feeds, sudden changes in feeding, allowing hot horses to drink too much water, and faulty teeth. Symptoms of colic include restlessness, pawing at the ground, kicking at the flanks, frequently lying down and getting up, and rolling. Animals passing manure have a better chance of recovering than animals that appear constipated. Keep the horse quiet. Watch him or her carefully to prevent injury. Do not let him or her lie down. Slowly walking the horse — DO NOT RIDE HIM — will sometimes help. If the animal is passing manure, prepare and administer the following mixture. Into a bucket put a one-pound coffee can of bran or half a sixteen ounce box of all-bran breakfast cereal. Add enough very hot water to make the mixture sloppy wet; then add the usual grain feed until the mash is only warm and damp. Finally, put in two tablespoons of baking soda and ten dissolved aspirins. If there is no improvement within thirty minutes after the mash is eaten, call a veterinarian.

If the horse is not passing manure, seems extremely sick, and signs of bloating are present, do not wait and do not feed the mash — call a veterinarian immediately.

Avoid colic by sticking to a regular feeding schedule and using high-quality feeds. Switch to new feeds and feeding schedules slowly.

R. Miscellaneous Information

Like other animals, horses are prone to internal parasite infestations. If left uncontrolled, parasites can cause colic and improper utilization of feeds. Keep your horse on a regular worming schedule. Many commercial preparations are available that can be mixed with feeds. Check to see what parasites the product you choose controls; quite a few commercial wormers do not help control bot fly infestations. Follow directions carefully and administer the proper dosage. Most wormers come in doses for a one thousand pound horse. The best way to approach parasite problems is to take a fecal sample to a veterinarian, who can then prescribe the exact dosage of the appropriate medication. Veterinarians will tube worm horses (pass a plastic tube into the stomach through which the worming medication is introduced); this is the best method.

ALL horses should be vaccinated against tetanus and against eastern and western encephalitis (sleeping sickness). If your horse travels a good deal and comes in contact with many strange horses, other vaccinations may be needed. Ask your veterinarian.

It is, of course, more troublesome to give medications to horses than to smaller animals. Some medications can be mixed with feed or given by injection. If intramuscular injections are required over a period of several days, the veterinarian can provide you with a supply of medication, sterile syringes, and needles, if you wish. He or she will show you how and where to administer the shots. Although you may be squeamish at first, after practice this is a fairly easy and painless process.

Horses are animals requiring a lot of care. Feed, living quarters and medical care will be more expensive than for smaller animals; be sure you can afford the time and money necessary to support a horse before buying one. When problems arise, don't skimp. Call a veterinarian when in doubt. Small problems, if untreated, can quickly cause more serious problems. Obtain a good book on horse care for reference. After being around your horse for awhile, you will develop an awareness about his or her normal behavior and be able to spot any abnormalities.

OTHER ANIMALS

When treating small animals such as mice, rats, hamsters, rabbits, or guinea pigs, use medication prescribed for cats (safer than those for dogs) if no specific one is available for your pet. Isolate sick animals and thoroughly scrub and clean their cages so other animals will not contract the illness. Know normal behavior and appearance of your pet so you can quickly detect problems.

If you have an animal other than a dog or cat, locate a veterinarian close by who is able to treat him or her. Most veterinarians specialize only in dogs and cats and do not treat other types of animals.

YOUR VETERINARIAN

For *any* type of animal, find a veterinarian with whom you feel confident and comfortable and stick with him or her. If a veterinarian knows you, he or she is more willing to attend emergencies during nonoffice hours (some veterinarians will not take on an emergency case unless the owner of the animal is a regular client). Have the telephone number of your veterinarian written down with other emergency numbers. Do not burden him or her with trivial questions, but feel free to ask any valid ones concerning your pet's health, treatment, or fees. Any veterinarian, if a good one, will be happy to answer such questions.

WILDLIFE

My advice here, in most cases, is DO NOT attempt first aid. Wild animals, especially baby ones, that appear injured or abandoned may not be; and in handling them you can be condemning them to death. If it is obvious an animal needs help, BE EXTREMELY CAREFUL. Those appearing dead or unconscious may instinctively snap or strike out when touched. Use heavy padding on your hands and arms before attempting to handle a wild animal. Put a blanket or coat over the animal, and remove him or her to a dark, warm, quiet place to recuperate. If the animal has merely been stunned, this will allow recovery time. If the injuries are more severe, chances are he or she will not live. Very few veterinarians treat wild animals. Try to locate a specialist in your area. Call zoos or the local chapter of the American Veterinary Medical Association for references. A book published by the Morris Animal Foundation, *Veterinarians for Zoo and Wild Animals*, is a brief guide to wild animal veterinarians around the country. If you can find a willing veterinarian, rush the animal to him or her.

A FIRST-AID KIT FOR ANIMALS

If you are interested in assembling an emergency treatment kit for animals, here are a few suggestions on items to include. This list is not meant to be all-inclusive; items may be varied according to what animals you will be likely to handle. The notations beside the following articles indicate for which animals they might be used: dog (d), cat (c), horse (h), wildlife (w), all animals (a).

Tweezers (a)

Roll of gauze, both 1" and 2" (a)

Small rectal thermometer (c,d)

Large rectal thermometer (h)

Scissors (a)

Nail clippers (c,d)

Snakebite kit (a)

Hydrogen peroxide (a)

Eye wash (a)

Burn ointment (tannic acid jelly) (a)

Sheet cotton (h)

Cotton balls (a)

Cotton-tipped swabs (a)

Adhesive tape, nonstick to fur (a)

Mineral oil (a)

Antiseptic powder (a)

Antiseptic solution (a)

Towel

Large gauze pads (a)

Band-aids, for you

Restraining stick (d)

Leash and collar (c,d)

Lead rope and halter (h)

Blanket (a)

Flashlight (a)

Petroleum jelly (a)

2" elastic bandage (a)

Pocket knife

Wire cutters (a, esp. h)

Canvas gloves (a)

Medicine dropper (a)

Milk of magnesia (c,d)

Carsick remedy (c,d—ask your veterinarian)

Aspirin (d,h)

Soap

Keep first-aid items in the trunk of your car. Large articles can be put in a box; put smaller items separate in a less bulky container, like a fishing tackle box, for easy access and transport.

PHYSIOLOGICAL DATA OF SELECTED ANIMALS

Species	Adult Weight Range	Age of Puberty	Gestation (Incubation) Period / Days	Normal Rectal Temp. (F)	Normal Heart Rate/Min.	Normal Respiration Rate/Min.
Dog	3-100 lbs.	7-12 months	54-65	101-102.5	80-120	10-30
Cat	F 3-8 lbs. M 4-12 lbs.	7-12 months	56-63	101.0-102.5	110-130	20-30
Horse	800-2500 lbs.	10-12 months	330-340	99-101.5	28-52	8-14
Goat	100-225 lbs.	6 months	140-160	101.5 - 102.5	70-90	12-30
Gerbils	60-200 gms.	60-120 days	21-24	100.8	260-600	65-90
Guinea Pig	F 350-600 gms. M 600-800 gms.	F 4-5 weeks	59-70	101-102.2	260-400	60-150
Golden Hamster	110-140 gms.	45-75 days	15-18	97.2-99.5	300-600	33-127
Rabbit	2-15 lbs.	3-8 months	30-32	101-103.2	123-304	35-56
Norway Rat	F 300-400 gms. M 250-300 gms.	30-70 days	20-22	99-101.5	261-600	65-113
Mouse	F 25 gms. M28 gms.	30-40 days	20-21	96.5-98.5	320-780	85-230
Canary	16 gms.	6-8 weeks	13	105-108	650-690	96-120
Parakeet	30 gms.	3 months	18	104-107.6	600-700	40-80
Parrot	100-700 gms.		21	105-106	140-200	36
Pigeon	1½ lbs.	5-8 months	13	109	140-220	25-30
Duck	7-10 lbs.	7 months	28-35	106-108	210-220	32-110
Goldfish	2-4 gms.	2nd year	3-5			

Note: Physiological data will vary according to age, temperament, species, and conditions under which the data are collected. These figures represent generalizations and averages.

Bibliography

Adams, Alexander B. *Handbook of Practical Public Relations*. New York: Thomas Y. Crowell Co., 1965.

American Humane Association. *The Animal Welfare Organization and the Law*. Organizational Guide Information Series. Englewood, Colorado: American Humane Association, 1968.

American Humane Association. *Organizing an Animal Welfare Agency*. Organizational Guide Information Series. Englewood, Colorado: American Humane Association, 1968.

Associated Humane Societies of New Jersey. "Vet's Advice Best." *New Jersey Humane News,* November 1975.

Carson, Rachel. *Silent Spring*. New York: Houghton Mifflin, 1963.

Chaloux, P. A. Letter to Howard Bragman. Washington, D.C.: Veterinary Services, Department of Agriculture, 1974.

Coleman, Sydney H. *Humane Leaders in America*. American Humane Association, 1924.

Congressional Quarterly Almanac, 1973. Washington, D.C.: Congressional Quarterly, Inc., 1974.

Dock, George, Jr. *The Audubon Folio*. New York: Harry N. Abrams, Inc., 1964.

Fish and Wildlife Service. "Selected List of Federal Laws and Treaties Relating to Sport Fish and Wildlife." revised. Washington, D.C.: Department of the Interior, 1973.

Friends of Animals. "Factory Farming." New York, 1976.

Hayes, Horace M. *Veterinary Notes for Horse Owners*. New York: Arco Publishing Co., 1964.

Kirk, Hamilton. *Index of Treatment in Small Animal Practice*. London: Bailliere, Tindall, and Cox, 1954.

Kirk, Robert W.; and Bistner, Stephen I. *Handbook of Veterinary Procedures and Emergency Treatment*. Philadelphia: W. B. Saunders Co., 1975.

Latimer, Heather. "First Aid." *Animal Cavalcade,* Nov/Dec 1974.

Lyles, Laurence L., ed. *Horseman's Handbook*. Santa Rosa, California: State Horseman's Association, 1971.

Maddox, Russell W.; and Fuquay, Robert F. *State and Local Government*. Princeton: Van Nostrand Co., 1962.

McCoy, J. J. *How to Live with a Dog*. New York: Berkeley Medallion Books, 1966.

McGinnis, Terri. *The Well Cat Book*. New York: Random House/Bookworks, 1975.

McGinnis, Terri. *The Well Dog Book*. New York: Random House/Bookworks, 1974.

Merck Veterinary Manual. 4th ed. Rahway, New Jersey: Merck and Co., 1975.

Mowat, Farley. *A Whale for the Killing*. Boston: Little, Brown and Co., 1972.

National Heart and Lung Institutes, National Institutes of Health. "Research Animals in Medicine." Edited by Lowell T. Harmison, Ph.D. Washington, D.C.: Department of Health, Education, and Welfare, 1973.

Niven, Charles D. *History of the Humane Movement*. London: Johnson Publications, Ltd., 1967.

Norwick, Kenneth P. *Lobbying for Freedom*. New York: St. Martin's Press, 1975.

Office of the Federal Register. *United States Government Manual, 1975/1976*. rev. ed. Washington, D.C.: National Archives and Records Service, General Services Administration, 1975.

Pegram, Louis J. "Puppy Feeding Techniques." *Purina Kennel News*, vol. 4, 1975.

Pinninger, R. S., ed. *Jones's Animal Nursing*. Oxford: Pergamon Press, 1972.

Point, Nicolas. *Wilderness Kingdom: The Journals and Paintings of Father Nicolas Point*. New York: Holt, Rinehart and Winston, 1967.

Rossow, C. F., D.V.M. "What to Do for the Pet in an Emergency." *Animal Cavalcade*, Mar/April 1974.

Simon, Noel; and Geroudet, Paul. *Last Survivors: The Natural History of 48 Animals Threatened with Extinction*. New York: World Publishing Co., 1970.

Singer, Peter. *Animal Liberation*. New York: New York Review Books, dist. by Random House, 1975.

Smithcors, J. F., D.V.M. "Doctor's Advice." *Animal Cavalcade*, Nov/Dec 1975.

Steele, Zulma. *Angel in Top Hat*. New York: Harper and Brothers, 1942.

Subcommittee on Fisheries and Wildlife Conservation of the Committee on Merchant Marine and Fisheries, House of Representatives. *Hearings on Legislation for the Preservation and Protection of Marine Mammals*. Washington, D.C.: U.S. Goverment Printing Office, 1971.

Subcommittee on Oceans and Atmosphere of the Committee on Commerce, United States Senate. *Hearings on S. 685, 1315, 2579, 2639, 2871, 3112, 3161 and Amendment 1048, Ocean Mammal Legislation*. Washington, D.C.: U.S. Government Printing Office, 1972.

Subcommittee on Fisheries and Wildlife Conservation and the Environment of the Committee on Merchant Marine and Fisheries, House of Representatives. *Hearings on Oversight of the Marine Mammal Protection Act of 1972*. Washington, D.C.: U.S. Government Printing Office, 1974.

Weber, William J. *Wild Orphan Babies*. New York: Holt, Rinehart and Winston, 1975.

Recommended Reading

TREATMENT OF ANIMALS

Amory, Cleveland. *Man Kind? Our Incredible War on Wildlife*. New York: Harper & Row, 1974.

Animals, Men and Morals: An Inquiry into the Mal-Treatment of Non-Humans. Edited by Stanley and Roslind Godlivitch. New York: Taplinger, 1972.

Batten, Peter. *Living Trophies: A Shocking Look at the Conditions in America's Zoos*. New York: Thomas Y. Crowell Co., 1976.

Caras, Roger. *Death as a Way of Life*. Boston: Little, Brown & Co., 1970.

Carson, Gerald. *Men, Beasts, and Gods: A History of Cruelty and Kindness to Animals*. New York: Scribner's, 1972.

Harrison, Ruth. *Animal Machines*. New York: Ballantine Books, 1964.

Leavitt, Emily S. *Animals and Their Legal Rights*. Washington, D.C.: Animal Welfare Institute, 1970.

Morse, Mel. *Ordeal of the Animals*. Englewood Cliffs, New Jersey: Prentice-Hall, 1968.

Olsen, Jack. *Slaughter the Animals, Poison the Earth*. New York: Simon & Schuster, 1971.

Regenstein, Lewis. *The Politics of Extinction*. New York: Macmillan, 1975.

Ryder, Richard D. *Victims of Science*. London: Davis-Poynter Ltd., 1975.

VANISHING WILDLIFE

Caras, Roger, *Last Chance on Earth: A Requiem for Wildlife*. rev. ed. New York: Schocken Books, 1972.

Curry-Lindahl, Kai. *Let Them Life: A Worldwide Survey of Animals Threatened with Extinction*. New York: William Morrow & Co., 1972.

Dorst, Jean. *Before Nature Dies*. Baltimore: Penguin Books, 1970.

Fisher, James; Simon, Noel; and Vincent, Jack. *Wildlife in Danger*. New York: Viking Press, 1969.

Guggisberg, C. A. W. *Man and Wildlife*. New York: Arco Publishing Co., 1970.

Laycock, George. *America's Endangered Wildlife*. New York: W. W. Norton & Co., 1969.

Matthiessen, Peter. *Wildlife in America*. New York: Viking Press, 1959.

McNulty, Faith. *Must They Die? The Strange Case of the Prairie Dog and the Black-Footed Ferret*. New York: Doubleday & Co., 1971.

Milne, Lorus; and Milne, Margery. *Cougar Doesn't Live Here Anymore*. Englewood Cliffs, New Jersey: Prentice-Hall, 1971.

Scheffer, Victor B. *A Voice for Wildlife: A Call for a New Ethic in Conservation*. New York: Scribner's, 1974.

Silverberg, Robert. *The Auk, the Dodo and the Oryx: Vanished and Vanishing Creatures*. New York: Thomas Y. Crowell Co., 1967.

Vanishing Species. Edited by Kathleen Brandes. New York: Time-Life Books, 1974.

ANIMAL BEHAVIOR

Ardrey, Robert. *The Territorial Imperative*. New York: Dell Publishing Co., 1966.

Bergman, Göron. *Why Does Your Dog Do That?* New York: Howell Book House, 1971.

Carrighar, Sally. *Wild Heritage*. New York: Ballantine Books, 1965.

Droscher, Vitus B. *Friendly Beast: Latest Discoveries in Animal Behavior*. New York: Harper & Row, 1972.

Errington, Paul. *Of Predation and Life*. Ames, Iowa: Iowa State University Press, 1967.

Fox, Michael W. *Between Animal and Man*. New York: Coward, McCann & Geoghegan, 1976.

Froman, Robert. *The Great Reaching Out: How Living Beings Communicate*. Cleveland: Collins, William, & World Publishing Co., 1968.

Gilbert, Bill. *How Animals Communicate*. New York: Pantheon Books, 1966.

Lorenz, Konrad. *King Solomon's Ring*. New York: Apollo Editions, 1952.

Sutton, Ann; and Sutton, Myron. *Animals on the Move*. Chicago: Rand McNally & Co., 1966.

Von Frisch, Karl; and Von Frisch, Otto. *Animal Architecture*. New York: Harcourt Brace & Jovanovich, 1974.

Von Frisch, Otto. *Animal Migration*. New York: McGraw-Hill, 1969.

Williams, Moyra. *Horse Psychology*. Cranbury, New Jersey: A. S. Barnes & Co., 1966.

PRIMATES

Mackinnon, John. *In Search of the Red Ape*. New York: Ballantine Books, 1974.

Schaller, George B. *The Mountain Gorilla: Ecology and Behavior*. Chicago: University of Chicago Press, 1963.

Schaller, George B. *Year of the Gorilla*. Chicago: University of Chicago Press, 1964.

Van Lawick-Goodall, Jane. *In the Shadow of Man*. New York: Houghton Mifflin Co., 1971.

AFRICA

Grzimek, Berhard; and Grzimek, Michael. *Serengeti Shall Not Die*. Huntington, New York: Fontana, 1959.

Myers, Norman. *The Long African Day*. New York: Macmillan, 1972.

BIRDS

Ames, Felicia. *The Bird You Care For*. New York: Signet Books, 1970.

Hyde, Dayton O. *Sandy: The True Story of a Rare Sandhill Crane Who Joined Our Family*. New York: Ballantine Books, 1968.

Sparks, John; and Soper, Tony. *Penguins*. New York: Taplinger, 1967.

ELEPHANTS

Douglas-Hamilton, Ian; and Douglas-Hamilton, Oria. *Among the Elephants.* New York: Viking Press, 1975.

WILD CATS

Adamson, Joy. *Born Free.* New York: Bantam Books, 1960.

Adamson, Joy. *Living Free: The Story of Elsa and Her Cubs.* New York: Bantam Books, 1961.

Adamson, Joy. *Pippa's Challenge.* New York: Harcourt Brace & Jovanovich, 1972.

Adamson, Joy. *Spotted Sphinx.* New York: Harcourt Brace & Jovanovich, 1969.

Eaton, Randall L. *The Cheetah: The Biology, Ecology, and Behavior of an Endangered Species.* New York: Van Nostrand Reinhold Co., 1974.

Mountfort, Guy. *Tigers.* New York: Crescent Books, 1973.

Schaller, George B. *Golden Shadows, Flying Hooves.* New York: Alfred A. Knopf, 1973.

Schaller, George B. *Serengeti Lion: A Study in Predator-Prey Relations.* Chicago: University of Chicago Press, 1972.

Singh, Arjan. *Tiger Haven.* New York: Harper & Row, 1973.

WILD CANINES

Dobie, Frank J. *Voice of the Coyote.* Boston: Little, Brown & Co., 1961.

Leslie, Robert F. *In the Shadow of a Rainbow: The True Story of a Friendship Between Man and Wolf.* New York: W. W. Norton & Co., 1976.

Mowat, Farley. *Never Cry Wolf.* Boston: Little, Brown & Co., 1963.

Ryden, Hope. *God's Dog.* New York: Coward, McCann & Geoghegan, 1975.

Van Lawick, Hugo; and Van Lawick-Goodall, Jane. *Innocent Killers.* New York: Houghton Mifflin Co., 1971.

DOGS AND CATS

Fox, Michael W. *Understanding Your Cat.* New York: Coward, McCann & Geoghegan, 1974.

Fox, Michael W. *Understanding Your Dog.* New York: Coward, McCann & Geoghegan, 1972.

Lorenz, Konrad. *Man Meets Dog.* Baltimore: Penguin Books, 1953.

Mery, Fernand. *The Life, History and Magic of the Cat.* New York: Grosset & Dunlap, 1968.

Mery, Fernand. *The Life, History and Magic of the Dog.* New York: Grosset & Dunlap, 1970.

HORSES

Blake, Henry. *Talking with Horses.* New York: E. P. Dutton & Co., 1976.

Dobie, Frank J. *The Mustangs.* Boston: Little, Brown & Co., 1952.

Green, Edward H. *The Law and Your Horse.* No. Hollywood, California: Wilshire Book Co., 1972.

Henry, Marguerite. *Mustang: Wild Spirit of the West*. Chicago: Rand McNally & Co., 1966.

Long, William G. *Asses Vs. Jackasses*. Beaverton, Oregon: Touchstone Press, 1969.

Naviaux, James L. *Horses in Health and Disease*. rev. ed. New York: Arco Publishing Co., 1976.

Roever, J. M.; and Roever, Wilfred. *The Mustangs*. Austin: Steck-Vaughn Co., 1971.

Ryden, Hope. *America's Last Wild Horses*. New York: E. P. Dutton & Co., 1970.

Wyman, Walker D. *The Wild Horse of the West*. Lincoln: University of Nebraska Press, 1962.

MARINE MAMMALS:

Carrighar, Sally. *The Twilight Seas*. New York: Weybright & Talley, 1975.

Davies, Brian. *Savage Luxury: The Slaughter of the Baby Seals*. New York: Taplinger, 1971.

Devine, Eleanore; and Clark, Martha. *The Dolphin Smile: Twenty-Nine Centuries of Dolphin Lore*. New York: Macmillan, 1967.

Fictelius, Karl-Erik; and Sjolander, Sverre. *Smarter Than Man? Intelligence in Whales, Dolphins and Humans*. New York: Ballantine Books, 1972.

Lilly, John C. *The Mind of the Dolphin*. New York: Doubleday & Co., 1967.

McNulty, Faith. *The Great Whales*. New York: Doubleday & Co., 1974.

Mind in the Water: A Book on Behalf of Whales and Dolphins. Edited by Joan McIntyre. New York: Scribner's and Sierra Club, 1974.

Nayman, Jacqueline. *Whales, Dolphins, and Man*. New York: Hamlyn, 1973.

Norris, Kenneth. *The Porpoise Watcher*. New York: W. W. Norton & Co., 1974.

Scheffer, Victor B. *The Year of the Seal*. New York: Scribner's, 1970.

Scheffer, Victor B. *The Year of the Whale*. New York: Scribner's, 1969.

Small, George L. *The Blue Whale*. New York: Columbia University Press, 1973.

Stenuit, Robert. *The Dolphin: Cousin to Man*. New York: Sterling Publishing Co., 1968.

Tryckare, Tre. *The Whale*. New York: Crescent Books, 1974.

MORE ABOUT ANIMALS

Carr, Donald E. *The Deadly Feast of Life*. New York: Doubleday & Co., 1966.

Derleth, August. *Forest Orphans*. Sweet Briar, Virginia: Ernest Edwards, 1964.

Gilborn, Alice. *What Do You Do with a Kinkajou?* New York: J. B. Lippincott & Co., 1976.

Hoover, Helen. *A Gift of the Deer*. New York: Alfred A. Knopf, 1966.

Hughes, Judy. *A Bird in the Hand and a Bear in the Bush: A Halfway House for Animals*. San Francisco: Chronicle Books, 1976.

Jaeger, Edmund C. *Desert Wildlife*. Stanford, California: Stanford University Press, 1961.

Johnson, Josephine W. *The Inland Island*. New York: Simon & Schuster, 1969.

Laycock, George. *The Alien Animals: The Story of Imported Wildlife*. New York: Natural History Press, Museum of Natural History, 1966.

Leslie, Robert F. *The Bears and I*. New York: Ballantine Books, 1968.

Mercatante, Anthony. *Zoo of the Gods*. New York: Harper & Row, 1974.

Milne, Lorus J.; and Milne, Margery. *The Balance of Nature*. New York: Alfred A. Knopf, 1960.

Powell, Eric; Bruun, Bertel; Kleiman, Devra; and Kypta, Brendan. *Animals of the World, North America*. New York: Hamlyn, 1970.

The World of Animals: A Treasury of Lore, Legend and Literature by Great Writers and Naturalists from the 5th Century B.C. to the Present. Edited by Joseph Wood Krutch. New York: Simon & Schuster, 1961.

ANIMAL CARE

Charles, Elizabeth. *How to Keep Your Pet Healthy*. New York: Macmillan, 1974.

Guthrie, Esther L. *Home Book of Animal Care*. New York: Harper & Row, 1966.

Heriot, Celia. *Handbook for Cat People*. New York: Universal/Award House, 1971.

Hickman, Mae; and Guy, Maxine. *Care of the Wild Feathered and Furred*. Santa Cruz, California: Unity Press, 1973.

Lewis, Howard J. *The Complete Book of Pet Care*. New York: Random House, 1956.

Purina Cat Care Center. *Handbook of Cat Care*. St. Louis, 1972.

Ritter, William. *Know Your Guinea Pig*. Know Your Pet Series #753. New York: Doubleday & Co., 1973.

Scheid, Dan W. *How to Buy a Healthy Horse and Keep Him That Way*. Fort Atkinson, Wisconsin: The Highsmith Co., 1972.

Spencer, Janet; Illeman, Mark; and Reilly, Steve. *A Guide to the Care of Injured Wildlife*. New York: National Audubon Society, 1974.

West, Geoffrey P. *Encyclopedia of Animal Care*. Baltimore: The Williams & Wilkins Co., 1975.

Whitney, Leon F. *The Complete Book of Cat Care*. New York: Doubleday & Co., 1973.

Index